Modern and Contemporary Spanish Women Poets

Twayne's World Authors Series
Spanish Literature

Janet Pérez, Editor

Texas Tech University

TWAS 858

Modern and Contemporary Spanish Women Poets

Janet Pérez

Texas Tech University

Twayne Publishers
An Imprint of Simon & Schuster Macmillan
New York
Prentice Hall International
London   Mexico City   New Delhi   Singapore   Sydney   Toronto

Twayne's World Authors Series No. 858

Modern and Contemporary Spanish Women Poets
Janet Pérez

Twayne Publishers
An Imprint of Simon & Schuster Macmillan
866 Third Avenue
New York, NY 10022

Library of Congress Cataloging-in-Publication Data
Pérez, Janet.
    Modern and contemporary Spanish women poets / Janet Pérez.
        p.   cm.—(Twayne's world authors series ; TWAS 858. Spanish literature)
    Includes bibliographical references and index.
    ISBN 0-8057-4627-7
    1. Spanish poetry—20th century—History and criticism. 2. Spanish poetry—19th
century—History and criticism. 3. Spanish poetry—Women authors—History and
criticism. 4. Catalan poetry—Women authors—History and criticism. 5. Galician
poetry—Women authors—History and criticism. I. Title. II. Series: Twayne's world
authors series; TWAS 858. III. Series: Twayne's world authors series. Spanish
literature
PQ6085.P37   1995
861.009'9287—dc20
                                                                                      95-22660
                                                                                           CIP

10 9 8 7 6 5 4 3 2 1

Printed in the United States of America

Paul Harrison Coon
In Memoriam

Contents

Preface

For Giambattista Vico, language—especially poetic language—was always, inescapably, a revision of previous language. Thus, poetic "originality" springs from prior texts, oral or written, directly or indirectly known, transcending mere intertextual allusion. As Harold Bloom explains, "Any poem is an inter-poem, and any reading of a poem is an inter-reading. A poem is not writing, but *rewriting,* and though a strong poem is a fresh start, such a start is starting-again."[1] Any poet, continues Bloom,

> is in the position of being "after the Event" in terms of literary language. His art is necessarily an *aftering,* and so at best he strives for a selection, through repression, out of the traces of the language of poetry; that is, he represses some of the traces and remembers others. . . . For poetry lives always under the shadow of poetry. The caveman who traced the outline of an animal upon the rock always retraced a precursor's outline. (4)

"Poetry" here means art, creative writing, but Bloom's description of creative process proves especially apt for lyric poetry, whose ancestry comprises centuries of oral transmission and reworking. Collective elements of poetic creativity subvert Romantic concepts of the poet-hero as solitary, inspired creator, moving ideal, individualized Art closer to artifice. By thus modifying the Romantic paradigm, Bloom and Vico offer a more realistic model, particularly befitting the creative process of women poets.

These critics wrote not apropos of women's poetry but the modern Western masculine canon. Their insights apply to women's writing in Spain, however: denied access to higher education, women relied for poetic precepts upon principles deduced via their own readings from the patriarchal canon. Judith Fetterley in *The Resisting Reader* observes that everyone, men and women alike, learns to read like a man (i.e., to adopt androcentric perspectives imbuing authoritative texts).[2] Unwitting internalization of phallocentric viewpoints inscribed in generic Western concepts of rationality and canonical critical discourse transforms women into what Fetterley terms "inmasculated" readers. As a "muted group," women learn the dominant idiom, expressing themselves within its parameters, adopting male viewpoints as a precondition for participating in scholarship (cf. Fetterley, xv, xvi). For women subjected to patriarchal norms of gender formation and androcentric education, male canonical models have prevailed; no gender-specific children's books existed prior to the late nineteenth century. Jonathan Culler's "Reading as a Woman"[3] suggests that the androcentric viewpoint that males and females absorb from canonical texts masks gender differences in reading, obscuring women's perspective: Masculinity inscribed in the text triggers women's socially conditioned inclination to adapt to male viewpoints (hence reading—or writing—as a woman involves considerable difficulty and conscious effort). Simone de Beauvoir defines woman as a being who exists as "Other" in a world where man is the "Subject," thus becoming an object even to herself (detached and alienated).[4]

The patriarchal socialization described by Fetterley and Culler together with internalized phallocentric values limit the possibilities of "woman's language," complicating the usefulness of that polemic. Both genders learn the same language, grammar, and syntax, and linguistic commonality intensifies in formulaic genres. Beth Miller concludes that

> men and women use much the same language in poetry and that gender-linked differences, when they occur, are mainly in the tenor—to use Richards' term—not significantly in the syntax or versification or other formal elements. . . . [W]e are on more defensible ground when we focus on content, even on elements such as theme and attitude, thought and statement, personae, poetic (or narrative) stance, and . . . allusion.[5]

Therefore, my examination of Spanish women's poetry seeks the feminine perspective and experience of life rather than gender-based language, emphasizing characteristic themes and concerns, women writers' frequent adoption of gender-neutral language or masculine personas—a common technique for making feminine writings more palatable to a predominantly male readership—and the circumstances of writing. Some writers deemed conservative today were considered scandalous in their time, so my study places women poets in their historical, social, cultural, and literary contexts, noting the impact of extraliterary factors, including the role of gender. Given frequent perjorative connotations, I avoid using "poetess" despite its being less cumbersome than "women poets."

Both Andrew Debicki and José Olivio Jiménez question the applicability of generational concepts to contemporary Spanish poetry.[6] Noting abundant "generations" crowded into a few years in the extant critical corpus, these critics decry overlapping chronologies, varying esthetics, and poets whose patterns of publication do not correspond to the "generation" into which they were born. Debicki stresses important developments in poetics and esthetics, independent of birth and publication dates, recommending modification of extant critical practice based upon the generational paradigm: fundamental changes in poetic attitudes and styles belong in the context of parallel currents in Western literature rather than Spanish literature's traditional isolation.

Compounding shortcomings of generational schemata, corresponding labels ignore the subsequent evolution of individuals and groups. Jiménez recapitulates major developmental events for twentieth century Spanish poetry, indicating esthetic significance and stressing simultaneous but divergent esthetic trends and the simultaneous presence onstage of members of three, four, or more "generations." Among directional changes transcending generational schemata, Jiménez cites postwar "rehumanization" (18) of so-called social poetry, its diverse chronological groupings and diverging esthetics. Like Debicki, Jiménez suggests seeking continuity rather than differences between generations, "affinities and proximities between literatures rather than ruptures and gaps" (18).

Generational caveats apply especially to women poets, often excluded from those standard reference works implicated in canon formation (anthologies, literary histories, genre studies) and deterred from participating in collective activities with male writers of a "generation."[7] Formulating their esthetics in solitude and writing within domestic confines, women seldom view themselves as belonging to a generation or movement, despite coincidences with major distinguishing characteristics of male writers of similar periods (Romantic, modernist, etc.).[8] Because women writers often begin publishing comparably late in life, birth dates (used to determine generational membership) prove less meaningful than publication dates. While reference to periods and movements provides a useful critical shorthand that I use as appropriate, women are not assigned to putative "generations" wherein their participation is marginal and from which canonical criticism excludes them.[9] I have organized my discussion chronologically, emphasizing first publication or esthetic affinities.

Selections for anthologies or encyclopedic works are necessarily arbitrary, and panoramic studies determine coverage arbitrarily at some point as well. I originally planned to cover women poets from Romanticism to the present, but I found that I needed to orient my discussion in earlier centuries, no matter how schematically. The numbers of poets and extent of their corpus proved so vast, however, that

I realized that undertaking such a chronological range would produce a reshuffled, annotated bibliography, permitting little individual
discussion. The enormous outpouring of women's poetry in the post-
Franco era requires separate treatment. Given significant modification in
prevailing Peninsular esthetics during the late 1960s, along with major
sociopolitical change, those women whose major poetic works appeared
thereafter will be studied in a second volume.

Within these parameters, I treat significant women poets individually,
with the maximum completeness allowable under page limitations.
Wherever possible I include Catalans, Galicians, exiles, expatriates, and
women poets who lived, wrote, and published in Spain, even if born elsewhere. Omissions result from my lack of linguistic expertise (in Basque
and vernaculars other than Catalan and Gallego), inaccessibility of relevant works, or an author's obscurity. Press runs of poetry are especially
small for women poets, who often publish with local publishers rather
than mainstream outlets. Insofar as feasible, coverage is proportional to
the poet's historical significance or quantity of production. Where critical monographs in English exist, my discussion suggests those sources.

This volume's scope as introductory overview precludes close readings, detailed textual analysis, and exhaustive discussion. Therefore, quotations are infrequent; translations are my own unless otherwise
indicated and render meaning rather than literal translation. Within the
constraints of the introductory biobibliographical panorama and limitations imposed by the extent of the corpus, critical methodology is eclectic, combining contextual and sociological approaches with New
Historicism, New Rhetoricism, feminist considerations, and occasional
mythic criticism. Modern and contemporary Spanish women poets are
situated within their sociopolitical and cultural contexts; relevant issues
of gender and identifying personal and individual nuances of numerous
poetic voices are placed in the foreground. While treatment of individuals rather than periods or generations may mask major esthetic patterns,
facilitating access to women usually excluded from canonical criticism
dictates minimizing attention to movements or groups. Not all women
are equally conscious of poetics; their exclusion from schools and "generations" often signifies distance from theory (cf. Carolina Coronado's
laments on the subject in Chapter 2). Many have published no formal
poetics, or if they have, these have been extemporized for anthologies or
derived ex post facto. Nevertheless, as poetics indicate what poets believe
their works attempt, poetics are discussed when available.

Spanish women's poetry as a holistic corpus remains terra incognita for many professional Hispanists and literary scholars, and my study attempts to address the interests of these scholars along with those of general readers, recovering a feminine canon and tradition heretofore largely unknown. Given Spanish women poets' perennial exclusion from the patriarchal canon and the paucity of relevant critical resources, generations of study will be required before any pretense of completeness can be made for the history of their work. To claim such exhaustiveness for a pioneering panorama would require a rashness I specifically disavow.

Acknowledgments

I am grateful to the Program for Cultural Cooperation between Spain's Ministry of Culture and United States' Universities for an indispensable grant to assist in purchase of materials for this study.

Thanks also to Texas Tech University for a faculty development leave for the purpose of completing the manuscript, and to the dean and staff of the graduate school for technical support and assistance.

And last but not least, my gratitude to my husband, Genaro, for his encouragement and understanding during the innumerable weekends devoted to this project.

Chronology

1916   Clementina Arderiu, *Cançons i elegies.*

1920   Clementina Arderiu, *L'Alta llibertat.*

1922   Herminia Fariña e Cobián, *Cadencias.*

1926   Maria Antònia Salvà, *Espigues en flor;* Concha Méndez, *Inquietudes;* Ernestina de Champourcín, *En silencio;* Carmen Prieto Rouco, *Horas de frebe.*

1927   Josefina de la Torre, *Versos y estampas.*

1928   Concha Méndez, *Surtidor;* Pilar de Valderrama, *Huerto cerrado;* Ernestina de Champourcín, *Ahora.*

1929   Carmen Conde, *Brocal.*

1930   Concha Méndez, *Canciones de mar y tierra;* Josefina de la Torre, *Poemas de la Isla;* Pilar de Valderrama, *Esencias.*

1931   Ernestina de Champourcín, *La Voz en el viento;* Herminia Fariña e Cobian, *Hosanna.*

1932   Concha Méndez, *Vida a vida.*

1934   Maria Antònia Salvà, *El Retorn: Poemes;* Carmen Conde, *Júbilos;* Josefina Romo Arregui, *La Peregrinación inmóvil.*

1935   Marina Romero, *Poemas "A";* Josefina Romo Arregui, *Romancero triste;* Roser Matheu, *La Carena.*

1936   Rosa Chacel, *A la orilla de un pozo;* Clementina Arderiu, *Cant i paraules* and *Poemes;* Ernestina de Champourcín, *Cántico inútil;* Josefina Romo Arregui, *Acuarelas;* Roser Matheu, *Cançons de Setembre.*

1938   Susana March, *Rutas;* Simona Gay, *Aigues vives/Eaux vives* and *La Lluita amb l'angel/Lutte avec l'ange;* Rosa Leveroni, *Epigrames i cançons.*

1940   Concha Méndez, *Lluvias enlazadas;* Josefina Romo Arregui, *Aguafuertes y otros poemas.*

1943   Pilar de Valderrama, *Holocausto;* Marina Romero, *Nostalgia de mañana;* Clemencia Laborda, *Jardines bajo la lluvia.*

1944   Concha Méndez, *Poemas, sombras y sueños;* Asunción Madera, *El Volcano silencio.*

1945   Carmen Conde, *Ansia de la gracia;* María Alfaro, *Poemas líricos;* Elena Martín Vivaldi, *Escalera de luna.*

1946 Clementina Arderiu, *Sempre i ara;* Concha Zardoya, *Pájaros del Nuevo Mundo;* Susana March, *La Pasión desvelada;* Dora Vázquez, *Palma y corona;* Celia Viñas, *Trigo del corazón.*

1947 Carmen Conde, *Mi fin en el viento, Sea la luz,* and *Mujer sin Edén;* Concha Zardoya, *Dominio del llanto;* Pino Ojeda, *Niebla del sueño;* María Beneyto, *Canción olvidada.*

1948 Maria Antònia Salvà, *Lluneta del pagès;* Angela Figuera, *Mujer de barro;* Clemencia Laborda, *Ciudad de soledades;* Pura Vázquez, *En torno a la voz;* Celia Viñas, *Canción tonta en el sur.*

1949 Angela Figuera, *Soria pura;* Luz Pozo Garza, *Anfora;* Roser Matheu, *Poems a la filla.*

1950 Angela Figuera, *Vencida por el ángel;* Gloria Fuertes, *Isla ignorada;* Josefina Romo Arregui, *Cántico de María Sola.*

1951 Carmen Conde, *Iluminada tierra;* María Alfaro, *Poemas del recuerdo;* Susana March, *Ardiente voz* and *El Viento;* Nuria Parés, *Romances de la voz sola;* Pura Vázquez, *Madrugada fronda* and *Desde la niebla.*

1952 Marina Romero, *Presencia del recuerdo;* Ernestina de Champourcín, *Presencia a oscuras;* Angela Figuera, *El Grito inútil;* Luz Pozo Garza, *El Vagabundo* and *O páxaro na boca;* Rosa Leveroni, *Presència i record;* María Beneyto, *Altre veu* and *Eva en el tiempo.*

1953 Concha Zardoya, *La Hermosura sencilla;* Angela Figuera, *Víspera de la vida* and *Los Días duros;* Elena Martín Vivaldi, *El Alma desvelada;* Susana March, *La Tristeza;* Cristina Lacasa, *La Voz oculta;* Roser Matheu, *Poems de la fam;* Celia Viñas, *Del foc i la cendra.*

1954 Marina Romero, *Midas: Poema de amor;* Concha Zardoya, *Los Signos;* Gloria Fuertes, *Antología y poemas del suburbio* and *Aconsejo beber hilo;* Pino Ojeda, *Como el fruto en el árbol;* Concha Lagos, *Balcón;* Angelina Gatell, *El Poema del soldado;* Carmen Prieto Rouco, *Violetas;* María Beneyto, *Criatura múltiple.*

1955 Concha Zardoya, *Desterrado ensueño;* Josefina Romo Arregui, *Isla sin tierra;* Carmen Barbera, *Despedida al recuerdo;* Concha Lagos, *Los Obstáculos* and *Al sur del recuerdo;* Celia Viñas, *Como el ciervo corre herido.*

1956   Asunción Madera, *Mi presencia más clara;* Trina Mercader, *Tiempo a salvo;* Carmen Prieto Rouco, *Lluvia menuda;* Pura Vázquez, *Mañana del amor;* Maria do Carme Kruckenberg, *Cantigas do vento, Los Parajes inmóviles,* and *Las Palabras olvidadas;* María Beneyto, *Ratlles a l'aire, Tierra viva,* and *Poemas de la ciudad.*

1957   Reyes Fuentes, *Actitudes;* Concha Lagos, *El Corazón cansado;* María Elvira Lacaci, *Humana voz;* Aurora de Albornoz, *Brazo de niebla;* Pura Vázquez, *13 poemas a mi sombra;* Maria do Carme Kruckenberg, *Rumor de tiempo;* Concepció Maluquer, *La Creu dels vents.*

1958   Angela Figuera, *Belleza cruel;* Gloria Fuertes, *Todo asusta;* Reyes Fuentes, *De mí hasta el hombre;* Concha Lagos, *La Soledad de siempre, Agua de Dios,* and *Arroyo claro;* Cristina Lacasa, *Los Brazos en estela;* Maria do Carme Kruckenberg, *Farol de aire.*

1959   Clementina Arderiu, *Es a dir;* Concha Zardoya, *Debajo de la luz* and *La Casa deshabitada;* Susana March, *Esta mujer que soy;* Nuria Parés, *Canto llano;* Julia Uceda, *Mariposa en cenizas.*

1960   Reyes Fuentes, *Sonetos del corazón adelante;* Concha Lagos, *Luna de enero;* Maria do Carme Kruckenberg, *Poemas inevitables.*

1961   Marina Romero, *Sin agua, el mar;* Asunción Madera, *Las Estancias vacías;* Clemencia Laborda, *Retorno a la provincia;* Reyes Fuentes, *Elegías del Uad-el-Kebir;* Concha Lagos, *Golpeando el silencio* and *Tema fundamental;* Acacia Uceta, *El Corro de las horas;* Aurora de Albornoz, *Poemas para alcanzar un segundo;* Cristina Lacasa, *Un Resplandor que no perdonó la noche;* Concepción Maluquer, *La Ciutat y les hores.*

1962   Angela Figuera, *Toco la tierra;* María Eugenia Rincón, *Tierra secreta;* Reyes Fuentes, *Romances de la miel en los labios;* Concha Lagos, *Canciones desde la barca* and *Campo abierto;* María Elvira Lacaci, *Sonido de Dios;* Julia Uceda, *Extraña juventud;* Aurora de Albornoz, *Por la primavera blanca;* Luz Pozo Garza, *Cita en el viento;* Maria do Carme Kruckenberg, *Poemas y canciones de aquí y de allá;* María Beneyto, *Vida anterior.*

1963   Concha Lagos, *Para empezar;* María Elvira Lacaci, *Al Este de la ciudad;* Angelina Gatell, *Esa oscura palabra;* Maria Mariño Carou, *Palabra no tempo.*

1964   Ernestina de Champourcín, *Cárcel de los sentidos;* Josefina Romo Arregui, *Elegías desde la orilla del triunfo;* Pino Ojeda, *La Piedra sobre la colina;* Cristina Lacasa, *Con el sudor alzado;* Maria do Carme Kruckenberg, *Tauromaquia en línea y verso* and *Memoria de mi sueño;* Celia Viñas, *Canto.*

1965   Concha Zardoya, *Corral de vivos y muertos;* Asunción Madera, *La Voz que me desvela;* Carmen Barbera, *Cartas a un amigo;* Simona Gay, *La Gerra al sol;* María Beneyto, *Poesía, 1947–1964.*

1966   Ernestina de Champourcín, *El Nombre que me diste;* Concha de Marco, *Hora 0.5;* Susana March, *Poemas;* Julia Uceda, *Sin mucha esperanza;* Cristina Lacasa, *Poemas de la muerte y de la vida;* Gloria Fuertes, *Ni tiro, ni veneno, ni navaja.*

1967   Concha de Marco, *Diario de la mañana;* Acacia Uceta, *Frente a un muro de cal abrasadora;* Aurora de Albornoz, *Frente a esos niños en hilera.*

1968   Concha Zardoya, *Hondo Sur;* Gloria Fuertes, *Poeta de guardia;* Julia Uceda, *Poemas de Cherry Lane.*

1969   Gloria Fuertes, *Cómo atar los bigotes al tigre;* Concha de Marco, *Acta de identificación;* Angelina Gatell, *Las Claudicaciones;* Cristina Lacasa, *Encender los olivos como lámparas.*

1970   Asunción Madera, *Continuada señal;* Elena Martín Vivaldi, *Diario incompleto de abril;* Concha Lagos, *Diario de un hombre;* Concha de Marco, *Congreso en Maldoror;* Acacia Uceta, *Detrás de cada noche;* Dora Vázquez, *Irmá: Poemas de ausencia.*

1971   Concha Zardoya, *Los Engaños de Tremont;* Trina Mercader, *Sonetos ascéticos;* Concha Lagos, *El Cerco;* Cristina Lacasa, *Ha llegado la hora.*

1972 Clemencia Laborda, *Tiempo del hombre, tiempo de Dios;* Elena Martín Vivaldi, *Durante este tiempo;* Concha de Marco, *Tarot.*

1973 Ernestina de Champourcín, *Primer exilio;* Gloria Fuertes, *Sola en la sala;* María Eugenia Rincón, *Frontera da la sombra;* Concha Lagos, *La Aventura;* Concha de Marco, *Las Hilanderas.*

1974 Ernestina de Champourcín, *Poemas del ser y del estar;* María Eugenia Rincón, *Boca sin tiempo;* Concha Lagos, *Fragmentos en espiral desde el pozo;* Concha de Marco, *Una Noche de invierno;* Aurora de Albornoz, *Palabras desatadas;* María Beneyto, *El Agua que rodea la isla.*

1975 Carmen Conde, *Corrosión;* Dora Vázquez, *Campo e mar aberto;* María Beneyto, *Biografía breve del silencio.*

1976 Elena Martín Vivaldi, *Cumplida soledad;* Concha Lagos, *Gótico florido;* Acacia Uceta, *Al sur de las estrellas;* Luz Pozo Garza, *Ultimas palabras/verbas derradeiras;* Maria do Carme Kruckenberg, *A sombra ergueita;* María Beneyto, *Vidre ferit de sang.*

1977 Elena Martín Vivaldi, *Los Arboles presento;* Julia Uceda, *Campanas en Sansuena;* Cristina Lacasa, *Mientras crecen las aguas.*

1978 Rosa Chacel, *Versos prohibidos.*

1979 Dora Vázquez, *Augas soltas.*

1980 Carmen Conde, *La Noche oscura del cuerpo;* Concha Lagos, *Teoría de la inseguridad* and *Por las ramas;* Acacia Uceta, *Cuenca, roca viva;* Maria do Carme Kruckenberg, *Cantares de mi silencio;* Celia Viñas, *Poesía última.*

1981 Elena Martín Vivaldi, *Nocturnos* and *Y será su nombre mar;* Julia Uceda, *Viejas voces secretas de la noche;* Cristina Lacasa, *El Viaje;* Luz Pozo Garza, *Concerto de outono;* Rosa Leveroni, *Poesia.*

1982 Carmen Conde, *Desde nunca;* Concha Lagos, *Elegías para un álbum* and *La Paloma;* Cristina Lacasa, *Opalos del instante.*

1983 Concha Zardoya, *Retorno a Magerit;* Gloria Fuertes, *Historia de Gloria;* Acacia Uceta, *Intima dimensión;*

Aurora de Albornoz, *Palabras reunidas;* Cristina Lacasa, *En un plural designio.*

1984   Pilar de Valderrama, *De mar a mar;* Concha Lagos, *Más allá de la soledad* and *Con el arco a punto;* Cristina Lacasa, *Ramas de la esperanza (Poemas ecológicos).*

1985   Elena Martín Vivaldi, *Tiempo a la orilla;* Concha Lagos, *En la rueda del viento;* Dora Vázquez, *Oración junto al camino.*

1986   Luz Pozo Garza, *Códice calixtino;* Maria do Carme Kruckenberg, *Cantigas pra un tempo esquencido.*

1987   Pino Ojeda, *El Alba en la espalda;* Susana March, *Poemas de la Plaza Real;* Nuria Parés, *Colofón de luz;* Acacia Uceta, *Arbol de agua.*

1989   Marina Romero, *Honda raíz.*

1990   Aurora de Albornoz, *Canciones de Guiomar.*

1992   Rosa Chacel, *Poesía (1931–1991).*

Prologue: A Silence of Centuries

Numerous contemporary Spanish women poets interviewed by Sharon Ugalde[1] responded negatively about belonging to a tradition or continuum of women poets, citing the scarcity of female figures in the male-dominated canon. Remarkably few female antecedents or "foremothers" were noted: Santa Teresa from the sixteenth century, the Mexican Sor Juana Inés de la Cruz from the seventeenth, Rosalía de Castro from the nineteenth, and Carmen Conde from the mid-twentieth. Yet most respondents characterized themselves as avid readers (especially of poetry), professing admiration for or friendship with other women poets. More than an avocation or profession, poetry for nearly all emerged as driving passion. Avoiding labels of feminist, these poets nevertheless treat themes that most observers class among "women's concerns" and adopt distinctly feminine perspectives. What explains, then, their curious "rootlessness," their gender alienation or ignorance of relevant feminine traditions?

Unawareness of past or present Spanish women writers, poets or otherwise, constitutes the norm rather than the exception. Educated Spanish speakers and professional Hispanists alike can mention few names. The complex historical and cultural causes of women poets' invisibility date back to the Middle Ages, if not before. As Angel and Kate Flores note in their introduction to *The Defiant Muse,* "Literacy . . . was long denied to women . . . and the Church, the dominant social force, considered women incapable of literacy, mentally as well as morally inferior to men."[2] These critics recall medieval misogyny resulting in numerous treatises warning against women—for instance, *Disciplina clericalis* (ca. 1100), the *Book of Deceits and Lechery of Women* (1253), the Arcipreste de Talavera's *El Corbacho* (ca. 1466), and *Repetición de amores* by Luis de Lucena (ca. 1497). Traditional *encierro* (cloistering) prevented women's access both to education and the larger world.

In Spain's misogynist or misogamist atmosphere and phallocentric society, literacy was the privilege of the nobility and clerics. Few potential writers (i.e., the small educated population) were women, and they lacked equal creative opportunity. For centuries, strong cultural taboos discouraged women's writing for publication (deemed an unseemly, immodest, "promiscuous" display of things best kept from public view).

Olivares and Boyce suggest that canonization of Santa Teresa (author of five books) barely 40 years after her death both generated and "authorized" feminine writing, accounting for the comparably large number of women poets in Spain's Golden Age.[3] But in patriarchal Spanish culture, Santa Teresa symbolized spirituality, not equality or greater freedom for women; she was a religious activist, not a feminist, although she defended women's right to education.

While feminism per se did not reach Spain until well into the twentieth century, feminine voices were raised centuries earlier to defend women's rights, as exemplified by Cristina de Pisán (1363–1431) and *La Ciudad de las damas* (The City of Women). Sor Teresa de Cartagena in the fifteenth century and Luisa de Padilla, Isabel de Liaño, Sor María de Santa Isabel, and especially Sor Juana and María de Zayas in the Golden Age figure prominently among female writers who championed certain rights for women, especially women's right to education and free choice in matrimony. Educated women in Spain before the modern age belonged almost without exception to the nobility or to religious orders (both strictly controlled women's behavior). Santa Teresa's example undoubtedly inspired her spiritual daughters, but most were motivated by religion, not esthetics. The relative freedom enjoyed by women during the Renaissance (from the late fifteenth century through the first half of the sixteenth) was withdrawn by traditionalist reaction during the Counter-Reformation in the late sixteenth century. Exemplifying the "new conservatism" after humanism's brief sway, Fray Alonso de Herrera echoes Fray Luis de León's century-old tract with *Espejo de la perfecta casada* (Mirror of the Perfect Wife) toward the end of the Golden Age.

Renaissance advances in women's education paralleled the growing popularity of books and private libraries (prerogatives of royalty and nobility) that became the epoch's status symbols. Humanism promoted reading; Queen Isabel I owned an extensive library, which helped establish feminine readership (and reading provided cloistered women—whether in convents or palaces—with important new entertainment and learning). Humanists including Luis Vives defended women's intelligence and intellectual potential as opposed to traditional marginalization, buttressed by the model promulgated by Fray Luis de León in *La Perfecta casada* (1583; The Perfect Wife), glossing Proverbs 31 (buttressing patriarchally inscribed norms as late as the nineteenth century). During the reigns of Ferdinand and Isabel and of Charles V, several women acquired renown for their erudition: a few exceptional women taught in universities, including Francisca de Nebrija and Lucía

Medrano. Beatriz Galindo ("La Latina") taught Latin to Isabel I; Luisa Sigea won fame for a letter written to Pope Paul III, composed in Latin, Greek, Arabic, and Syrian. A respected Latin poet, Sigea taught 13 years at the Portuguese court but ended her life in penury. Juliana Morell reportedly defended philosophical theses at age 13, mastering 14 languages and various humanistic and musical arts by the time she was 15. But neither female humanists nor coeval women writers typify Spain during any past century. As Electa Arenal and Stacey Schlau explain, "Few women of the period [Golden Age] wrote, but nuns were a great exception to that rule."[4] One cultural historian suggests that the proportion of writers to literacy was much higher among women than men: "[Women] poets at that time included all of the women of culture in Spain."[5] Culture, however, was neither easily available to women nor acquired without prolonged effort and extraordinary determination.

The norm was denial of education to women and girls. Ana Navarro cites the popular adage *ni moza adivina, ni mujer latina* (neither soothsaying maids nor educated women), recalling that baroque theater ridiculed feminine erudition. Lope and Calderón contributed to undermining the image of educated women, while Quevedo satirized women humanists more cruelly (cf. "la culta latiniparla" [the Latin-speaking woman]). Nor was mockery limited to Spain, as seen in Molière's comedy *Les Précieuses Ridicules*. Unsurprisingly, women writers resorted to anonymity or male pseudonyms or refrained from publication (others were ordered by confessors or superiors to destroy their works). Those who "broke the rules" by publishing and acknowledging their gender were alternately ridiculed or patronized for writing (almost) "like a man" while meeting with generalized scholarly neglect. Women writers were routinely excluded from patriarchal literary histories and panoramic reference works (though Santa Teresa, the Mexican-born Sor Juana, Pardo Bazán, and various additional "token women" constitute exceptions). Better than most in its coverage, the fourth edition of the Bleiberg and Marías *Diccionario de literatura española* (1972) includes both Latin American and Spanish authors from the Middle Ages to the present but lists only 30 women among more than 550 writers (1.8 percent).

Typically, works of literary historiography and criticism emphasizing genres or periods either ignore women completely or include one or two token representatives of the "second sex." Women writers have been studied more frequently in the post-Franco era, but most continue to be ignored by phallocentric "mainstream" critics, as shown by a significant study of Spanish Golden Age poetry released at the end of 1993. Arthur

Terry's *Seventeenth-Century Spanish Poetry: The Power of Artifice* (1993) treats Góngora, Lope, Quevedo, and Sor Juana as major poets but excludes Fray Luis de León (1527–91), Fernando de Herrera (1534–97), San Juan de la Cruz (1542–91), and Santa Teresa (1515–82), since he opted to "cover" the seventeenth century (baroque) but omit the sixteenth century (Renaissance). Sor Juana is the only woman acknowledged, although Terry includes some 20 additional males, from relatively well-known poets Villamediana and Antonio Hurtado de Mendoza to the obscure Fernández de Andrada (1575?–1648?), "otherwise unknown" save for one poem dedicated to the unknown "miniaturist" poet Francisco de Rioja (134). Several pages each treat Luis Carrillo de Sotomayor (1582/3–1610), Medrano, Arguijo, and Rioja, who all died young or ceased writing early (cf. 122). Terry omits Peninsular women: contemporaries Ana Caro, María de Zayas, Catalina Clara Ramírez de Guzmán (whose *Poesías* [1930] were edited by Joaquín de Entrambasaguas), Luisa Sigea, Luisa de Carvajal, "Marcia Belisarda" (pseudonym of Sor María de Santa Isabel), Leonor de la Cueva y Silva, Antonia de Mendoza (Countess of Benavente), and Sor Marcela de San Félix (illegitimate daughter of Lope de Vega). When distinguished Hispanists from supposedly progressive countries ignore women late in the twentieth century, the problem clearly transcends Spain's traditional misogyny or Hispanic machismo.

Omitting feminine authors, except from works on women, seems paradigmatic in canonical criticism. In silencing their voices (and existence), Terry follows well-established practice—for instance, classic anthologies such as the otherwise judicious compilation of Elias Rivers, *Renaissance and Baroque Poetry of Spain* (1966), which includes only Sor Juana (not literally Spanish), or Dámaso Alonso's *Poesía española: ensayo de métodos y límites estilísticos* (1957). These critics follow long-established patterns for anthologies, as reflected in Howard Mancing's 1986 essay "A Consensual Canon of Hispanic Poetry."[6] Beginning with the Middle Ages and including both Spain and Spanish America, Mancing's "canon" names more than 220 poets, only 10 of them women (half being Spanish American). Surveying 100 anthologies selected as most representative after consulting some 150 published between 1940 and 1980 (see 76–78), Mancing's "Consensual Canon" for Spain deems only Santa Teresa, Carolina Coronado, and Rosalía de Castro clearly canonical, given their inclusion in some 20 anthologies (excluding compilations specialized by gender, groups, themes, regions, generations or specific types, he omits most collections where women poets appear). Carmen Conde, the only Peninsular woman poet mentioned after Rosalía, appears under "Other Poets," meaning that her work figures in fewer anthologies than necessary for being deemed canonical.

Mancing observes that "literary anthologies—along with academic surveys of literature, which are usually based on the anthology—contribute more than anything else to canonization . . . yet the concept of literary anthologies is problematic at best" (54). Indeed so; most anthologies within the Peninsula during the period surveyed were subject to varied political considerations, produced to promulgate specific views of poetry or promoted friends of the anthologist. Unfortunately, a canon based upon real or imaginary consensus of anthologies simply perpetuates exclusionism, and no meaningful relationship exists between how often poets appear in anthologies and their relative importance: Santa Teresa, for example, was listed in 37, while her relatively minor contemporary Gutierre de Cetina appeared in 41 (total anthological mentions would make Darío Castilian's most significant poet). Scores of other anthologies falling beyond Mancing's parameters are similarly exclusionary, and anthological bias has sparked countless polemics: one recent example appears in Víctor García de la Concha's "La Renovación estética de los años sesenta,"[7] which criticizes many anthologies and denounces bias in José María Castellet's *Nueve novísimos poetas españoles* (1970; Nine of the Newest Spanish Poets) and others.

Male critics alone do not bear responsibility for women's absence from the canon. Eminent women Hispanists usually confine themselves within patriarchally established bounds. Thus, for example, Biruté Ciplijauskaité in *El Poeta y la poesía (Del Romanticismo a la poesía social)* (1966) covers more than a century without treating any woman in detail (three pages are devoted to Angela Figuera, but Rosalía de Castro, Carmen Conde, and Gloria Fuertes each receive only passing allusions during discussions of male poets). Concha Zardoya largely omits women poets from her critical volumes on the Generation of 1898 and the Generation of 1927 (brief treatment of Conde appears in later editions). Fanny Rubio's post-Franco anthology covering the period 1939–80 includes three women, but scores exist, often as prolific or significant as many of the male poets included. Perhaps fearing accusations of gender bias, women critics rarely exceed token inclusion of women in works purporting to represent the canon. Perpetuating patriarchally inscribed boundaries of generational canons, androcentric focus and the consequent silencing of women's voices continue in recent and respectable scholarship; additional examples exist ad nauseam.

Omission of women transcends scholarly investigations of specific periods; the silencing observed in Golden Age and early-twentieth-century studies also shrouds women writers of the eighteenth and nineteenth centuries. As recent an anthology as Walter Dobrian's multivolume *Poesía española: Neoclasicismo y Romanticismo* (1988) omits women of the stature of Carolina Coronado and Gertrudis Gómez de Avallaneda, including only Rosalía de Castro. Canonical studies of twentieth-century postwar poetry similarly neglect women (excepting Figuera and Fuertes), improving somewhat in the post-Franco era—that is, the past two decades.

Ample reasons exist for considering women (especially women writers) a silenced group. Adam Jaworski notes that "silence has been a prescribed state for women for centuries, as exemplified in the well-known admonition by Saint Paul: 'Let the women keep silent in the churches, for they are not allowed to speak'" (2 Corinthians 14:34).[8] Jaworski denounces the "*great silence* over women's achievements in a patriarchally-controlled history" (119).[9] Especially relevant is the conclusion of this male sociolinguistic theorist that "on a sociopolitical level, the silencing of women as a group has . . . worked so well that even the significant voices of many women in the past have been silenced and have become forgotten" (120). Logically, young poets interviewed by Ugalde were unacquainted with their roots.

Modern literary history, sparked by Romanticism, produced pioneering bibliographical works on Spanish women writers. Early investigators of women's literary history in Spain included Diego Ignacio Parada y Barrero's *Escritoras y eruditas españolas* (1881), followed by Juan Pedro Criado y Domínguez's *Literatas españolas del siglo XIX: Apuntes bibliográficos* (1889). Parada cites slightly fewer than 400 women writers in all genres, largely writers on religious topics (probably nuns); Criado y Domínguez covers only the nineteenth century. Manuel Serrano y Sanz attempted to compile information on Spanish women writers from the early fifteenth century to Romanticism in *Apuntes para una biblioteca de escritoras españolas desde el año 1401 al 1833* (1903–1905), amassing biographical and bibliographical or manuscript data on some 1,100 women writers, predominantly authors whose works never saw the light of day, or did so only briefly before slipping into oblivion. Navarro states that of the nearly 1,300 writers (*sic*) cataloged by Serrano y Sanz in *Apuntes,* approximately 100 are included in the Royal Spanish Academy's *Antología de poetisas líricas* (1915). Serrano y Sanz also contributed another genre- and gender-specific anthology, *Antología de poetisas líricas* (1915).

María Antonia Vidal's *Cien años de poesía femenina española e hispanoamericana* (1943) begins with the nineteenth century and expands its focus to include Spanish America. Carmen Conde (poet, critic, and the first Spanish woman admitted to that classic "old boys' club," the Royal Spanish Academy) edited two volumes on women poets: *Poesía femenina española (1939–1950)* (1967) and *Poesía femenina española (1950–1960)* (1971). Studies of women and writers in the vernacular or "minority" languages have proliferated since Franco's death in 1975, leaving little doubt that, obstacles notwithstanding, women poets existed throughout much of Spanish history. Classic anthologies and bibliographies undoubtedly saved many women writers and works from total oblivion. But whether languishing forgotten in convent archives or clinging to marginal existence as out-of-print editions on obscure library shelves, writings by women typically found few readers and fewer exegetes. Furthermore, gender-specific studies may perpetuate women's exclusion from studies of the genre per se—usually specialized studies of men. Nor can gender-specific studies of women offset centuries of oppressive silence when women's achievements have been written off or written out of the history of literature, education and science. Jaworski paraphrases Dale Spender: "Probably the best indicator that the process of silencing women has been successful is that many women themselves do not perceive any kind of feminist tradition in their lives and work" (120).[10] Spanish women poets' ignorance regarding their predecessors thus exemplifies the prototypical situation of oppressed groups (racial and ethnic minorities, political opponents of tyrants and dictators, etc). Denying access to the media figures prominently among mechanisms of oppression, with censorship in Spain being one such mechanism. Women writers have also suffered extragovernmental oppression in social, cultural, and other forms.

Economic factors have aggravated the "invisibility" of Spanish women poets. Small potential markets make publishers reluctant to risk money on unknown poets (especially women) or to invest in large print runs, advertising, and promotion. A poet's being female simply compounds difficulties peculiar to the genre. Similar limitations affect secondary literature: aimed at bibliographers and specialists, the works of Parada y Barrero and Criado y Domínguez have themselves become bibliographic rarities. Works of Serrano y Sanz are almost equally rare, and Vidal's *Cien años,* printed 50 years ago, is long out of print.

Although the lyric enjoyed greater popularity in medieval times and Spain's Golden Age than today, poetry has essentially been a "minority" genre since the Renaissance. Because poetry frequently seems elitist or hermetic, "average" readers avoid it, as do many critics. Such disincentives, the silence concerning women writers, and women writers' exclusion from the phallocentric canon augment gender isolation or alienation, explaining contemporary women poets' unawareness of their foremothers and common poetic heritage. Despite changes in the post-Franco era, few women poets find their situations significantly improved today. Yet gender-specific studies during the last 100 years document continuing production by Iberian women poets since before the Christian era.

Chapter One

Buried Roots

Identifiable antecedents of today's women poets are as old as Sappho in the fourth century B.C. Angel and Kate Flores's Introduction to *The Defiant Muse* affirms that "on the Iberian Peninsula songs and poems by women date from the time it was a colony of the Roman Empire" (Flores and Flores 1986, xiv). The Floreses mention Pola Argentaria (contemporary of Martial), the poet and Stoic philosopher Teofila, and Serena; Ana Navarro gives essentially the same information. Women poets of Roman Hispania in the late empire obviously wrote in Latin and thus (like those writing in Arabic) are not, strictly speaking, Spanish women poets.

Clara Janés recalls the prominence of women poets in the courts of Provence—women who both wrote and protected troubadours. She indicates that 21 women are known to have written poetry in southern France from 1160 to 1250 (12), while coeval Spain had women poets in Andalusia writing in Arabic, among them al-Abbadiyya, Butayna, and Hafsa al-Rumaykiyya.[1] Poetry and song were "habitual activities" of Muslim women in Andalusia (Janés, 13). Several scholars believe that the *jarchas* (two or four lines in Hebrew or Spanish added to Arabic strophic poems) comprise the "most characteristic genre of the early European lyric in the vernacular: women's folk songs, which also include the German *Frauenlied,* the French *chanson de femmes,* the Castilian and Catalan *cantar de doncella,* and the Galician-Portuguese *cantiga d'amigo"* (Flores and Flores 1986, xv).

Significant recent contributions chronicling Spain's women poets have expanded historical horizons for Peninsular women's poetry. No fewer than four studies and anthologies of Hispano-Arabic women poets appeared between 1983 and 1989.[2] María Jesús Rubiera Mata's 1989 volume affirms that upper-class Hispano-Arabic women destined to veiled seclusion and cloistering escaped only if the family had no sons, or if they were the only daughters; some who avoided the harem and remained single include classic Hispano-Arabic poets Wallada-la Omeya and Hafsa ar-Rakunieyya (8). Poorer women and slaves enjoyed more "freedom," working as laundresses, prostitutes, hairdressers, singers, fortune-tellers, teachers, spinners and weavers, midwives, and go-betweens.

A few women earned fame practicing medicine in Córdoba in the ninth century; others were herbalists, blood-letters, or practitioners of similar remedies. "Wise women" were learned in the law or were scribes. Elementary education, apparently customary for upper-class women, included reading, writing, and studies of poetry and the Koran (daughters were educated at home, probably by women).

Cultural orality resulted in poetry's accessibility to the illiterate and blind, but even so, women's poetry was normally confined to the home or transmitted by male relatives (the two best-known classic Hispano-Arabic women poets were linked by marriage or kinship to male poets). Wallada was of royal blood, as were Butayna Bint 'Abbad (known beyond the harem only via capture and enslavement) and Umm al Kiram Bint Sumadih from Almería. Only one or two poems of each survives. Sometimes their poems were preserved via biographies of male peers (as with Nazhun Bint al Qa'i, facile improvisor of satiric verse in response to male poets' works).

Creation of amorous passion was an art, game, and cultural event in medieval Arabic society. Songs and poetry aided in seduction (later recording or celebrating it); thus *cantoras* (female singers) were carefully educated, often acquiring repertoires with hundreds of songs and poems. Cultured *hetairas* (usually captured Christians) were highly prized, with educations that included logic, philosophy, geometry, music, astronomy, grammar, prosody, literature, and calligraphy (15). The most valued accomplishment of *hetairas* was music, especially playing the lute, but the second most desired talent was poetry, with several being famed for their prowess.

In classic Arabic poetry (largely of Bedouin origin) authors' names were usually known, while popular poetry was anonymous, employing different meters. Typifying indigenous poetic genres was the popular *moaxaja* or *zéjel*, with which the *jarcha* is associated. These compositions ended with glosses of popular song or verse in local vulgar Arabic or regional Romance dialect, written in Arabic or Hebrew characters. Hence the *jarchas* were not deciphered and transcribed for centuries; discovery of their Romance language origins and relationship to the *cantigas d'amigo* belongs to the twentieth century. Themes, usually women's love songs, express the speaker's own desire. This form's ancient origins, traced back through the *albas* of Provence to archaic Greek, have remoter antecedents in the Mesopotamian cult of Ishtar/Astarte (forerunners of Venus/Aphrodite). Traces occur in Roman lyrics and rites of spring, and in medieval songs in Vulgar Latin.[3] Severely censured and vilified by the Church as diabolic, erotic, and obscene, these lyrics were deemed evil not only as vestiges of paganism but especially as expressions of feminine desire, proscribed by patriarchal Judeo-Christian traditions. The *moaxaja* inherited reputed shamelessness and obscenity. Daring language in the anonymous *jarchas* must be read in the context of homoerotic culture, wherein most *moaxajas* (i.e., the body of the poem preceding the final gloss) celebrate ephebes; the gloss, in the feminine voice, summons the lover back from the handsome adolescent's charms. Rubiera suggests that within Arabic courtly love lyrics, adopting feminine voice might indicate the (male) lover's final humiliation (23).[4]

The *cantigas* in Galician and Portuguese developed as women poets emerged in Provence during the twelfth century, flourishing in the thirteenth and fourteenth, before lyrics in Castilian. The genre's several variants included *cantigas de escarnio* (songs of invective and satire), *cantigas de Santa María* (songs to the Virgin Mary), *cantigas de amor* (men's love songs in troubadour style to an unattainable lady), and the *cantigas d'amigo,* sad plaints by female speakers, betrayed or abandoned. Logically, early literature in Catalan should likewise have included women poets. Catalan literature, like Galician, developed before Castilian, flourishing until the end of the fifteenth century. National unification under Ferdinand and Isabel (with the conquest of Granada in 1492) saw Castilian proclaimed the official national language with decline of the vernaculars and near demise of Galician. By this time, however, the lyric had begun to emerge in Castilian, along with the first known women writing in this language.

Florencia Pinar (contemporary of Ferdinand and Isabel) authored poems included in Hernando del Castillo's *Cancionero general;* an increasing number of poems now attributed to women are being culled from various *cancioneros* ("songbooks" or poetic anthologies of the Renaissance).[5] Antonio Rodríguez-Moñino's index of the *Cancionero general* identifies three poems by Florencia Pinar, one by Florencia, and 12 by Pinar, probably all by the same poet, suggesting unusual productivity and prominence in her day, since many *cancionero* authors are not known by name, and others are represented by fewer poems. Peter Broad stresses that Pinar is the *only* woman in the section of *poesía culta* (learned as opposed to popular poetry).[6] He considers Pinar skilled in manipulating conceits of the courtly love tradition without arid intellectualism yet capable of complex word play, intertextual allusion, and innovation. Pinar, deemed the "only truly personal feminine voice distinguishable in the *cancioneros*" (Pérez Priego, 20), exemplifies the century's amatory current, celebrating the idealized, distant, unattainable beloved; characteristic courtly poems constitute prolonged laments over rejection and belabor the topos of amorous suffering. Pinar's only theme is love, whether abstract, generic, universal, or courtly; she uses the first person, concrete detail, atypical realistic images, and strong sexual undertones. Her extensive play of concepts and artifice, repetition of homophones, and use of ellision, paronomasia, antitheses, and paradox anticipate aspects of the baroque. Navarro stresses Pinar's formal versatility, veiled eroticism, spontaneity, and baroque devices.

Improved general availability and awareness of early poetry in Castilian result from recent publication and cataloguing of manuscripts and codices of the fifteenth, sixteenth, and seventeenth centuries, together with hundreds of rare books and incunabula. Numerous editions by José J. Labrador Herraiz and Ralph DiFranco of *cancioneros* from the sixteenth century are expanding knowledge of little-known or partially explored primary sources, establishing links between "families" of manuscripts via annotations and descriptive articles.[7] In 1993 these investigators published *Tabla de los principios de la poesía española (XVI–XVII),* alphabetically listing more than 30,000 poems by first lines from 118 manuscript and printed sources. Their brief Introduction mentions the preponderant love theme, with variants including old-fashioned, angry, cruel, sweet, false, mad, perfect, youthful, unhappy, and true love (xvi). Other researchers have cataloged the content of fifteenth-century manuscripts and are doing an inventory of poetic manuscripts in Spain's National Library and Palace Library. Such listings seldom cite authors' names (excepting occasional single-author manuscripts) and do not distinguish on the basis of gender, but extant investigations indicate that women poets treated canonical themes.

During poetry's fifteenth-century flowering, few works are identifiably *by* women; most are *about* women. Much *cancionero* poetry was anonymous; other poems were attributed only to "Una Dama" (A Lady). The Flores anthology mentions Catalina Manrique and Marina Manuel from the *Cancionero general,* citing scholarly belief that certain lyrics "found in the *Cancioneros* were originally composed by women and attributed to the men who collected, refined, or glossed them" (Flores and Flores 1986, xv). The Flores critical anthology adds the names of Queen Ana, wife of Enrique II; "Vayona"; and Beatriz Galindo, who tutored Queen Isabel I (Flores and Flores 1984, 11–14). The anthology of women poets in the *cancioneros* for the Instituto de la Mujer adduces a dozen names and some 20 compositions of varying length. Besides the

Cancionero general, Miguel Angel Pérez Priego studies the *Cancionero musical de palacio,* the *Cancionero musical de la Colombina,* and *Cancionero de Upsala,* affirming that these four "songbooks" demonstrate the presence of women poets throughout the fifteenth century and their activity in all major centers of poetic creativity in the Renaissance courts of Enrique III, Juan II, Leonor de Navarra, Enrique IV, and Isabel I. The more recent anthology by Luzmaría Jiménez Faro mentions another fifteenth-century woman poet, María Sarmiento, who in 1428 founded the Hospital de Santiago in Vitora, together with her husband, Hernán Pérez de Ayala; some of her *octavas* survive (cited briefly by Pérez Priego). Frequent feminine contributors to the *cancioneros* included the queens' ladies, "poets of circumstance," commemorating weddings, christenings, jousts, and celebrations. Pérez Priego singles out Doña Mayor Arias with her lament for her husband's departure to Samarkand and the court of Tamerlane.

Love's variants constitute the dominant topos of the *cancioneros;* other traditional themes include work songs, May songs, drinking songs, soldiering songs, elegies, and songs of pilgrimages, welcome, religious celebrations, and weddings. Amorous notes dominate, with the enamored maiden's voice frequently heard (Pérez Priego, 27). Citing studies by Leo Spitzer and P. Dronke, Pérez Priego affirms (in accord with Navarro and Gangutia) that the feminine love song underlies all universal folk poetry, as documented by examination of ancient songs of Russia and Scandinavia, ancient China and Egypt, grafitti in Pompeii and North African lyrics. Late-fifteenth-century *cantares* and *villancicos* (popular counterparts of the *cantigas d'amigo)* revolve around personal feelings of love, desire, absence, lament, and joy. Dialogue, repetition, *estribillos* (tag lines), and parallelistic constructions were popular features, as were glosses and *romances* (ballads)—popular forms used in feminine love songs.

Navarro's anthology of sixteenth- and seventeenth-century women poets, sponsored by the Ministry of Culture's Institute of Women, provides 39 names of Golden Age women known to have written poetry (Janés's anthology represents 41 from these centuries, not entirely duplicating Navarro). Downplaying the poetic significance of Santa Teresa, to whom some 40 poems are attributed, Navarro affirms that Teresa's lyrics lack the vigor and accessibility of her prose. She praises Sor María de la Antigua, an illiterate lay sister who dictated "more than 1,300 notebooks," including numerous poems in the ascetic vein. Navarro emphasizes Luisa de Carvajal y Mendoza (1566–1614), religious reformer who refused both marriage and the alternative of the nunnery, proselytizing for the Catholic Church in England where, despite being jailed, she founded a religious community. Among the seventeenth century's best women poets of religious passion, Carvajal is singled out by Julián Olivares and Elizabeth S. Boyce for her depictions of mystic encounters. Another religious activist, Sor Jerónima de la Asunción (1555–1630) from the Convent of Clarisas in Toledo, founded a convent in Manila as well as cultivating religious poetry. "Spiritual daughters" of Santa Teresa include Sor Luisa de la Ascensión (1565–1636)—ecstatic, visionary, and polemical—and Sor Isabel de Jesús, author of spiritual poems. The Flores and Flores anthology emphasizes Catalina de Erauso (1592–1625), the tempestuous "Monja Alférez" (Nun Sergeant) who dressed in male garb and participated in New World exploration and conquest (1984, 15). Jiménez Faro notes sixteenth-century contributions of Luisa Sigea (b. ca. 1530 in Toledo), anticipating techniques of Quevedo; Sor María San José (b. 1548), disciple of Santa Teresa; Sor María de la Antigua (b. ca. 1540s in Cazalla de la Sierra, Seville); Sor Hipólita de Jesús Rocaberti (b. in Barcelona 1549), a Dominican nun; Sor Ana de San Bartolomé (b. 1549 in Avila); Sor Jerónima de la Asunción (b. 1555 in Toledo), who entered the Convent of Santa Isabel; and Cayetana Ossorio, who wrote *Huerto del celestial esposo* (Garden of the Heavenly Spouse) and an exposition of Psalms following the Cistercian breviary.

Sor Marcela de San Félix (1605–87), the illegitimate daughter of Lope de Vega and likewise a poet, dramatist, and religious, reportedly composed some five volumes, including an autobiography. Everything except her poetry was burned at her confessor's direction. Sor Marcela's poems depict the serene convent garden, cloistered solitude, Church festivals, meditations, and other aspects of convent life such as theatrical performances, both sacred and profane. Her *Poesías místicas* (Mystic Poems), preserved in the convent of Trinitarian Nuns in Madrid, treat specifically religious themes: worldly appetites, death, the Nativity, and sacraments. The Electa Arenal and Georgina Sabat de Rivers introduction to Sor Marcela's works stresses that women's independence and originality were tolerated at best but never encouraged.[8] Sor Marcela considers problems of illegitimacy and self-legitimation (causes of personal suffering, perhaps explaining her professing as a nun at 16). She adapts ascetic traditions to express both autonomy and sublimated sensuality. Her dramatic poetry upholds asceticism, mortification, and self-discipline as means of overcoming carnal appetites and selfish desires. Besides Sor

Juana, Navarro privileges the "late mystic" Sor Gregoria de Santa Teresa (d. 1736) and Sor María do Ceu as final representatives of seventeenth-century religious poetry.

The second lyric current in women's poetry of the Golden Age, the worldly or profane lyric, has courtly and Italianate veins. Poetic contests included such feminine participants as "Lucinda Serrana," Isabel de Figueroa, and Clara de Barrionuevo. "Devotion to the throne" informs works inspired by births, deaths, weddings, journeys, and other royal family events; frequent elegies commemorated deaths of prominent figures. Such compositions, lacking real personal emotion, are "poetry of circumstance," composed largely of word play and twisted conceits. Another thematic nucleus consists of religious solemnities (unlike religious poetry per se, these poems treat ceremonies and pageantry, beatification, canonization, or acquisition of sacred relics).

Many Golden Age women poets used pseudonyms of classic origin (not all authors' identities have been established). Among names singled out by Navarro, Cristobalina Fernández de Alarcón, the "Muse of Antequera," was famed for her prodigious facility of versification, freshness of form, and beautiful baroque imagery, resulting in luminous, brilliant poems revealing secret and profound sentiments. Jiménez Faro terms Alarcón exceptionally well-educated, and a relatively abundant poetic corpus survives. Writing of platonic courtly loves, she used conceits, puns, word play, and baroque rhetoric and techniques. Some of her amorous verse, however, apparently expresses real passion. Epigones of Góngora include Ana Ataide, Sor María Sallent, and Gregoria Francisca de Salazar; Catalina Clara de Guzmán represents *culteranismo* in Catalunya (Navarro, 54).

Pseudonymous secular poetry written by nuns is exemplified by Sor María de Santa Isabel, who cultivated both religious and sentimental themes, the latter as "Marcia Belisarda" (her descriptions of mystic encounters are praised by Olivares and Boyce, who likewise cite works in this category by Sor María de la Antigua, Sor Marcela de San Félix, Sor Violante del Cielo [or do Ceu] and Ana Francisca Abarca de Bolea [61]). Marcia Belisarda's 138 secular poems, notable for their metric virtuosity (exhibiting classic and popular forms from ballads and folk songs to Gongorist sonnets and more exotic verse), use bold language; others express nostalgia and melancholy. Fusion of popular with cultured forms and themes appears in the works of Ana Abarca de Bolea, abbess of Casbas (seventeenth century). Outstanding technical mastery and varied themes render her an exemplar of baroque poetry, incorporating mythological, historical, religious, and cultural allusions and themes of the *culteranistas*, descriptive and narrative ballads.

What Navarro terms "nature poetry" or poetry of "botanic" inspiration (celebrating the beauty and variety of flowers) formed yet another thematic nucleus, typified by Leonor de la Cueva y Silva. Many women cultivated satiric poetry, notably Francisca Paez de Colindres. But poetic fortunes and results varied: Ana Caro Mallén—celebrated for her theater—proved less successful poetically. Friend of María de Zayas (who collected both their works), Caro wrote *Décimas y sonetos en loor de doña María* (Poems in Praise of Lady María [presumably Zayas]). María de Zayas, the period's best-known woman writer after Santa Teresa, sprinkled poems throughout her novellas, as did Mariana de Carvajal. Jiménez Faro terms Antonia de Mendoza, countess of Benavente (d. 1656), a "magnificent poet" and emphasizes Catalina Clara de Guzmán, of Zafra, whose poems mention various sisters (and one canto celebrates the charms of her brother Pedro). Guzmán cultivated *romances* on the themes of nature, winter, fountains, and courtly love. An unsuccessful poetic venture cited by Navarro is Bernarda Ferreira de la Cerda's rhymed epic, *La España libertada* (Spain Liberated), which begins with the Arabic invasion and details the Reconquest—not typical "women's poetry." Also attributed to Ferreira are two chivalric novels, *Palmerín de Oliva* and *Primaleón,* and several plays.

The most extensive study and anthology of women's poetry in Spain's Golden Age to date is *Tras el espejo la musa escribe: Lírica femenina de los siglos de oro,* edited by Julián Olivares and Elizabeth S. Boyce. Women writing in the sixteenth and seventeenth centuries were inevitably influenced not only by male poets, the editors note, but also by pastoral novels and books of chivalry. Coeval literature, imbued with codes and conventions of courtly love, used more or less exclusively the male voice with all but the pastoral mode. Essentially lacking models other than the masculine, women writers could imitate male discourse, adopt and adapt it, or subvert it. Various sociocultural factors may explain the relative dearth of female voices: (1) access to universities was all but nonexistent (Salamanca opened its doors briefly to women in the sixteenth century but soon closed them again); (2) education made daughters harder to marry; (3) scorn and satire targeted the erudite woman "who studied Latin";[9] (4) women's silence was equated with modesty, chastity, and virtue, while speaking out (or writing, and especially publishing—the masculine domain) sufficed to class one as a "public woman"; and (5) moralists inveighed against women's reading.[10]

These authors concur that convents—paradoxically—offered women more freedom than lay life. With convents the only socially acceptable alternative to marriage, women lacking any religious zeal fled masculine "protection" to study or pursue literary and artistic aspirations. Others (orphans abandoned at birth) were raised in convents; illegitimate daughters were often interned in infancy, while others, unmarriageable by reason of illegitimacy, chose to make the convent their home. Nonconforming females of any age might be interned against their will. Electa Arenal and Stacey Schlau state that convents became prisons for the "dishonored" or "disobedient" and sanctuaries for the studious, who had little access to higher education (3). Women remaining in the world legally belonged to men, with no possessions of their own, while autonomy and self-development were possible in the convents, even though fanatical and ignorant clerics considered women's "meddling in philosophical profundities" dangerous and inappropriate: "No institution in Europe has ever won for the lady the freedom of development that she enjoyed in the convent."[11] Thus convent populations grew disproportionately large and often had waiting lists. Royal convents provided considerable luxury and freedom for noble women; Santa Teresa directed her reforming zeal against this situation. Conversely, women reared "in the world" frequently suffered gender inferiority complexes. But while women wrote largely in convents, religious demands obviously conflicted with literary growth (or devotion to literature conflicted with devotion to God). Artistic expression, except as testimony of faith, was censured, and superiors silenced, destroyed, or prohibited writings for religious reasons. Yet convent archives now offer the best source for reconstructing these women's history.

Nun poets treated by Arenal and Schlau (all Carmelites) include María de San José, whose poetry exudes a distinctly masochistic air: "I long to suffer endlessly / for I delight in torment / . . . / because there is delight in anguish" (44). Another Teresa among the saint's spiritual daughters (see "Another Teresa" in Arenal and Schlau, 112–17) and sisters María and Cecilia Sobrino Morillas (María de San Alberto and Cecilia del Nacimiento [131–67]) likewise composed poetry; only Cecilia enjoyed literary recognition, and, ironically, part of her work was long attributed to San Juan de la Cruz, because her heightened sensuality, playfulness, and familiarity with rhetorical devices led critics to conclude the author was a man (143–44). Cecilia's more conventional ascetic verse praises solitude, contemplation, and transformation.

Conflicts notwithstanding, many nuns achieved modest renown as poets. Although Marianist poems might seem logical vehicles for

women's religious poetry, especially after seventeenth-century stimulus
to the cult of the Virgin, Marianist verse proved less common than
poems to or about Christ, and poetry celebrating the Nativity and
Eucharist. Many nuns described mystic encounters employing nuptial
and erotic imagery, and some penned profane love lyrics (the most
famous example, Mexican Sor Juana Inés de la Cruz, overshadows
Marcia Belisarda and Sor Marcela de San Félix). Women poets adapted
courtly love conventions to voice desire for intellectual freedom, fame,
autonomy, and escape from male domination. Olivares and Boyce
explain that women writers encountered discourse conventions dominated by the masculine voice, and recognizing the need to "feminize" their
writing, they adapted as models religious poems by males expressing
humility, abnegation, and contrition, or the erotic discourse employed by
mystic writers (Marcela de San Félix is one example; cf. Arenal and
Schlau, 239–43). By contrast, burlesque uses of the courtly lyric to criticize male shortcomings used masculine voice to rhapsodize on passionate love of food, for example. Traditional *querellas femeninas* required no
adaptations; these criticized the social status of women and censured
masculine behavior toward women (especially inconstancy, traditionally
associated with the female). Burlesque verse, a minor genre for male
poets, provided a major vehicle for women.

Early women poets in Castilian employed strategies still used by
today's women poets (as attested to by several interviews in Ugalde),[12]
with language that is largely gender-neutral, both in terms of speaker
and recipient, and constructions without gender-specific pronouns,
adjectives, images, or other referents. Women poets resort to "cross-gender writing," wherein female speakers deliberately elect masculine voice,
either ironically or to feign acceptable gender roles and observe poetic
decorum in treating taboo topics (sexual desire, desire for power, or intellectual pursuits). Some women poets use pseudo-masculine narrators or
commentators, manipulating masculine perspectives to imply approba-
tion for women or praise for themselves. Intertextuality and male interlocutors (via replies to masculine poems) provide other strategies.
Subverting reader expectations—via parodic inversion of standard outcomes for the form employed, self-mockery, or ironic burlesque—constitutes yet another option.

Olivares and Boyce identify conventions or situations that allowed
women to speak: alerting other women (e.g., daughters) of dangers
posed by men, "confessing" to mothers or confidantes, and the satirico-
burlesque tradition. Pastoral works exhibited some "equality of gender"

in speech, with women experiencing liberation from established social codes when assuming shepherdess roles. Certain stereotypes—including the *mujer varonil* (a "tomboyish" woman, usually rejecting marriage), *la bella cazadora* (modeled on the chaste huntress, Diana), and the Amazon—likewise facilitated women's linguistic access. Sometimes, especially daring material assumes the guise of dreams. Cruz and Whitnall postulate a distinctive diction traditionally associated with the female—for instance, complaints against men directed to the mother, expressions of disenchantment or rejection.[13]

Women poets working in the Basque language (Vascuence or Euskera) are a case apart. Euskera, the language of some three million Basques in northern Spain and southern France (mainly in the Pyrenees), remained an oral medium until almost the present day. Ibon Sarasola in his post-Franco history of Basque literature affirms that no literary content exists in works in Euskera before the twentieth century, since most texts were religious—written by priests—or else folkloric.[14] Ecclesiastical monopoly of written works in Euskera from feudal times until the present resulted from near total illiteracy in the Basque area, intensifying the cultural marginalization of women and impeding their intellectual development. Thus a recent scholar notes that Basque poetry per se (including that by male authors) is "a literary form unknown in the Hispanic ambient"[15] and largely a byproduct of Romanticism. The sociopolitical and religious situation of Basque women was especially deplorable given the fanaticism and intolerance characterizing Basque Catholicism. Few Basque women's names are associated with literature before this century, and most wrote in French or Spanish.

Since the late Middle Ages, most Basques have been necessarily bilingual, and Julia Otxoa in her pioneering anthology of Basque women poets defines Basque literature to include works by Basques in Castilian (12), arguing that common cultural factors weigh more than the language of expression. Otxoa notes the presence of texts in Euskera in the tenth-century monastic codex, *Glosas Emilianenses,* and the appearance in 1545 of the first book written in Basque, but she stresses oral tradition: myths, legends, funeral laments, couplets, tales, ballads, proverbs, lullabies, and other songs and poems. Traditional *bertsolarismo* (spontaneous improvisation) dates from the Middle Ages: it is an art in which Basque women were elegiac poets par excellence. Women elegists of the Renaissance cited by Otxoa include Sancha Ochoa de Ozaeta, Emilia de Lastur, Usua de la Torre de Alós, and Gabriela Lohitegui. In the late eighteenth century Sor María Luisa (a nun) gained fame for her Basque religious songs; in the nineteenth century Rosario Artola was celebrated as a *bertsolari* (improvisational versifier), together with lesser contemporaries Cristina Mardaraz and Arantxa Loidi.

Archaic Basque poetry had little in common with early Castilian verse (epics, ballads, and elegies), exhibiting more similarities to Old French lyrics (16). Otxoa includes as Basque writers three illustrious women from the fifteenth- and sixteenth-century courts of Navarre: Marguerite de Navarre and her daughter Juana de Labrit and granddaughter Marguerite de Valois, cultivated women who wrote in French, defended women's rights, and fomented vernacular culture. Otxoa also claims Basque ancestry for Sor Juana Inés de la Cruz (23), citing her poetry to Vizcaya (neither Sor Juana's culture nor her language were Basque). Female illiteracy in the seventeenth and eighteenth centuries was 96 percent in Vizcaya, compared to 80 percent in the general population (Otxoa, 25). Nor did eventual establishment of schools open cultural doors to women: "schools were opened, but not minds" (Otxoa, 25).

Spain's eighteenth century has traditionally been considered a plunge to cultural depths following heights achieved during the Golden Age (1545–1681), a cliché that contemporary criticism is now reevaluating. Literary quality and quantity undeniably diminish, however, both in the male canon and writings by women, becoming more prosaic and essayistic than otherwise. Josefa Amar y Borbón (1753–1803) wrote an important study on women's education and the significant *Discurso en defensa del talento de las mujeres, y de aptitud para el gobierno y otros cargos en que se emplean hombres* (Defense of Women's Talent and Aptitude for Government and Other Posts Held by Men).

María Gertrudis de Hore y Ley (1742–1801), famed as "la hija del Sol" (daughter of the Sun) for her beauty and intelligence, was born to Irish parents in Cádiz. Married at 20, she lived thereafter in Madrid's high society, later seeking and receiving permission from her husband (1779) to enter the convent. She took the veil at Saint Mary's in Cádiz (Fernán Caballero's explanation alleges a secret lover's murder as the cause). Her poetry, composed during two decades prior to entering the convent, was preserved by her bishop when Hore wanted to burn it. Jiménez Faro states that shortly after entering the convent, Hore left for the New World. Hore's poetry expresses baroque *desengaño* (disillusionment), primarily in the lines "Nada en el mundo dura / todo lo acaba el tiempo" (cited by Jiménez Faro, 59; "Nothing in this world lasts / Everything is finished by time"). Vanities rejected include worldly pleasure, concerts, theater, dances, and parties. Hore's manuscripts are preserved in the

Biblioteca Nacional; some poems were printed by Manuel Serrano y Sanz, and others appeared in 1875 in *Poesía lírica del siglo XVIII,* edited by Leopoldo Augusto de Cueto. When canonical male representatives of the period were still unknown, Hore's poetry was widely imitated, especially her Anacreontic verse. She also favored the sonnet, hendecasyllables, and *endechas* (short lyric dirges), writing works full of melancholy and love of nature. Concern and compassion for animals and criticism of human cruelty appear alongside pre-Romantic depictions of gloomy ruins, crumbling cemeteries, and nightscapes. Other poems describe life in Madrid, her son's death during an epidemic, and her decision to enter a convent.

Margarita Hickey Pellizzoni (1757–93), born in Barcelona of Irish/Italian ancestry (her father was an army officer from Dublin; her mother was a Milan opera singer), became a defender of women, a poet, and a translator of French classical theater. Married early to an elderly nobleman from Navarre and widowed at 26, the talented beauty never remarried, opting instead (ca. 1779) for literature and research in geography. Her *Poesías varias sagradas, morales y profanas o amorosas* (1789; Sacred, Moral, and Profane or Amorous Poems) contain autobiographical substrata and protests against unjust treatment of women. Often critical of the opposite sex, she portrays men in acerbic tones, using such adjectives as ignorant, stupid, and clumsy. Hickey believed women were capable of better work than men in the arts and sciences (for which she was deemed eccentric) and affirmed in one poem that women daily and hourly "outstrip men in the arts and sciences / If they apply themselves to studying" (Jiménez Faro, 57). Yet she also composed love poetry, and her sonnet defining love exemplifies baroque polarities and paradoxes, hyperbaton (the deliberate disruption of normal word order), and skillful rhetorical manipulation. Significantly, she wrote that "el alma, como espíritu / carece de sexo" ("The soul, being spirit / has no sex"). Her favorite metric forms include *endechas,* sonnets, and ballads. Her beautiful love sonnets contrast with treatment of divine love and compositions treating the "war of the sexes" and men's shortcomings. Epic poems praising military heroes and some translations from Racine and Voltaire were published in the same volume (with the pseudonym "Antonia Hernanda de la Oliva," due to personal, confessional content in some poems). Hickey's lyric accomplishments hold only limited historical interest, but her views on the feminine condition merit contemporary attention.

María Isidra Quintina de Guzmán (1768–1803), allegedly the first woman to earn a doctorate at the University of Alcalá de Henares (at 17,

in 1785), was sponsored by King Carlos III. Her controversial election to
the Real Academia Española in 1784, seen as royal favoritism, was hotly
contested. Guzmán married the Marquis de Guadalcázar in 1789 and
bore three children, but she also authored treatises on the Aristotelian
system. She was named honorary professor of modern philosophy at the
University of Alcalá, dying of tuberculosis at 35. Her poetic works
reflect strong classical influences.

María Rosa Gálvez (1768–1806) produced *Obras poéticas* (1804; Poetic
Works), predominantly neoclassical theater, anticipating aspects of
Romanticism. María de las Mercedes Gómez Castro defended women's
talent, although her work was censored. Other women poets of the eigh-
teenth century noted by Jiménez Faro include Joaquina Tomaseti de
Aranda, a Cádiz-born poet of circumstance, and María Nicolasa de
Helguero, who was born in Palencia and married the Marqués de San
Isidro. Widowed, she entered the convent of Huelgas, where her aunt
had been abbess. Helguero wrote elegies, including octaves to a brother
killed in battle against the Algerians. Repression of women's voices continued throughout the eighteenth century (Flores and Flores 1984, 20).
Although eighteenth-century women writers were primarily poets, they
were neither numerous nor prolific. As with canonical male writers, a
clear hiatus exists between the Golden Age and Romanticism.

Chapter Two
The Nineteenth Century

In the Introduction to *Las Románticas*, Susan Kirkpatrick identifies 1841 as the date when Spanish women "began to make themselves heard" (1), initiating an ongoing tradition of women's writing in Spain.[1] Actually, Vicenta Maturana de Gutiérrez (1793–1857), the best-known woman writer during the reign of Fernando VII, began publishing nearly two decades earlier, first an anonymous novel (1825), then a signed one four years later. Her poetry collections include *Ensayos poéticos* (1828; Essays in Poetry), containing pastoral odes, sonnets, and a variety of traditional forms, and *Himno a la luna: Poema en cuatro cantos* (1838; Hymn to the Moon: Poem in Four Cantos). The latter, a long prose poem, is considered one of the earliest appearances of that genre in Spain, and it clearly anticipates Romanticism in its emphasis on emotions and impressions. Her loyalty to Fernando VII was such that following his death in 1833 she went into exile in France, where *Himno a la luna* was published, as well as *Poesías de la señora doña Vicenta Maturana de Gutiérrez* (1841), the most nearly complete edition of her poems.

Carolina Coronado's first poems appeared in Madrid in 1839, her first collection in 1843. In 1840, after the first Carlist war, major Romantic poetic works appeared, including Espronceda's *Poesías; El diablo mundo* and works by Zorrilla and Rivas appeared in 1841, plus the Catalan *Poesias* of Maria Josepa Massanés and the *Poesías* of Gertrudis Gómez de Avellaneda (omitted from some Spanish literary histories owing to her birth in Cuba—controlled by Spain until 1898). The 1840s—the height of Peninsular Romanticism and propitious for liberal reforms—witnessed establishment of the Madrid Ateneo and Liceo Artístico y Literario.[2] Spanish women began writing for the press, reading French and Spanish Romantic writers, including Mme de Staël and Georges Sand (Kirkpatrick, 34–35). Poetry, lyric or dramatic, was Romanticism's dominant mode and the most prestigious genre until the novel's definitive triumph in the 1870s. Cultural acclaim accorded celebrated women poets belied their political and legal disempowerment.

In the 1840s Spanish women lacked civic or judicial equality: married women could not undertake contracts or legal action without spousal

15

permission, and upon marriage they relinquished control of any proper-
ty. Lacking the vote, they were political nonentities (women in Spain
were legally perpetual minors, wards of their husbands, until post-
Franco constitutional reforms). Romanticism's exaltation of individual
rights, prior gains in the Enlightenment, and advancement through rev-
olutionary process would not filter down to Spanish women's daily lives
until well into the twentieth century.

Although Spain experienced new ways of thinking, new concepts of
the self, and new kinds of subjectivity, no feminist movement per se
existed there during the nineteenth century (despite advocacy by
Concepción Arenal and Emilia Pardo Bazán near the century's end);
general schooling for girls was nonexistent, and even Queen Isabel II
learned only "adornments," including music and dancing. According to
María del Carmen Simón Palmer, "Spanish women writers had no
choice but to educate themselves, reading whatever they could get their
hands on."[3] The wealthy and convent-educated learned domestic skills
and social graces along with religious training; others studied rudiments
at home with their mothers, similarly educated. Elena Catena affirms
that 90 percent of Spaniards were illiterate in the 1840s (15).
Nineteenth-century Spain's best-known women writers (excepting
Pardo Bazán) were middle-class provincials who lived under economic
and emotional hardship and traveled little.

Patriarchal ideologies confining women within the home postulated
domestic ambients of loving tranquility, self-abnegating devotion, and
gentleness and nurturing, not favoring female intellectual activity.
Departures from traditional gender roles invited censure for immorality
and "unfeminine" activity; aspiring women poets faced hostile literary
and social traditions, cultural environments adverse to women writers
and intellectuals, even Romanticism's concept of the (male) poet.
Necessarily writing largely for masculine readers imbued with conservative patriarchal values, women writers often used masculine pseudonyms, maintaining low profiles. Most women included in the 1992
Antología poética de escritoras del siglo XIX cultivated other genres but also
wrote some poetry.[4] Women writers' common enemy (traditional censure of women's writing) produced special kinships. Several expressed
particular devotion to the Virgin Mary, not as saint but as a woman
who had (like many of them) suffered the death of a child; Mary thus
acquired traits of the muse for women poets.

Carolina Coronado

Slightly younger than Massanés or Avellaneda, Carolina Coronado received prior attention for her poetry. Born in the Extremaduran village of Almendralejo to a petit bourgeois family of vineyard owners near the provincial capital of Badajoz, Coronado lived to almost 90. Valis gives Coronado's dates as 1820–1911; standard sources give her birth date as 12 December 1823, echoing the 1850 biographical sketch by Angel Fernández de los Ríos that Valis reproduces.[5] Valis (51n1) and Fernando Manso Amarillo (15–17) note that Coronado's baptismal certificate is dated 1820 (Manso reproduces the handwritten document). Manso mentions three sisters and four brothers (13). Nonagenarian Coronado witnessed Romanticism, its passing, and that of her own fame, as well as the triumph of realism, naturalism, modernism, and the Generation of 1898. Tutored at home, she wrote retrospectively in 1909, "All I really studied were the sciences of needlepoint and Extremaduran lace-work, which can be at least as complex as the Latin legal code."[6] Actually, Coronado was autodidactic, learning French and Italian on her own; Juan Eugenio Hartzenbusch's prologue to her first poetry collection indicates she read everything that she could find or borrow, struggling to memorize the book so she would not need it again.[7] Coronado learned to speak English and Portuguese, and biographer Pérez González terms her a virtuoso of the piano and harp (22), a claim reaffirmed by Jiménez Faro.

Individual accomplishments notwithstanding, the brevity of women's education posed serious obstacles for female would-be writers unacquainted with classical rhetoric and poetics. Coronado lamented familial restrictions on reading and her unfamiliarity with Spanish versification. The widespread, popular stereotype of *el ángel del hogar* (the angel in the house) was premised upon denial of female intellect and sexuality.[8] This feminine paradigm—maternally loving but otherwise passionless, essentially irrational but deficient in reason—needed little education. Coronado recalls family prohibitions of further study and provincial ridicule of women's presumption in daring to write.

Coronado began publishing within this oppressive environment when (assuming 10 percent of the Spanish population was literate) only a fraction of potential readers were women.[9] Writing strictly for women would reduce the market to perhaps 2 or 3 percent of the population.

Present theories of implied readership suggest a sociological imperative to include male readers or write for a mere handful. After "A la palma" (To the Palm Tree) appeared in Donoso Cortés's Madrid periodical, *El Piloto,* in December 1839, Coronado published her best-known work in newspapers (collected as *Poesías* in 1843). Her poetry belongs mostly to the 1840s; she wrote poems only sporadically between her marriage in 1852 and her death. She published her first poem when allegedly only 16 (based on the traditional birth date). Lauded by famed Romantic Espronceda, she was collaborating in Latin American newspapers within four years. But publishing books was not easy; nearly a decade elapsed before her second collection, and—excepting María del Pilar Sinués (1835–93), the first writer of sentimental feminine *romances*—few Spanish women lived by writing before the twentieth century.

In 1852 Coronado married American diplomat Horace Perry, then secretary of the U.S. legation in Madrid, thereafter maintaining a fashionable Madrid salon. Manso indicates that the pair had an Anglican wedding in Gibraltar and a Catholic ceremony in Paris. Coronado, moderately conservative politically, enjoyed cordial relations with Queen Isabel II. More progressive regarding women and children's rights, Coronado also opposed intolerance and religious fanaticism and offered asylum to participants in a failed revolution (1866). Furthermore, she took part (with feminist Concepción Arenal) in anti-slavery campaigns of the Madrid Abolitionist Society, headed by Gómez de Avellaneda. Coronado's grandfather, a distinguished liberal politician, died during persecution by absolutists under Fernando VII (Pérez González, 19).[10] Her father, imprisoned for his political ties, suffered under the same regime (Torres, 9). During the first Carlist war (1838) Coronado sewed the flag for a batallion defending Isabel II's right to the throne (Pérez González, 36). Her defense of women, the intellectual sisterhood of women writers, and the rights of wives and children springs equally from the Romantic movement and her family's liberal tradition.

Coronado usually receives short shrift as a minor Romantic poet, transitional figure from Romanticism to realism, or civic poet (she also wrote several moderately successful novels, unsuccessful theatrical works, and miscellaneous essays).[11] Along with José Zorrilla, García Gutiérrez, Gertrudis Gómez de Avellaneda, Enrique Gil y Carrasco, and Ramón de Campoamor, she exhibits a less combative Romanticism than Rivas, Martínez de la Rosa, and Espronceda. Intimate, Arcadian thematics anticipate post-Romantics Gustavo Adolfo Bécquer and Rosalía de Castro. Coronado's most important poetry springs from an eclectic background, comprising neoclassical heritage and Romantic ambience.[12] Classic influences include the mystics, San Juan de la Cruz, Santa Teresa, and Fray Luis de León (cf. her erotico-religious language).

Traditional criticism emphasizes Coronado's poetry of nature and flowers, conventionally "feminine" motifs seen in early titles such as "A las nubes" (To the Clouds), "Al otoño" (To Autumn), "A una estrella" (To a Star), and "A una gota de rocío" (To a Dewdrop). Botanical motifs include "A la amapola" (To a Poppy) and poems to the jasmine, sunflower, lily, rose, and sedum. Coronado celebrates birds, meadows, and other idyllic motifs. Neoclassic pastoral tradition allowed her to expand poetic space beyond household confines without directly challenging contemporary standards of femininity (Kirkpatrick, 213). Her repetitive resurrection motif originated in 1844, when she was erroneously declared dead after an attack of catalepsy (Valis, 7), a disease associated with mental disorders. She suffered several cataleptic seizures; social acquaintances described her as nervous, bizarre, lachrymose, hysterical, superstitious, and given to visions and fetishes (Valis, 22–23). Personal tragedies exacerbated her emotional disturbance: after her infant son died in 1854 and her 16-year-old daughter in 1873, the family retired to Perry's mansion in Lisbon.

Notwithstanding idyllic motifs and the pathetic fallacy, one critic believes Coronado attempts to transcend Romanticism, bridging the gap between poets of the 1850s and those afterwards (like Campoamor).[13] Both use less rhetorical language; Coronado avoids the trivial reality and quotidian discourse of Campoamor. Navas Ruiz praises her spontaneity and simplicity, noting influences of the Bible and Espronceda;[14] Vicente Llorens stresses her internal struggle, preferring her religious poetry.[15] Gerardo Diego considers her a "responsible" poet who celebrated progress and was deeply concerned with politics, defying pigeonholing.[16]

Diego's insight is significant, for Coronado is often dismissed as bland, girlish, and simplistic, yet she was socially active, collaborating in decidedly feminist 1840s periodicals. Liliana Trevizan discusses Coronado's overtly adaptive but covertly conflictive relationship with the patriarchally delimited canon.[17] Trevizan contrasts militant or consciously feminist poems and Coronado's solidarity with other women poets with compositions illustrating Coronado's need for masculine patronage. Some of her attitudes still appear modern—for instance, feminist pacifism in "Sobre la guerra" (1845; On War)[18] and protest in "A Claudia" (1846), which rejects women's reification and marginalization. The sonnet "A la abolición de la esclavitud en Cuba" (1869; To Abolishing

Slavery in Cuba) shows Coronado's liberalism; Ramón Gómez de la Serna included it in his sensationalistic biography *Mi tía Carolina Coronado* (1942; My Aunt Carolina), stressing deathlike epileptic trances, manias, phobias, and Coronado's keeping Perry's embalmed body unburied for 20 years.

Manso's rhetorical analysis of Coronado's poetry identifies zoological and botanical images and those designating natural phenomena and elements, artificial objects, trades and supernatural beings. Other sections focus upon metrics, synesthesia, adjectivation, and hyperbatons. Coronado preferred standard Spanish metrics and versification, often *arte menor* (lines of two to eight syllables): tetrasyllables, pentasyllables, heptasyllables, hendecasyllables, and octosyllables. Her predominant strophes were quartets, followed by *redondillas,* sometimes in the same composition. She avoided tercets, using few five-line verses except the *lira,* and favored the *romance* (ballads), leaving 15 sonnets plus more than 50 *octavas italianas,* which were popular with Romantics.

Critics usually divide Coronado's poetry into three periods: youthful works written before 1843, those from 1843 to 1852 (the largest group), and works from 1852 until her death. The first and last groups are smaller and more homogeneous, with the former comprising juvenilia whose common denominators are nature and Romantic motifs and the later oft-mentioned civic compositions. Her apprenticeship poems establish similarities between the lyric self and nature (a ruse permitting the expression of prohibited sentiments while avoiding direct challenge to dominant gender ideologies). Coronado's best, most mature pieces from the second period continue with introspective Romantic themes and add nostalgia and historical themes; she wrote a number of feminist, satiric, political, and social poems during this period. Circumstantial pieces commemorate such events as a railroad inauguration and the first dirigible flight (in 1844). More imaginative compositions address legends, fantasy episodes, religious topics (miracles by the Virgin), ancient and modern kings and heroes, and fellow poets. Love poetry and philosophical meditations were also significant themes.

The Alberto cycle sparked polemics as to whether Alberto was real or simply a poetic pretext. These approximately two dozen pieces (dated 1845–49 in Badajoz and Elvas) recount an implied narrative from discovery of the beloved through love's development, to separation, the sorrow of absence, the significance of the beloved's portrait, and emotional letter-writing. Ultimately the poetic persona hears of Alberto's death at sea. Another less unified group of poems portrays the poet's relationship with her youngest brother, Emilio.

The majority of Coronado's poems are feminine; the minority are feminist. Kirkpatrick notes that "Coronado's lyrical voice is coded much more explicitly [than Avellaneda's] as feminine according to cultural gender conventions" (209). Coronado usually wrote and behaved as patriarchal society demanded, accepting traditional definitions of lady-like behavior, renouncing preeminence, avoiding passion, and suppressing ambition, rage, and violence. But "El Marido verdugo" (The Executioner-Husband), treating wife abuse, depicts male brutality and the lacerated, bleeding wife in sarcastic, scornful tones. Defending victimized women, Coronado abandons pseudo-conformity for open indignation. Kirkpatrick observes that Juan Eugenio Hartzenbusch declined to publish the poem in *Poesías* (231), speculating that this sparked other poems of protest (Manso believes Coronado's most intense feminist activity corresponds to 1845). Strangely, no critic has linked Coronado's devotion to the Virgin of Bótoa with "El Marido verdugo"; legend connects the image's miraculous apparition to divine vindication of an innocent wife, victimized by husbandly suspicion (retold in one of Coronado's rare narrative poems, "La Encina de Bótoa" [The Bótoa Oak]). Coronado's religious poetry could thus disguise protests, deflecting patriarchal censure.

Feminist readers should consult Coronado's poems to sister poets (including Robustiana Armiño, Vicenta García de Miranda, Angela Grassi, María Josepa Massanés) celebrating the essential sisterhood of women writers. "La Flor del agua" (The Water Flower) implicitly identifies water flowers—sinking, rising, tossed by currents—with female poets. Coronado laments the feminine poet's unhappy lot, appealing to sisterhood and mutual support, motifs repeated in "¿Adónde estáis, consuelos de mi alma?" (Where Are You, My Soul's Consolation?)[19] Other poems to women poets include "A la señorita de Armiño," "A Elisa," "A Lidia," and "Yo no puedo seguirte con mi vuelo" (I Can But Follow You from Afar), supposedly a tribute to Avellaneda. Valis affirms that "lyric sisterhood" and feminine solidarity "saved" Coronado and other contemporary women poets, helping them resist society's hostility (12–13); Kirkpatrick concurs (79–86).

Likewise addressing women poets, "Cantad hermosas" (Sing, Beauties) suggests women are now less oppressed; interestingly, the suffering envisioned is strictly intellectual and artistic. Coronado unfailingly defends women's right to self-expression, sometimes ironically, as in the humorous ballad entitled "La Poetisa en un pueblo" (1845; The Woman Poet in the Small Town): "¡Ya viene, mírala! ¿Quién? / Esa que saca las coplas. / Jesús, qué mujer tan rara. / Tiene los ojos de loca . . . . / ¿Será verdad que ella sola / hace versos sin maestro?" ("Look, there she comes! Who? / That woman that writes couplets. / Jesus, what a weird woman. / She has the eyes of a madwoman. . . . / Can it be true that she/ writes verses without a teacher?" [Torres, 5]). Valis comments that *poetisa* was a cultural stereotype (14), and women poets were also ridiculed in other cultures.[20]

Elsewhere, Coronado's protest against women's lot turns bitter. "Libertad" (1846; Liberty), inspired by electoral reforms (see Kirkpatrick, 236–37), denounces women's disenfranchisement, inquiring, "¿De qué nos vale, / Si son los tiranos nuestros, / No el yugo de los monarcas, / El yugo de nuestro sexo?" ("What good does it do us / If the tyrants of women / Are not the monarchs, but our sex?" [Torres, 140]). "La Desgracia de ser hijos de España" (1847; The Misfortune of Being Spanish) anticipates Antonio Machado's poem "El Mañana efímero" (Ephemeral Tomorrow), juxtaposing the poet's idyllic, Arcadian vision with the decadent economy obliging the poor to work like animals. This poem ironically exposes contradictions between literary escapes to nature and impoverished rural reality, anticipating Realism and Naturalism.

Coronado also challenges the establishment in the 23 "Poems to Alberto" (first published in the 1852 edition). Kirkpatrick argues that Coronado's expression of desire, although platonic, exemplifies "tension between the desire-driven, egocentric self projected in Romantic discourse and the passionless, other-directed female subject defined by bourgeois gender ideology" (34). Even conventionally Romantic poems, such as one describing a violent storm witnessed from a ruined medieval mountaintop fortress, "En el Castillo de Salvatierra" (In Salvatierra Castle [Torres, 167–70; Kirkpatrick, 237–39]), comment on women's lot. Evoking centuries witnessed by these forgotten towers, Coronado envisions women enslaved or imprisoned there affirming, "Ni un eslabón los siglos quebrantaron / De nuestra anciana y bárbara cadena" ("The centuries broke not one link / Of woman's ancient, barbarous chain" [Torres, 167]). Coronado was traditionally little studied save by specialists in Romanticism or the regional literature of Extremadura; Kirkpatrick and Valis bring contemporary perspectives to bear upon textual production, resuscitating this forgotten feminist pioneer. Commemorative publications from Extremadura during the 1980s include Gregorio Torres and Isabel María Pérez González. Valis cites a biographical study I have not seen, and three other articles in English are available.[21]

A Catalan Romantic: María Josepa Massanés

María Josepa Massanés (b. 19 March 1811 in Tarragona), the daughter of an engineering corps captain whose mother died when she was five, was raised by paternal grandparents in Barcelona.[22] Although her old-fashioned grandparents discouraged early literary interests, her father encouraged further education. Condemned to death as a liberal (1830), he fled to France, leaving his invalid mother and young daughter penniless. Working as a seamstress, Massanés studied Latin, French, and Italian, reading classic authors. Upon her father's return (after Regent María Cristina pardoned the exiles, prompting Romanticism's triumph in 1833), Massanés lived more comfortably. Publishing poems in various periodicals, she gained recognition with *Poesías* (1841), which Kirkpatrick terms the first book of poetry published by a woman in the Romantic era. In 1843 Massanés married Ferrán González de Ortega, living in Madrid until 1845. During the 1850s and 1860s she wrote *Flores marchitas* (1850; Wilted Flowers), didactic works on education, and an unfinished drama concerning the conquest of Valencia.

With restoration of the "Jocs Florals" (competitive vernacular poetry festivals, 1859), Massanés commenced writing more in Catalan, joining the vigorous Renaixença (Catalan Renaissance). Despite criticism of her Catalan as defective, she won several prizes, becoming admired and respected by Catalan and international critics. When political change in 1869 ended her husband's military career, she opened a private girls' school. Despite the deaths of her husband and one adoptive son and economic reversals, she remained active, writing and maintaining literary contacts until her death 1 July 1887. Catalan poems published in periodicals between 1860 and 1881 were collected in the posthumous *Poesies* (1908). Dolors Monserdá de Macia wrote what is considered the best biographical source and the earliest critical overview.

Massanés received tributes from Catalan poets and critics but was neglected by mainstream (Castilian) critics, some of whom debated writing's advisability for women. Massanés staunchly defended women's right to write, supporting feminine "emancipation." Ricardo Navas Ruiz suggests in his Introduction to the 1992 anthology of her poetry that Massanés is "possibly the first woman within the Hispanic literary

tradition to debate the problem of women's right to write" (18). Navas
Ruiz stresses the authorial prologue to Massanés's *Poesías,* which reflects
incipient feminine rebellion against traditional gender-role limitations,
already aggressively presented in "La Resolución" (1837; Resolution
[Kirkpatrick, 129–34]). This poem satirizes patriarchal social values
marginalizing women, sarcastically listing insults inflicted upon women
writers: stupid, mad, visionary, intellectual.

Massanés usually cultivated conventional themes: religion (biblical
characters and events), love, family, maternity, friendship, patriotism, love
of homeland (both Spain and Catalunya). Support of Catalan causes
inspired poems to the red beret (symbolizing Catalan nationalism),
Barcelona, and local landmarks, while denouncing fratricidal civil wars.
She anticipated the Generation of 1898, treating national decadence,
breaking with tradition in condemning Spain's colonization of the Indian.
Sincere religiosity underlies poems treating biblical themes, charity, peace
and consolation, praising God in nature, evoking morning prayer and
examining social dimensions of religion. Devotion to the Virgin and love
for humanity—constant notes—reinforce her poetry's simplicity, univer-
sality, occasional rural serenity, intimate suffering and solitude. Massanés
abandons conventional visions of the feminine: her poetic personas, unlike
idealized Romantic heroines, break with prevailing erotic codes, presenting woman as subject rather than object—with real desires, aspirations,
eroticism, and pragmaticism (Navas Ruiz, 26–27).

Subtly ridiculing Romantic stereotypes and neoclassical rhetoric,
Massanés burlesques clichéd discourse in "Romance" (118–22), a lengthy
ballad. She addressed poetic creativity and praised other poets, echoing
Romantic conceptions, and cultivated poetic legends and circumstantial
and historical themes. Her most mature collection, written after
Romanticism's decline and published posthumously, attracts readers
today with its modernity and realism, reflecting such problems as poverty,
illness, and social injustice. Massanés depicts both rural and urban life,
preferring the latter. Like Rosalía de Castro, Massanés wavers between
two languages and cultures and suffers because of their conflicts.

Minor Poets of Romanticism and the Mid-Century Era

María del Carmen Simón Palmer's bibliography of nineteenth-century
Spanish women writers listing almost 5,000 publications demonstrates
that the traditional silence imposed upon women was broken definitively

in the Romantic period.[23] Modernization of the publishing industry, growth of the bourgeoisie, and the emergence of a bureaucratic, professional middle class created a "mass" readership, and periodicals appeared catering to women readers. Few women writers openly supported political equality, but most defended feminine literary rights. While patriarchal cult.ire and the phallocentric canon still denied feminine literary or intellectual equality, certain elements of Romanticism—privileging instinct and emotion over reason and discipline, exalting spontaneity and the natural, untutored, picturesque, or folkloric—coincided with prevailing notions of the feminine psyche, favoring women's use of the pen. In unprecedented numbers women writers seized their historic opportunity.

Most women writers cautiously implied conformity with traditional gender roles, emphasizing religiosity, conservative ideologies, and patriarchal virtues (motherhood, maternal love, fidelity and abnegation). They neither demanded equality nor externalized erotic desire, ambition, or excess love of liberty; instead they cultivated uncontroversial themes (nature, childhood innocence, changing seasons, the hours of dawn and twilight) and imitated male writers in representing women as flowers and doves. Erotic experience, if mentioned, might be attributed to others, or treated as dream, history, or legend (surrogate expressions of amorous fantasy produced several historico-legendary *romances* modeled upon Rivas and Zorrilla). Love themes were broached with extreme caution, and love experience was often placed within religious contexts (the most significant exception being Avellaneda). Counterbalancing a dearth of personally experienced love or eroticism came a wealth of poetry portraying relationships between women—mother-daughter bonds, sisterly love, and special spiritual kinship—dealing with frustrations and sometimes difficult, bitter struggles (cf. Kirkpatrick 1992 and Valis).

Nineteenth-century women writers' general opposition to slavery (not widespread in peninsular Spain) reflects patriarchal "enslavement" of women. Identification with socially oppressed, exploited, marginal figures—a Romantic topos for male writers (cf. sentimental treatments of pirates, paupers, bandits, prostitutes, and orphans)—implied identification with the slave. Later nineteenth-century conservative reaction against Romanticism and liberalism reinforced dominant gender stereotypes. Concurrent decline in women writers reflects spreading Victorian values in Europe generally, in Spain particularly, as women's expression was again strictly circumscribed.

Lesser-known mid-century women poets include Robustiana Armiño (1821–90), Vicenta García Miranda (1816–?), Rosa Butler y

Mendieta (1821–?), Dolores Cabrera y Heredia (1826–?), Amalia Fenollosa (1825–69), Rogelia León (1828–70), Enriqueta Lozano de Vílchez (1829–95), María Verdejo y Durán (1830–54), and Victorina Bridoux (1835–62).[24] Neither social nor ideological common denominators exist: these women were convent-raised orphans, poverty-stricken seamstresses, and members of the aristocracy, united only by their desire to write.

Angela Grassi and Pilar Sinués de Marco actively echoed patriarchal norms, promoting traditional idealized gender models among women readers. Neither was primarily a poet, although both published poetry. Grassi (1823–83), born in Italy but raised in Barcelona, began publishing at 16—a play, historical romance, poetry collection—producing various successful dramas and some 18 sentimental, pedantic, moralizing, lachrymose novels, plus sporadic poetry. She collaborated with Coronado in the periodical *El Pensamiento,* briefly supporting a protofeminist movement (later renounced). Moving to Madrid in the 1850s, she directed the journal *El Correo de la Moda* (in which her novels were serialized). She aimed at feminine readers, attempting to improve her audience morally and intellectually. Advocating Christian values, virtue, domesticity, platonic love, and friendship, Grassi believed woman's role was to regenerate and redeem, promoting moral values. Her *Poesías de la señorita doña Angela Grassi* (1851; Poems by Miss Angela Grassi), employing traditional meters and inspirational tones, treat religious themes—odes to the Virgin, hymns, and elegies. *Poesías* (1871) reprints previous poetry and adds new compositions, including new themes: unrequited love, Spanish history, autobiographical episodes.

Sinués (1835–93), facile novelist of customs and editor of women's magazines, was best known for *el ángel del hogar* (she published a magazine, collection of novelettes, and advice to women under this rubric). She also wrote poetry, especially verse legends: *Mis vigilias* (1854; My Vigils) and *Luz de luna* (1855; Moonlight). Other verse collections include *Cantos de mi lira* (1856; Songs from My Lyre) and *Amor y llanto* (1857; Love and Tears). *Flores del alma* (1860; Flowers of the Soul) contains lyric poetry; a personal anthology, *Mis poesías* (My Poems), appeared in 1855. Sinués espoused the traditional forms and values found in Grassi.

Another woman fiction writer and director of children's magazines, Faustina Sáez de Melgar (1834–95), turned to poetry after her children's deaths, composing *La Lira del Tajo* (1859; Lyre of the Tagus) and patriotic poetry published as *Africa y España* (1859).

Gertrudis Gómez de Avellaneda

Born 23 March 1814 in the Spanish government's provincial administrative center of Puerto Príncipe in Central Cuba, Gertrudis Gómez de Avellaneda was among five children of an aristocratic Spanish naval officer and a wealthy Cuban woman. Her parents were cultured slaveholders, well educated and socially prominent.[25] Only the future poet and her brother Manuel survived infancy; their father died when Tula (as family and friends called her) was eight. Her mother remarried, but Tula, who had idealized her father, emotionally rejected her stepfather (Catena, 8). She criticized her stepfather, but an 1836 visit to his relatives took her to Spain, where she would spend most of her life. Conflicts with her stepfather's relatives prompted visits to Andalusian relatives of her biological father in Seville, where her poetic and literary activities began.

Avellaneda was tall, slim, and ardent, an unconventional dark beauty whose sensual attractiveness brought admiring suitors, while her intelligence, aggressiveness, independence, frankness, and volatility repulsed or alienated many. More liberated and more controversial but also more celebrated, she enjoyed more literary triumphs while suffering more public censure (Catena [13–15] notes Avellaneda's problems because of local prejudice against women writers). Her literary fortunes were offset by misfortune in love, with the most intense passions of her life spent on men who spurned her. Ignacio de Cepeda, whom she met in Seville in 1838, remained a reluctant suitor for some 15 years; their relationship was repeatedly interrupted or suspended. Avellaneda's passionate love affair with conservative politician, accomplished womanizer, and mediocre versifier Gabriel García Tassara produced an illegitimate daughter born in 1845—a sickly child who died a few months later, while Tassara refused to recognize her and continued his diplomatic career. Avellaneda's love letters have appeared in English translation.[26] In 1846 she married another politician and unsuccessful Romantic dramatist, Pedro Sabater, then civil governor of Madrid, already terminally ill; he died within months and the grieving widow entered a convent in Bordeaux while recuperating. There she composed prayers and religious poetry, published as *Devocionario* (1975; Prayer Book).

In 1853, with two collections of poetry, five novels, and some 10 successful plays, Avellaneda's admission to the Royal Spanish Academy was denied because women were ineligible. Her second marriage, to Colonel

Domingo Verdugo (1855), was celebrated in Madrid's Royal Palace (indicating her literary prestige and Verdugo's political standing). This otherwise happy marriage suffered from misfortune: in 1858 Verdugo was wounded in a mysterious stiletto attack from which he never fully recovered, dying in Cuba in 1863. Avellaneda was triumphantly received in Cuba in 1860, adding to her literary successes in Spain; when she died in 1873, however, she was already forgotten. The centennial of her birth sparked mild critical interest.

Avellaneda incorporates Romantic exaltation of art and its divinely given creative powers but emphasizes feminine attributes (peace, love, harmony), implicitly identifying feminine poets with the spirit of poetry. She combines superior poetic attributes with "womanly" traits (gentleness, beauty, emotion, soulfulness), stating that "women who choose to cultivate their artistic vocation must sacrifice the security and comfort available to women who adopt the traditional feminine role" (Kirkpatrick, 186). "Insisting on the equivalence of the male and the female subject" (187), she rejects misogynist assumptions of feminine inferiority.

Kirkpatrick notes that male Romantic poets employed avian images—Shelley's skylark, Keats's nightingale, Musset's pelican—as externalized representations of the intimate self, and that Avellaneda adapted the turtledove, butterfly (187–89), and finch. While expressing feminine desire, Avellaneda makes it lead to annihilation (realistically reflecting the double standard) and fragmentation of the feminine subject. Woman's subjugation via desire is represented by caged birds, imprisoned by phallocentric culture. Appropriating conventional parallels between the lyric self and nature, Avellaneda communicates alienation (the wind-blown leaf becomes a metaphor for the self). She figures the lyric self "in ways that exhibit different and more extreme forms of alienation than do the lyrical selves of her male Romantic colleagues" (Kirkpatrick, 202). Internal division, instability and questioning, characterizing Avellaneda's Romantic poetry, sometimes convey anger, fury, and rage, "the antidote to feminine weakness" (204).

Raimundo Lazo[27] emphasizes Avellaneda's treatment of love's varied manifestations (personal reactions, passion, mysterious sentiments, eroticism, divine love, mystic assimilations), nature at its most grandiose and tempestuous or idyllic, religion, philosophical reflections, poetry and other poets, travel, daily life, circumstantial poetry, and "egophilia" (39). Lesser motifs include tedium, insomnia, melancholy, botanical and ornithological images, translations and imitations of other poets, and social customs or types (such as the fisherman).

Avellaneda allegedly began writing poetry following her mother's remarriage; *Poesías* (1841), dedicated to her mother, contained 45 poems, including seven translations, dated 1836–41. Passionate and jealous, Avellaneda shared archetypal Romantic interests in medieval history and legends. Attracted by the period of conquest and discovery, writing frequently on patriotic themes, she expressed love for both Cuba and Spain, dedicating numerous poems of circumstance to the royal family, especially the Queen Regent and Queen Isabel II (women's governing Spain during the Romantic era probably facilitated women's access to cultural institutions). Avellaneda's second edition of *Poesías* (1850), dedicated to Isabel II, contained 129 poems of varying lengths.

Hugh A. Harter stresses Avellaneda's "formidable career as a playwright . . . unsurpassed, if equalled, by any other woman in the history of the theater" (Preface), noting that she was publicly acclaimed as the greatest woman poet of all Spanish literature. In 1852 alone, five of her dramas were produced. Her novels were less well received, but she departed from Romanticism's medieval preoccupations, addressing such contemporary issues as abolition, divorce, crime and punishment, women's rights, and social problems. Besides poetry, Avellaneda produced six novels, 15 full-length dramas, various shorter plays, assorted essays and short stories, an extensive correspondence, and collections of legends. After Verdugo's death she visited the United States (1864), toured Europe, returned to Seville, befriended "Fernán Caballero" (novelist Cecilia Böhl von Faber), and prepared her *Obras completas* (Complete Works) in five volumes (published 1869–71), consisting of one volume of poetry, two of drama, and two of prose.

Avellaneda's poetry depicts both love's exultation and ecstasy and the depths of disillusionment and pain, a "compendium or panorama of styles in Hispanic poetry from late neoclassicism through romanticism" (Harter, 50). Relying upon intuition rather than precepts, she signed no manifestos and wrote no formal *ars poética*. Influences included major French, English, Spanish, and Latin American poets (especially Romantics)—Hugo, Lamartine, and Heredia along with Petrarch and Byron. Although fond of sonnets, Avellaneda employed varied metric and rhyme schemes; Harter sees her as anticipating Bécquer (71–72). Like other Romantics, she favored polymetric compositions: for instance, "La Noche del insomnio y el alba" (Night of Insomnia and the Dawn

[Catena, 75–79]) begins with lines of one and two syllables: "Noche / Triste / Viste / Ya" ("Sad night, you've already seen"). Next come strophes of three- and four-syllable lines: "Brindándole / Al mundo / Profundo / Solaz" ("Giving to the World Profound Solace"). Then five-syllable lines: "Mas siempre velan / Mis tristes ojos" ("But my sad eyes forever keep watch"). And finally verses of six, seven, and eight syllables, progressively building to 16-syllable lines. Impressive technical accomplishments include the sonnets "El Recuerdo importuno" (Importunate Memory [Catena, 87]) and "A Dios" (To God [Catena, 136]), exemplifying skillful control of form and idea.

Cuba's mountains, savannah, Edenic jungles, and exotic flora and fauna inspire poems, while Spain elicits poetic portraits of the Basque region and Castile (Avellaneda also wrote poems to France and Poland). Faith imbues lyric prayers, elegies, poems of peace and spiritual anguish, poems to Christ and the Virgin Mary, and treatments of eternity, redemption, resignation, renunciation, and biblical themes. Philosophical meditations center upon foreboding and death, destiny and fate; illness, despondency, abulia, liberty, melancholy, and the orphan state inspire personal reflections. The life-as-a-journey topos combines with self-identification as "La Peregrina" (pilgrim or wanderer). Time, occasionally represented by sun, moon, stars, and sea, appears in memories of adolescence and Arcadian innocence, plus its darker side, being-toward-death. Other poems treat the deaths of the poet's husbands, loss, doubt, hope, grief, the war of the sexes, pride and victimization, and angel/demon motifs.

Avellaneda "epitomizes Romanticism, oscillating between extremes of passionate love and religious devotion"; she excelled in the "control and use of verse, lyric or dramatic" (Harter, Preface). Possibly overpraised at the height of her career, she was unjustly consigned to oblivion thereafter. Contemporary interest in women writers is rediscovering this so-called Spanish Georges Sand.

Rosalía de Castro

Rosalía de Castro, born 24 February 1837 in Santiago de Compostela (Galicia), was the child of unwed parents, hidden away by her mother, María Teresa da Cruz de Castro y Abadía, who was of traditional, minor Galician nobility (the name Castro dates to Celtic [pre-Roman] fortified towns in Northwest Spain). Mystery originally surrounded Castro's birth; besides scandal attached to a 33-year-old spinster's illegitimate child, this case involved sacrilege. The father, José Martínez Viojo (then 39) is variously termed seminarian, presbiter or priest; he served as chaplain in Iria Flavia (from whose church the poet, known simply as Rosalía, was buried) in nearby Padrón.

Conflicting accounts of Rosalía's little-known earlier years concur that she lived in nearby Castro Ortuño until acknowledged by her mother when the girl was between 10 and 13 (perhaps following a grandparent's death).[28] This imprecision reflects the secrecy veiling noble "scandals" and the disregard for upbringing and education of females. During adolescence, Rosalía attended a school sponsored by the Sociedad Económica de Amigos del País (Economic Association of Friends of the Country) rather than receiving the convent education customary for young ladies. The name implies low-cost schooling with emphasis on Galicia and things Galician (*país* here means region). Her studies included music, drawing, and French; she excelled in writing,[29] guitar, and theater, performing in productions at the Santiago Lyceum during the cultural revival spurred by Romanticism, known in Galician as the Rexurdimento (restoration).

At 19, Rosalía moved to Madrid (1856). Having commenced versifying almost as soon as she learned to write, she published six rather extensive Romantic poems as *La Flor* (The Flower) early in 1857. In May the volume was reviewed by Manuel Martínez Murguía, a Galician journalist, critic, and historian, who identified echoes of Espronceda and Zorrilla, lauded the author, and augured future fame. Murguía, Rosalía's future husband, asserted he was unacquainted with her, but scholars express doubt. Their engagement was announced later that year, and the marriage celebrated in Madrid in 1858, with the newlyweds living in Galicia. Alejandra, their first daughter, was born the next year in Santiago, shortly before Rosalía's first novel, *La Hija del mar* (1859; Daughter of the Sea), appeared. Marina Mayoral indicates that this novel depicts the "Electra complex," as two women—mother and daughter—compete for the hero, who prefers the younger.

Rosalía's precarious health meant no more children for a decade. Five or six other children were born between 1868 and 1877, with the last daughter being stillborn.[30] Rosalia's difficult pregnancies culminated in uterine cancer. Murguía's career and literary pursuits favored her artistic development. Himself a creative writer, he encouraged her, seemingly accepting her superior talent, having her poems published when she modestly expressed reluctance. Critics and biographers disagree whether the marriage was happy, given poetic themes of solitude, pain, and sorrow. Numerous separations ensued when Murguía took positions in Madrid and elsewhere, leaving Rosalía in Galicia with the children.[31] His career as government archivist, repeatedly interrupted by changes of power, meant periodic unemployment, and the family suffered financial straits.

Rosalía's second lyric collection, *A mi madre* (1863; To My Mother), inspired by her mother's death, appeared shortly before her first major success, *Cantares gallegos* (1863; Galician Songs), composed in the rural Galician dialect when the poet was experiencing intense homesickness while living in Simancas (Old Castile), where Murguía headed the National Historical Archive. Rosalía's second lyric tribute to Galicia was composed during renewed residence in Simancas in the early 1870s: *Follas novas* (1880; New Leaves), her last major work in Galician, preceded her final significant poetry collection, *En las orillas del Sar* (1884; On the Banks of the River Sar), published only months before she died in July 1885. Filled with motifs of suffering and death and written with full awareness that her illness was terminal, these poems express Rosalía's love of life and tragic sense of mortality.

Critics often term women writers autobiographical, and Rosalía's life clearly shapes her lyrics (her fiction is more imaginative). She wrote *cuadros de costumbres* (sketches of manners), inspired by Galicia during nearly two decades, collected as *Costumbres gallegas* (Galician Customs) and *El Domingo de Ramos* (Palm Sunday), both published in 1881. Many poems of Galician inspiration constitute lyric variants of *costumbrismo*. Other important motifs originate in personal experience: physical pain and maternal tragedies inspired expressions of suffering, maternal grief and loss, exacerbating the poet's melancholy—possibly innate, augmented by childhood separation from her mother and living in various homes before age 13. Lacking a paternal figure, she suffered a "psychic orphan state" (Albert, 35).[32] Basilio Losada suggests in his Prologue to the centennial anthology that Rosalía suffered a "lifelong complex as a bastard," citing the "weight of her illegitimate birth."[33] Identification with victims of social injustice reflects Rosalía's marginal status as illegitimate and her inevitable awareness of her mother's suffering after being seduced, impregnated, and abandoned.[34]

Observers noting maternal aspects of Rosalía's work emphasize her gentle strength and themes of loss and sorrow. More feminine than feminist, her work reflects acceptance of traditional gender roles as wife and mother and relegation to the domestic sphere. Neither aspiring to legal or political equality of the sexes nor demanding personal autonomy and liberation, she limits herself to affirming women's artistic and intellectual rights, terms matrimony a social necessity (*OC,* 1526–27) but does not militate against it, and probably experienced diminished literary discrimination thanks to Murguía's support.[35] Sensitive and retiring, despite what she deems her "asperity of character" (*OC,* 1526–28), she was wounded by provincial prejudice. Her "Letter to Eduarda" advises the putative friend to renounce writing: society will not forgive her presumptuousness and will even attribute her successes to her husband's having written them (*OC,* 1526–28). Rosalía insistently combatted the low esteem in which Spain held Galicia. Remote, mountainous, backward, and poor, Galicia has much the same relationship to the rest of Spain as Appalachia or the Ozarks to the United States, and its people are stereotyped as hillbillies—ignorant and coarse.

Rosalía's first two poetry collections are brief, intensely emotional, and somewhat atypical, lacking the characteristic Galician themes and forms of her most famous lyrics. *La Flor,* six long Castilian poems replete with Romantic motifs (fate, doomed love, despair, lost innocence, hostile destiny, disillusionment, grief, treachery, deception), uses solitary, lugubrious settings, phantoms, mysterious personages, and Gothic ruins and dark cemeteries. Nature at its most violent and pathetic and the confessional mode repeat Romantic models. Grief in *A mi madre* is unmistakably genuine, but this elegiac collection resembles later works only in "universal" meditations on death and life's brevity. Rosalía describes her mother compassionately as having loved and suffered intensely, always forgiving (*OC,* 252), tenderly depicting her as victim; she laments not appreciating her mother's love and sacrifice.

The significance attributed to *Cantares gallegos* transcends commercial success. This collection is credited with reviving popular Galician literature via glosses and imitation. The poet sings of Galician lakes, mountains, fields, fjordlike *rías,* flora, fauna, twilight, solitude, clearings, riverbanks, ancient traditions, myths, folklore, and customs. Galician lyric poetry reached high artistic levels in the thirteenth and fourteenth centuries, before lyric tradition emerged in Castilian, but during 500 years Spain's rulers systematically discouraged regional vernaculars or dialects; writers whose first languages were "minority" tongues wrote largely in Castilian for political and economic reasons. Not until Romanticism's passion for the Middle Ages and fondness for folklore did the vernacular literatures undergo revival, lasting until the Spanish Civil War. Unlike Catalan, whose stronger socioeconomic base and larger number of speakers supported continuous linguistic cultivation and literary production, Galician came close to being assimilated. Lacking grammar books and dictionaries to maintain linguistic precepts and uniformity, Galician had no literary histories. Alive largely as oral tradition, Galician was not "literary"; Rosalía and other poets of the Galician revival, unaware of medieval Gallego-Portuguese lyrics, believed they were working in a peasant dialect requiring adaptation for literary expression. Yet much of what Rosalía wrote evoked medieval lyrics, forgotten by the educated but kept alive by uneducated villagers.

Rosalía presents epic, celebratory visions of Galician archetypes (lusty country lads, robust farm girls, aged beggar women, itinerant bagpipe players), revered religious images, pilgrimages, dances, and joyous folk festivals. Her Preface describes popular Galician poetry as "all music and vagueness, all laments, sighs and sweet smiles, sometimes murmuring with mysterious forest winds, sometimes shining with the sun's rays serenely falling on swollen rivers running solemnly beneath the flowering willows" (Barja, 14), proclaiming her desire to "sing the beauties of our land in that soft, sensitive dialect considered barbarous by those unacquainted with its ability to surpass all other languages in harmony and sweetness" (16). Indignantly, she denounces those who speak ill of Galicia. Some poems protest hardships suffered by Galician harvesters and the migrant farmworkers who wander across Castile and live in subhuman conditions. Galician customs (reflecting contemporary trends to realism) appear in samplings of village humor, rustic jokes and tricks, paraphrasing traditional *romances,* wherein joyful sensuality contrasts with miracles by the Virgin Mary and collective rural celebrations. Patriotic defense of Galicia accompanies social themes of exile and emigration.

The *Cantares* use dialogue and monologue with skillful artlessness, achieving natural effects, or gloss popular folk motifs (cf. Kulp-Hill, 41–45) and then give brief narratives or meditations, strongly cadenced and evoking mill songs, tambourine songs, and dance rhythms. Traditional Spanish metrics—*copla, seguidilla, romancillo, endechas*—appear with other lines of *arte menor* (eight or fewer syllables). Assonance predominates, with occasional consonant rhyme. The *Cantares* had 13 independent editions (aside from six reprintings in the complete works) as of the 1985 centennial (Losada, 16); illiterate Galician peasants can recite these poems by heart.

Follas novas disconcertingly switched from popular rhythms and spontaneous humor to metaphysical depth and more personal, intimate tones, although poems recalling the *Cantares* also appear (cf. Losada,

17–19; Alonso believes their inclusion breaks the unity of protest and despair). Galicia becomes the background for distinctly existential themes, anticipating Unamuno (solitude, anguish, being-toward-death), with motifs of suffering, misfortune, and pain. Several critics consider *Follas novas* and *En las orillas del Sar* precursors of *modernismo* (Spanish modernism); Rosalía experiments with uncommon metric combinations and broken rhythms, attaining surprising technical virtuosity. Castilian critics Menéndez Pelayo, Clarín, and Valera ignored her completely (Losada, 18), however.

Written during ill health, difficulties and sadness, *Follas novas* reflects these travails; the Preface affirms that the muse of our times is sorrow. With independence recalling Unamuno, Rosalía rejects categorization as "literary woman" or poetess (Kulp-Hill, 53), reiterating her devotion to simple, natural poetry. Motifs of superstition and religion continue, but quaint, festive customs and picturesque types yield to poverty, hunger, and suffering—by Galicia, its women and the poet herself; esthetic distance is achieved by using various poetic personas. Subjective, intellectual, and spiritual concerns and Rosalía's personal experience acquire greater visibility. The collection's 139 poems, loosely organized in five groups ("Reveries," "Intimacy," "From the Land," "Miscellany," and "Widows of the Living and Dead"), support assertions that they were not originally intended as a book.

Love turns more somber in *Follas novas:* separation, disappointment, sacrifice and unrequited passion replace hope, fidelity, and euphoric erotic fulfillment (cf. Kulp-Hill, 60). The final section (Widows of the Living and Dead), important to those critics who consider Rosalía a social poet, presents the heartbreaking forced departure from home and family to escape poverty and lack of opportunity, plus the powerful drama of women left behind. The poet struggles against despair and emotional pain, attempting to escape life's chaos and instability, groping toward inner wholeness. Alone, bewildered, soul-sick, and afraid, she wavers between flight and fight. Road and journey symbols represent the fantasy of escape. Solitude, the passing of time, and religious preoccupations (search for immortality, crisis of faith and doubt) culminate in poems referring to suicide. In the struggle against guilt and madness, life triumphs, but sorrow remains.

Before Rosalía's only significant collection in Castilian, *En las orillas del Sar,* her health deteriorated rapidly (she died of cancer in 1885). She turned to another linguistic medium, more patterned discourse, and disciplined artistic expression, perhaps for therapeutic reasons, to distract

herself from her physical pain. Considerable thematic and metric continuity exists between the last two works, but *Sar* exhibits more unity,
order, and artifice with less colloquialism. Tones become quiet, dignified,
detached, and resigned as the poet confronts death, viewing suffering as
inseparable from life's meaning. Colors, voices, protests, lighting, and
nature in its varied portraits and symbols are muted in *Sar*. Like Antonio
Machado, Rosalía uses conventional imagery—road, river, falling leaves,
sunset, or winter evoke traditional associations and connotations—but
underlying emotions, philosophical and metaphysical reverberations, and
intense suffering convey special power. Both poets treat profound
themes in simple, lucid, popular language, deceptively prosaic yet irre-
ducibly lyric.

Less natural syntax, hyperbatons, repetitions, parallelisms, contrasts
and paradoxes convey a baroque air. Winter motifs reveal a preoccupation with death, characterized by the shadow effects of light and darkness. There is a sense of fleeting and phantasmal reality. Bitterness,
longing, and despair characterize an autumnal world of sad omens,
empty nests, devastated gardens, dry fountains, felled trees, dark clouds,
and cold, twilight, and chimeras. Many poems treat death explicitly
(depicting ways of dying); others approach it symbolically, via fading
stars or dying fires: "Ya siente que te extingues en su seno, / llama vital
que dabas / luz a su espíritu, a su cuerpo fuerzas / juventud a su alma"
("Now she feels your extinction in her breast / vital flame who once gave
/ light to her spirit, strength to her body / youth to her soul").[36] The
poet ironizes concerning "eternal" romantic love (cf. 83–84) and inconstancy (85–87, 149–50).

The Galician river Sar near Rosalía's girlhood home evokes rivers'
conventional meanings: passing time, life's journey, progress toward the
unknown. More remote but still appropriate, mythic parallels with the
rivers Styx and Jordan allude to the moment of death. Temporal
motifs—day, night, seasons, hours—and symbols (river, sea, fount, road)
multiply as awareness of mortality intensifies. Dreams proliferate, along
with meditations on poetry's capacity to recapture happier moments and
repulse despair. The significant "Santa Escolástica" (97–101) recalls a
quasi-mystical experience revealing connections between beauty, poetry,
and divinity when, for Rosalía (as for Juan Ramón Jiménez), these fuse in
the divine essence.

Rosalía de Castro, revered after her early death, became synonymous
with the Galician revival, gaining the distinction—uncommon for
women poets—of inspiring imitators and followers. Her Galician work

fared better with Catalans than Castilians; evaluations by mainstream Castilian critics rest primarily on *Sar,* which established her eminence. As Kathleen Kulp-Hill notes in her Preface, Rosalía is cited with Bécquer as one of the "two best and most enduring poets of Nineteenth-Century Spain." Rosalía's simpler expression and social concerns link her to postwar "social poets," making her the most "contemporary" nineteenth-century woman poet.

The Franco regime identified vernacular languages with sedition, prohibiting their use for many years, and exercising discriminatory censorial control over publication in those languages. Vernacular legality was restored when 1970s reform of Spain's educational system authorized study of the regional tongues. Transition to democracy under King Juan Carlos brought an explosive renaissance of vernacular languages and literatures, accompanying numerous local autonomy movements. Critical studies on Rosalía burgeoned owing to historical confluence: cessation of censorship, publishing "booms" in vernacular literature and criticism, and the centennial of Rosalía's death in 1985 inspired conferences, homages, and symposia on her life and works.

Other Minor Poets

Victòria Penya d'Amer (1827–98), born in Ciutat de Mallorca, participated in the first "Jocs Florals" (poetic jousts) held in the island, winning a prize for *Amor de mare* (1865; A Mother's Love). She contributed to several periodicals during the Catalan Renaissance, including *La Renaixença, Lo Gay Saber,* and *La Ilustració Catalana.* Sometimes moralizing and religious in her poetry (as well as sentimental), she held editorial positions with *La Ilustración católica* and the women's periodical *El Pensil del Bello Sexo.* Romantic influences are evident: she frequently treats medieval and chivalric themes—tragic love and deaths from heartbreak—in addition to her fascination for folklore. The posthumous *Poesies* (1909) also contains several Marian poems.

Micaela de Silva y Collás (1809–84) wrote under the pseudonym "Camila Avilés." Born in Oviedo, she lived in Barcelona and Madrid and studied languages (she translated Manzoni). *Un Novio a pedir de boca* (1963; A Sweetheart Made to Order), a posthumously published satire in *octavas reales,* describes the ideal suitor (virtues include honesty, decency, and fidelity) and paints the man to be avoided (womanizer, gambler, wife-abuser, glutton, wastrel, and narcissist). *Emanaciones del alma* (1885; Emanations from the Soul) was compiled from Silva's poems in the periodical press and published in a single-volume collection following her death.

Today's readers, postmodern or postcontemporary, may be disconcerted by nineteenth-century women poets. Recipients of an education that silenced women's existence and concerns or dismissed them as trite, these poets predictably adopted masculine techniques and motifs. But they also proved capable of adapting male poetic conventions to express specifically feminine attitudes and problems. Women poets contributed significantly to the Catalan and Galician revivals, influencing poetry's move away from Romanticism's overblown rhetoric and stereotyped themes and settings and toward more flexible expression and realistic concerns. Twentieth-century women poets may indeed write without knowledge of these foremothers, not because precedents are lacking, but because gender equity plays no part in canon formation.

Chapter Three

Poets at the Turn of the Century

Poetic productivity declined as Romanticism subsided; prose writers supplanted poets and lyric dramatists. Only three lyric poets from the post-Romantic era retain importance today: Gustavo Adolfo Bécquer (1836–70), Rosalía de Castro (1837–85), and Ramón de Campoamor (1817–1901). The latter, comparably prosaic and realistic, deemed "philosophical" by contemporaries, remains marginal in poetic development from late Romanticism to modernism. End-of-the-century male poets, early modernists preceding the Generation of 1898 (the most prominent being Salvador Rueda [1857–1933], Francisco Villaespesa [1877–1936], and Tomás Morales [1884–1921]), managed only modest renown. The triumph of realism and naturalism accompanied poetic decline. Lyric activity languished under resurgent patriarchal conservatism, with renewed restrictions, diminished visibility, and declining numbers of women writers. Susan Kirkpatrick's anthology of nineteenth-century women's poetry samples lyric compositions by six women from the turn-of-the-century, compared with the 14 women from the Romantic period and nine from post-Romantic years.

Minor Poets

Rosario de Acuña (1851–1923), primarily a dramatist, provoked controversy with her progressive ideas: male-female equality, female heroism, anticlericalism, civil matrimony, and freedom of thought. Acuña also wrote short stories, essays, and poetry, including *Ecos del alma* (1876; Soul Echoes); *Morirse a tiempo* (1880; To Die on Time), an imitation of Campoamor; and the comic *Sentir y pensar* (1884; Feeling and Thinking).

Concepción Estevarena y Gallardo (1854–76), born in Seville—then a cultural center—suffered economic straits and orphanhood, dying young of tuberculosis. Her only collection, *Ultimas flores* (1877; Last Flowers) was posthumously assembled by friends. Major themes include the struggle for life, ambition, doubt, suffering, desire, and love of liberty.

Blanca de los Ríos de Lampérez (1862–1956), cultured and well-to-do, began writing in adolescence. *Esperanzas y recuerdos* (1881; Hopes and

Memories), her first poetry collection, appeared three years after her first novel. She was influential as a literary scholar, novelist, short-story writer, and editor of the conservative literary magazine *Raza Española* (1919–26). A lifelong friend of Sofía Casanova, she represents the tendency (condemned by the Generation of 1898) to idealize Spain's past.

Josefa Ugarte Barrientos (1854–91), precocious playwright and folklorist, collected traditional legends, retelling them in verse in *Recuerdos de Andalucía* (1874; Memories of Andalusia) and *Páginas en verso* (1882; Pages in Verse). Ugarte won several poetry contests, and her highest achievements were posthumously published as *Poesías selectas* (1904; Selected Poems).

Poets Writing in Catalan and Galician

Kirkpatrick covers only Castilian, omitting several poets who wrote largely or partly in Catalan and Galician (except Filomena Dato Muruais, who wrote in Castilian and Galician). Dolors Monserdà de Macia (1845–1919) displayed interest in social issues, working-class problems, and conditions affecting women. This Catholic liberal wrote novellas, novels, plays, and poetry in Catalan, contributing significantly to the Renaixença (Catalan Renaissance). Known for realistic fiction, she first published brief poems on her daughter's death, entitled *Ma corona* (1877; My Wreath)—predictably religious and sentimental. In 1888 she published *Poesies catalanes,* whose patriotic, historical, and folkloric topics center upon the regional "nation" of Catalunya. More personal, intimate poems treat maternal, domestic, religious, and philosophical themes. *Poesies* (1911) reprints works from the previous volume, adding new material; neither edition constitutes a complete compilation. Various interim compositions won prizes in Catalonian Jocs Florals (poetic contests). Monserdà also wrote plays in verse.

Catalan Renaissance figure Agnès Armengol de Badia (1852–1934), pianist, composer, folklorist, and feminist, was an emotional poet writing exclusively in Catalan. Her *Lays* appeared in an anthology edited by Joan Roca i Bros, *Volum rimas* (1879), with *Ramell de semprevives* (1891; Bouquet of Succulents) followed by a long religious poem, *Redempció* (1912; Redemption). The Catalan past inspires nostalgic *costumbrismo,* idealizing village life, religious celebrations, songs, dances, serenades, and legends, comparable to Rosalía de Castro's poems of Galician life and customs. Important collections are *Sabadellenques i altres poesies* (1925; Sabadell Verses and Other Poems), depicting past and present customs of Sabadell, and *Rosari Antic, tradicions i records* (1926; Antique Rosary, Traditions, and Memories), drawing upon childhood observations of regional tales, songs, ceremonies, and legends, plus classical writers remembered from the poet's upper-class French school. Armengol also treats nature, religion, and her own history.

Another Catalan revival poet, Joaquima Santamaria i Ventura de Fabrigues (pseudonym of Agnès de Valldaura), traditionally Catholic, contributed to the debate over women's "place" with *Breus consideracions sobre la dona* (1882; Brief Consideration of Women). She produced at least two poetry collections, *Fullaraca: Prosa y vers* (1879; Dry Leaves: Prose and Verse) and *Ridolta: Aplech de poesies* (1882; Water Flower: Bouquet of Poems). Less productive poets in Catalan are Emília Sureda (1865–1904), whose *Poesies mallorquines* (Majorcan Poems) appeared in 1905, and Antònia Gili i Guell (1856–1909), from the wine-growing Villafranca del Penedès (Barcelona), who published *Poesies* in 1899.

Caterina Albert (1869–1966; pseudonym of Víctor Catalá), known primarily for rural naturalist prose, is the major woman writer of the Catalan revival. Novelist, playwright, and poet before turning to prose fiction, Albert gained attention for her poetry and drama (several theatrical monologues were written in verse). By contrast with her "vulgar" naturalistic novels, her stylized poetry betrays modernist influences. Inspired by Guimerà, Oller, and Maragall among earlier Renaixença writers, she was reclusive, apparently traumatized by the revelation of her gender and identity. Sensitive and shy, Albert published the poem *El Llibre nou* (The New Book) in 1898 and subsequently produced several poetry collections, including *Els cants del mesos* (1899; Song of the Months), 12 poems with symbolist and impressionist elements. *El Llibre blanc* (1905; The White [or Blank] Book), reprinted in her *Obres completes* (1951–72), was much admired for lyric qualities and impeccable form.

Clara Corral (1847–1904), a Galician follower of Rosalía whose only collection is *A Herminia* (1881; To Herminia), treats primarily amorous themes and love of Galicia. Filomena Dato Muruais, born in Orense (Galicia) in the mid-1800s, exemplifies the Galician literary revival sparked by Rosalía de Castro. Dato collaborated in various literary periodicals, contributing articles and poems to *El Heraldo Gallego,* and wrote *Follatos: Poesías gallegas* (1891; Foliage: Galician Poems) in Galician. Kathleen March states that Dato published four additional poetry collections in Castilian.[1] Kirkpatrick indicates that these included *Penumbras* (1880; Shadows), *Follatos* (1891; Foliage; in Galician), *Romances y cantares* (1895; Ballads and Songs), and *Fe* (1911; Faith), late religious poetry published when the poet was blind. "Defensa das mulleres" (1887; In Defense of Women) received the most important of several awards garnered by Dato. She died in Moruxo in 1926.

Francisca Herrera Garrido (1869–1950) belonged to the conservative upper class and, like her more accomplished contemporary Sofía Casanova, lived largely outside Galicia. Herrera, who wrote both in Galician and Castilian, spent some three decades in Madrid. As disciple of Rosalía, Herrera contributed to the Galician revival; literary history remembers her more for her narratives. Although forgotten from the Republic onward, nine of her titles from 1913 to 1928 appear in Carolyn Galerstein,[2] including short stories, four or five novels, and three volumes of poetry. The title of *Sorrisas e bágoas* (1913; Smiles and Tears) reflects their emotional sentimentality. *¡Almas de muller . . . Volallas na luz!* (1915; Women's Souls . . . Sparks in the Light!), termed very "feminine" (March, 9) and explicitly compared to Rosalía's *Cantares gallegos,* represents all significant facets of Herrera's poetry. Favoring dialogue, her poems are less lyrical than narrative or dramatic, portraying essentially the same rural Galician ambient as Rosalía de Castro, stressing the struggle for existence and humble virtues of the peasants and villagers, especially rural women. These pieces, albeit "not direct declarations of women's strength, are nonetheless illustrative of women's worth, both . . . [social and] sentimental" (March, 9). Herrera emphasizes country people's generosity, strength, dignity, and perseverance, thereby anticipating postwar "social poetry." After *Flores do noso paxareco* (1919; Flowers from Our Bird Cage) Herrera turned to fiction. Imbued with Catholic dogma and the patriarchal mystique of *el ángel del hogar,* she defended traditional values; much esteemed in her day, she was elected to the Royal Galician Academy.[3]

Sofía Pérez Casanova de Lutoslawski

Quite easily among Spain's most remarkable women of any century, Sofía Casanova (1861–1958) was a poet, journalist, and brilliant foreign correspondent during World War I and the Russian Revolution. Pioneering feminist, social worker, prolific novelist, translator, and the author of children's books, short stories, and essays, she also wrote plays and political commentary. After marrying a Polish nobleman in 1887 she lived most of her 95 years outside Spain.

Born 30 September 1861 to an aristocratic Galician family near Almeiras (La Coruña), she spent her childhood in one of Europe's most backward areas. Left to support herself and three small children, Casanova's mother provided the model of an independent, resourceful woman. The family moved to Madrid during the Bourbon Restoration, where the beautiful, talented young Casanova attracted noble patronage. She enrolled at the Madrid Conservatory, studying drama, literature, music, and declamation.

Fluent in Galician, Casanova knew Portuguese well and studied French (especially Alfred de Musset's sorrowful Romanticism), but she wrote in Castilian, espousing serene Parnassist ideals. Symbolist influences appear in her rhetoric of vagueness: things are distant, misty, dim, undefined, and indefinable. Casanova was familiar with works of Gertrudis Gómez de Avellaneda and Carolina Coronado but "idolized" Rosalía de Castro.[4] Despite lifelong love of Galicia, she felt stifled by the reactionary provincial atmosphere. Madrid, however, delighted her, and the elegant blond, green-eyed beauty entered select social and literary circles. The epoch's major poet, Ramón de Campoamor, became her official mentor; friends included prominent playwrights Zorrilla, Echegaray, and Joaquín Dicenta, plus poets Salvador Rueda and Blanca de los Ríos. Casanova read her poetry at court, and the monarchs subsidized her first book, *Poesías* (1885).[5]

These 37 early poems, imbued with Romantic rhetoric, were gentler, more subdued, evoking Bécquer. For Casanova, Galicia is background, not leitmotiv. The "pessimism" perceived by Campoamor and Pérez de Ayala is not unrelieved: some lighthearted poems seem playful, despite sentimentalism, nostalgia, and melancholy; others depict doomed love— for instance, "Drama vulgar" portrays a girl's suicide after her fiancé's death in an Andalusian mining accident. Many poems address an unidentified "tú" (thou); in others the youthful persona terms herself alone, sick, bitter, abandoned, and sad. But she also mentions dreams of love and glory. In prototypical Romantic fashion, Casanova uses Gothic settings: ruined castles, Romanesque chapels, cemeteries, the ancient city of Toledo. Yet she celebrates progress, paints fishermen and miners, exalts the dignity of work—themes closer to realism and naturalism than Romanticism. Sometimes the speaker adopts a masculine voice to praise elusive beauties or lament rejection; turning philosophical, she depicts dialogues between youth and age, faith and doubt. Casanova cleverly twists clichés in "De un idilio" (Concerning an Idyll): the enamored persona suggests that the joy of requited love would be fatal, preferring to receive no response. Feminist notes in "Al trabajo" (To Work) echo labor themes ("redeeming the working class"), pointedly recalling women and children (forgotten in union platforms) and affirming that real progress demands that women no longer need marry to survive, but can be truly free.

Intelligent, sensitive, culturally active, Casanova was not attracted to Spanish matrimony and *encierro* (cloistering) of wives; her ideal (modeled on legendary Gaelic poet Ossian) was a heroic northern bard. Shortly after publishing her *Poesías,* she met Wicenty Lutoslawski, a Polish nobleman, polyglot, and philosopher-scholar visiting Spain. Espousing contemporary theories of eugenics, Lutoslawski was a mystic Polish nationalist (Poland, ruled by Russia, Germany, and Austria-Hungary, was his entire family's crusade). Lutoslawski wrote philosophy in seven languages and knew several more. A highly intelligent and messianic manic-depressive, he sought a foreign wife to fulfill legendary prophecy by fathering Poland's savior. Appalled by his ideas yet attracted by his intelligence, Casanova overcame family opposition and married Lutoslawski in 1887, agreeing to learn and speak only Polish in their home. For eight years, she traveled in Portugal, England, and France and lived in Estonia, Poland, Russia, and Kazan (in Russian Central Asia). She returned to Galicia to recuperate after a daughter died (Lutoslawski fanatically deemed doctors unnecessary). They lived four years in a fishing village near La Coruña, where Casanova's fourth daughter and last child was born. Estranged from her husband (for "failing" to bear a son), she devoted herself to writing, charitable works (promoting health care for Galician peasant women), and visiting regional women writers, including Pardo Bazán, Fanny Garrido, and Filomena Dato Muruais (Alayeto, 38).

Fugaces (1898; Fleeting Things)[6] includes 14 poems reprinted from *Poesías;* 60 previously unpublished poems convey travel impressions, especially reactions to the frozen gloom of arctic winters and snow-covered steppes. Silence, darkness, dim pale shapes, clouds, ice, and Siberian winds fill the poet's landscapes, sometimes crossed by limping, half-frozen beggars. Playing with her infant daughters, Casanova fears for their future; she returns briefly to the Romantic mode in "Tempestad de una tarde de verano" (Tempest on a Summer Afternoon), an extended trope (and pathetic fallacy) wherein nature mimics a lovers' quarrel and reconciliation. She abandons convention by suggesting permanent damage to the delicate flowers of sentiment rather than renewed beauty in the calm after the storm (reflecting growing marital conflicts and estrangement). Several poems are dedicated to friends, her mother and brothers, Lutoslawski's siblings, and other writers (mostly women).

Polish landscapes introduce memories of Andalusia, Castile, Galicia, Spanish customs, and Spanish holidays. "Jadwiga" vows never to forget the daughter whose death she will mourn forever. Modernist influence informs poems on art and beauty that reveal that Casanova has lived intensely, experienced despair, borne four children, and suffered her daughter's death and conjugal disaster. Emotional and intellectual maturation produces increased depth and power; earlier pessimism acquires density from her suffering and disappointment. As Ofelia Alayeto observes, "Hopelessness is the prevailing mood."[7]

From 1899 to 1905 the Lutoslawski home in Cracow became one of Poland's most fashionable literary salons; Casanova, personally acquainted with numerous Polish writers, translated many to Spanish. Permanently separated from her husband in 1912 (he married a young disciple in 1906), Casanova—a fervent Catholic—maintained her wedding vows, supporting her children by writing. During some seven decades in Eastern Europe, she was Spain's principal interpreter of Russia and Poland, producing essays, travelogues, and fiction and more than 830 articles for *ABC,* then Madrid's most influential daily. From 1905 to 1914 she reestablished herself in Madrid, receiving the distinction (rare for a woman) of election to the Royal Galician Academy (1906) and the Modernist Academia de Poesía Española (1911), founded by Manuel Machado and Francisco Villaespesa. *El Cancionero de la dicha* (1911; Songbook of Happiness) appeared at this time.[8]

Prefaced by eight sonnets from modernist poets (including Villaespesa, Manuel Machado, and her brother Vicente), *El Cancionero de la dicha* contains selections from earlier collections, plus 33 new compositions, 14 grouped under the title rubric, and 19 subtitled "Los Días de hoy" (The Present Days). These modernist poems are less confessional and autobiographical, emphasizing metric and formal experimentation. Casanova avoids decadence, preferring spiritual and moral concerns, light, music, unrealized ideals, beauty, death, fin-de-siècle tedium, disillusionment, and boredom. Several poems describe paintings; others evoke historic national heroes. Modernist motifs—roses and lilies, pagan gods and nymphs, and pale princesses—could sometimes be mistaken for Rubén Darío's, as in "Princesa de las Nieves" (Snow Princess): "Di a la rubia Princesa de las tierras nevadas / el secreto doliente de las cosas calladas / que cual tumba contiene nuestro amor ideal" ("I gave the pale princess of the snow-covered lands / the tormented secret of things left unsaid / which keeps like the tomb our lost ideal love" [105]). "Pagana" portrays the moonlit garden and fountain, marble statuary and gallant idyll in the stereotyped lexicon of Hispanic modernism. Allusions to Poland replace other modernists' orientalism; Casanova neither invents exotic settings nor pretends to be acquainted with them.

Casanova was much admired by Campoamor, Manuel and Antonio Machado, Eugenio D'Ors and Ramón Pérez de Ayala; one of her plays was produced in Madrid's premier Teatro Español on request of Benito Pérez Galdós. Other admirers included Don Antonio Maura (president of the Royal Spanish Academy), Jacinto Benavente, and Torcuato Luca de Tena, founder of *Blanco y Negro* and *ABC* (her longtime publisher). Celebrated for her chronicles of war and revolution, she triumphantly returned to Spain in 1919, receiving Spain's highest medal for service to humanity, La Gran Cruz de Beneficencia. Nominated for a Nobel prize (1925) and among few women mentioned in the Espasa Calpe encyclopedia (1913), she received equal space with Pardo Bazán (two pages) and was included in Polish reference works.

An avowed pacifist, Casanova became Spain's first female foreign war correspondent during World War I and volunteered as a Sister of Charity in Red Cross hospitals in Warsaw, nursing wounded Germans and Russians. Then 52 years old, she worked 10 and 12 hours daily, writing articles at night for *ABC* (1914–15) that were smuggled out of the country. The only Spanish journalist on the eastern front, she attempted objectivity, truth, and compassion, standing firm in her convictions though most Poles disagreed with her pacifism and support of Jews; her criticisms of Spain's support of Gemany offended many Spaniards. Evacuated to Russia after the fall of Warsaw, she witnessed the Russian Revolution, boldly interviewing Trotsky in October 1917. The only Spanish reporter covering World War I, the Russian Revolution, and World War II and its aftermath, Casanova was confined behind the iron curtain for her last 20 years and was essentially forgotten by her death. Her modernist poetry has long since passed from fashion, while male modernist poets have remained in the canon. Her more personal, heartfelt pieces in *Fugaces* convey universal sentiments underlying all great poetry. For historical reasons as well as her poetic concerns and the artistic difficulties she overcame, Casanova deserves to be better remembered.

The Most Important Mallorcan Poet

Maria Antònia Salvà (1869–1957), self-taught Catalan modernist inspired by Majorcan oral traditions and the island's rural *glosadors* (improvisational folk poets), is deemed the best poet of the Majorcan school. Like Armengol de Badia, Salvà concentrates on island landscape and history, depicting folkloric motifs, religious festivals, rural customs, peasant culture, ancestral traditions, and idyllic country life. Relatively conservative and Catholic, Salvà avoids ideological entanglements, depicting regional foods, children's games, island miscellany, manor settings, saffron flowers, and the sea at dawn. Enamored of little animals (especially baby chickens) and regional flora, she paints them lovingly in poetry and prose.

Salvà's poetic production spans a lifetime, beginning with *Poesies* (1903), continuing through *Espigues en flor* (1926; Wheat in Bloom), *El Retorn: Poemes* (1934; The Return), and ending with *Lluneta del pagès* (1948; Mirror of the Peasant). These, plus lesser collections and additional poems, appear in a six-volume edition of *Obres de Maria Antònia Salvà* (1948–55). An anthology entitled *Al cel sia! {poeta Maria Antònia Salvà}* (1981; And She'll be a Poet in Heaven) appeared during the post-Franco rediscovery of vernacular writers. Xesca Ensenyat's Prologue indicates that Salvà was born on 4 November 1869 in Palma, losing her mother in infancy. Catalan poet Miguel Costa i Llobera (their parish priest) encouraged the child and became her mentor; they traveled to famous Mediterranean sites of the ancient world during 1907, which inspired numerous poems.

Salvà expresses love of nature rather than human love; her poetry exhibits sensitivity for subtle shadings, refined sensibility, and vague longings characterizing the Majorcan school, enhanced by her femininity. Human love appears in her elegies to poet Emília Sureda, a beloved friend who died prematurely. Salvà wrote without esthetic ideology, without intellectual pretensions, employing minute, detailed realism, reflecting daily happenings in rural life. Reserved, discreet, upper-class, and religious, she was appalled by "immodest" Paris fashions; her correspondence with Miquel Ferrà criticizes new styles. These attitudes conditioned her to welcome the Franco revolt as "salvation" from the supposed chaos of Republican anarchy, but Salvà could not accept Francoist repression of Catalan; she collaborated in clandestine homages to Guillem Forteza and other cultural figures, perpetuating Catalan's literary viability.

Salvà composed poems to the Virgin, family servants of her childhood, a seamstress casually glimpsed, and female relatives (including nuns) and saints, albeit without feminist consciousness or intent. Other compositions celebrate religious architecture—a hermitage, church portal, convent, family sepulchre—or revolve around the Church calendar

(New Year's Day, Easter, Christmas, saints' days, Ascension), as in *Cel d'horabaixa* (Sky at Twilight). Religiosity imbues poems on blessing the fields, Christ, pastoral advice, humility, grace, the priest's rosary, church bells, contemplation of sacred art, and the hand of Providence in daily events. Salvà's lyrics celebrate childhood, physical and spiritual beauty, and children's innocence, leading Carles Riba to term her poetry "maternal without maternity" (cited by Ensenyat, xxvi).

Minor Vernacular Poets

Maria Gracia Bassa (1883–1961) used the pseudonym "Gracia B. de Llorens"; her Catalan poetry includes *Esplais de llunyania* (1919; Expanses of Distance) and *Branca florida* (1933; White Flowered). Anna Canalias (1866–1934), born in Zaragoza, likewise wrote in Catalan, publishing *Liriques* (Lyrics), *Natura, Sonets erudits* (Erudite Sonnets), and *Poesies* (no dates found). Maria Ibars Ibars (1892–1965), a Catalan poet from Denia (Valencia), published *A l'ombra del Montgó* (1949; In the Mountain's Shade). Interestingly enough, most of the women's poetry published between the end of Romanticism and the vanguard era (beginning in the late 1920s) was written in the vernaculars or by women who were bilingual.

The turn-of-the-century era produced several women recognized as poets during their lifetimes, all quickly forgotten and none in the canon today. While none have been judged of major stature when measured by the yardstick of history, neither do male poets of these same years loom large, yet the canon has better preserved their memory. In reconstructing the history of Spanish poetry in this epoch, especially regional history and that of poetry in the vernacular languages, these women merit considerably more study than they have yet received.

Chapter Four
Poets between the Wars

Canonical studies of twentieth-century Spanish poetry include no women in the Generation of 1898, Peninsular variants of *modernismo*, or the so-called *novecentistas* (Generation of 1914). Nor do women figure among the Generation of 1927 (Alberti, Aleixandre, Alonso, Cernuda, García Lorca, Guillén, Salinas, etc.). Gerardo Diego's classic *Poesía española contemporánea* (1932, 1934) recognized only two women: Josefina de la Torre (b. 1910) and Ernestina de Champourcín (b. 1905), who began publishing in the 1920s, coinciding with early publications of the Generation of 1927. Both maintained friendships and common interests with male poets of that group. Torre's poems occupy more space in Diego's anthology, but de la Torre no longer enjoys esteem comparable to Champourcín's. Because they began writing in these years, sharing similar tenets and friendships with the Generation of 1927, Rosa Chacel and Clementina Arderiu (born a decade earlier) merit prior consideration.

A European Modernist

Born in Valladolid (Castile) in 1898, Rosa Chacel moved with her family in 1908 to Madrid. She attended school briefly, disliked it, and thereafter was tutored by her mother. Limited formal studies concentrated on sculpture and painting at the ancient Escuela Superior de Bellas Artes de San Fernando in Madrid. When her delicate health dictated renouncing work in the unheated old building, she joined the Madrid Ateneo (Atheneum or private library), devoting herself to reading literature. During the 1920s, she became a disciple of José Ortega y Gasset, intellectual and cultural mentor of the rising generation, contributing regularly to his prestigious *Revista de Occidente*. Her first published poems figured among these collaborations.

Chacel married fellow painter Timoteo Pérez Rubio (1922), traveling extensively in Europe and residing in Italy. Returning to Spain in 1927, Chacel befriended new intellectual and literary figures and began publishing in *Ultra* and *Hora de España*. Her first novel, drafted in Rome, was inspired by Joyce's *Portrait of the Artist as a Young Man: Estación: Ida y vuelta* (Station: Round Trip). Similar European modernist influences characterize Chacel's subsequent work. One collection of verse appeared in Spain before the Civil War interrupted publication. Chacel's prose (novels, short fiction, and essays), like the poetry written throughout her life, incorporates poetic norms of the Generation of 1927—less experimentally, with more classical elements. Recognizing differences vis-à-vis prevailing esthetics, she withheld poems written over the years. Chacel and Rafael Alberti were the last survivors of their generation; critics consider her the period's most important woman prose writer.

Chacel became more active politically during the war, signing Loyalist manifestos and helping to organize the Frente Popular. She joined protests against imprisonment of Miguel Hernández and contributed poems to the Loyalist (Republican) magazine, *Hora de España*, composing 30 Gongorine sonnets, *A la orilla de un pozo* (1936; By the Shore of a Well), not in the neo-Gongorine mode but following Góngora's original, Latinized syntax. These feature numerous hyperbatons, relatively obscure classical allusions, and an exceptionally learned lexicon. Encouraged by Juan Ramón Jiménez, Manuel Altolaguirre published the collection in May 1936. Chacel's prologue recounts that the inspiration for the collection originated during conversations with Rafael Alberti in which both lamented contemporary neglect of classical form. Chacel intended to use the sonnet as a vehicle for the "most abrupt, incongruent images . . . practicing the inextricable liberty given us by Surrealism, its poetic essence."[1] Some celebrate contemporary literati: Alberti, María Teresa León, Luis Cernuda, Pablo Neruda, María Zambrano, Arturo Serrano Plaja, Manuel Altolaguirre. Personal relationships prompt the inclusion of "secret" confidences—memories and images from various friendships that exalt distinctive, individual traits. Chacel reminisces that many poems were composed mentally, beginning at age 12 or 13 when she took long, silent walks with her father (255–56). The sonnet lends itself to mental composition and storage. Chacel's war poems show directional change; shortly afterward she ceased publishing poetry for several decades. Donna Kirchner's article in the *Dictionary of Literary Biography* indicates that the "food sonnets," with others by Neruda, Alberti, Cernuda, and Juan Gil-Albert, were intended to aid the Republican government in exile by extolling Valencian products. Kirchner notes military imagery, celebrating defense of the home front. Chacel published occasional poems in Argentine periodicals (*La Nación, Sur, Realidad*), plus stories, reviews, and articles that were republished in *Los Títulos,* treating contemporary poets Cernuda, Alberti, and Gil-Albert. Kirchner argues that "Chacel presents poetry as a process, a silencing of conscious thought that tries to approximate the sublime, the unspeakable" (67).

Versos prohibidos (1978; Forbidden Verses) contains five epistles without fixed strophic form, varying from six lines to three pages, unrhymed pieces resembling blank verse, predominantly hendecasyllables or 14-syllable alexandrines. Other metric subgroups include sonnets and odes. The title refers to Chacel's having "prohibited" them herself for esthetic reasons, believing them too facile. Some appeared earlier in newspapers and periodicals, but most are previously unpublished. The collection consists of "Moral and Pious Epistles," "Circumstantial Sonnets," "Odes," and "Other Poems." The epistles treat ethical or philosophical inspiration, faith, religiosity, separation, and vague, undefined menace. Most were composed between 1933 and 1937 (themes of menace and separation reflect civil upheaval and the Civil War). "Epístola Moral a Serpula," treating truth (inspired by her friendship with Concha de Albornoz), appeared in *Hora de España.* Chacel considered herself an expatriate rather than an exile during some three decades in Latin America while the Franco regime controlled Spain. Having lived several years in Rome before the war, her art was essentially apolitical, but her family could not live in Spain given her husband's Republican partisanship (collaborations in Loyalist periodicals probably made Chacel persona non grata as well). Her poetry, consistently abstract, never mentions politics or exile; typifying the epoch's "pure poetry," autobiographical material is minimal.

The "Other Poems" section includes free verse and pieces published in Chacel's youth, plus previously unpublished compositions. They follow neither chronological nor thematic order, although subgrouped by form; reflecting Chacel's cosmopolitan wanderings, date lines include Paris, 1938; Greece, 1941; and New York and Montevideo. The poet depicts her studies of art, classic sketching, charcoal drawings and design, and chilly classrooms and textbooks. Contemplating the Hudson River evokes memories of the Nile, Seine, and Tiber as the water becomes fluid beauty, reflecting electric stars. Word paintings include the zoo in La Plata, places in Cuba, Rio de Janeiro, museums, ruins, and archaeological areas (inspiring attempts to re-create life there). "A Teresa" recalls the genesis of Chacel's biography of Teresa Mancha, tragic lover of Espronceda. Another significant poem treats solitude, which Chacel says taught her how to express herself.

The "Circumstantial Sonnets" vary in inspiration from Delacroix's painting to epigraphs for her novels, reflections of exile, and an "Ode to Hunger." Others treat death, anguish, abandonment, and lost happiness of days past (not her own but in classical antiquity). Chacel avoids the confessional mode; poems containing personal substrata, depersonalized by use of the plural, ostensibly relegate emotion to another time or place (e.g., oblique evocation of Spain's civil conflict via the Trojan War and Joan of Arc). "On the Battlefield" mentions puddles of blood but remains so "pure" and abstract that no textual evidence links it to the Spanish Civil War or to any identifiable war. Practitioners of "pure poetry" followed geometric models, aspiring to create lyric polyhedrons, depersonalizing and reifying people and emotions. Chacel's four-page "Ode to Joy" similarly dehumanizes joyfulness: "crystal, purest carbon prism, invulnerable to hammer blows. / Impassive to tears, / it pretends, as they do [to be] / water in polyhedric quietude" (137). Only the final lines contain personal notes: "never, never, nevermore / can we reach the threshold / of your sanctuary, never penetrate your dawn" (137). "Ode to Joy," the last composed of the *Versos prohibidos,* was written after the death of Chacel's husband (not mentioned). Elsewhere, she explains that only from great sorrow could she write clearly about happiness. "Epistle to Julián Marías" contemplates nature with intertextual references to Renaissance poet Garcilaso. Chacel explicitly rejects facile word play, confessing failure to avoid "an elegy on the suffering of our Spain" (151). The next two pages provide exceptional autobiographical references. "The Orchids" recalls reaching and leaving the "Land of Orchids" (considering the decades Chacel spent in Brazil and Argentina, surprisingly few allusions occur). "Lady of the Night" evokes an encounter in Rio, but its abstractness could picture any metropolitan setting.

While in South America, Chacel did translations from Italian, French, German, and English, including works of Rilke, Mallarmé, Camus, and Racine. Chacel's translation of Stéphane Mallarmé's "Herodias" in *Poesía (1931–1991)* reveals her own poetics: Mallarmé's theories emphasized rigor, abstraction and density, luminosity, and concentration and hermeticism. Similar qualities characterize Chacel's verse; she, too, eschews anecdotal and descriptive content (excepting highly suggestive objects), generally omitting Romanticism's lyrical "I," separating her poems from external phenomena and rendering them irreducible to experience. Both poets make extensive use of metaphor, syntactical displacement, and subdued puns, using varied forms of negation.

Chacel averts hints of *écriture féminine,* steering clear of gendered topics and distinctly feminine voice. Late twentieth-century critics view her not primarily as poet but as "dean" of Spanish women writers. Kirchner states that Chacel "assumed the status of poet laureate of Madrid in 1980"; in 1988 she won the National Prize for Literature. Active in her nineties, she twice won the Premio de la Crítica (1976 and 1977) and was nominated for the 1985 Cervantes Prize, the Spanish language's most significant recognition. Blindness during her terminal illness interrupted her writing shortly before her death on 27 July 1994.

Clementina Arderiu

Representing Catalan culture and traditions is Clementina Arderiu i Voltas (1899–1976). Born in Barcelona to a petit bourgeois family, she studied music, French, and Italian. Her silversmith father offered little encouragement for her literary interests. While still an adolescent, she met in 1912 her future husband, Catalan humanist and poet Carles Riba; he became her teacher, mentor, and then suitor. Arderiu recalls her father's laments when young poets began to frequent the house, because "those oddballs would give his business a bad name." Arderiu began working in the first Montessori School in Barcelona about the time she married (1916); Riba served as translator for Montessori's public lectures. Arderiu's first slim lyric collection, *Cançons i elegies* (1916; Songs and Elegies), eclectic in character and esthetically uneven, reflects her apprenticeship. Echoes of Renaissance Catalan writers yield to lively interest in living things, profound awareness of the richness of silence and solitude, and constant, hope-filled faith. Arderiu's originality is not thematic (constants include religious experience, love, and daily life) but results from her personal, idiosyncratic feminine voice and discourse and her optimism and gentle exuberance.

Postsymbolist influences imbue *L'Alta llibertat* (1920; High Liberty), containing 85 compositions; Arderiu also draws upon Catalan culture, folklore, and oral tradition. Some maturation but no significant thematic changes occur; the poet retains her apparent naïveté, deceptive simplicity, and unassuming soft voice. Among influences she has mentioned Catalan poets Josep Carner and Bofill i Mates; other critics add Ausias March, Roiç de Corella, and traces of Petrarch. Arderiu concisely expresses feminine joys and sorrows, the miracle of birth, love for her husband and son, and personal pleasure in silence and solitude. These first collections were incorporated in *Poemes* (1936), *Poesies completes* (1952) and *Obra poètica* (1973). Sixteen years followed, during which maternity (four children born between 1921 and 1928) and child-rearing absorbed the poet's energies. *Cant i paraules* (1936; Song and Words) appeared when Riba was teaching Greek at the University of Barcelona and the couple had begun to enjoy modest security. During the Civil War they remained in Catalunya, but when Barcelona fell in January 1939 Arderiu joined Republican refugees fleeing on foot to France; after four years in refugee camps they returned to Spain (1943) to find they had lost everything. War experiences inform what many consider Arderiu's best book, *Sempre i ara* (1946; Now and Always), which won the 1938 Joaquim Folguera Prize but remained unpublished during wartime. Arderiu's characteristic themes—daily routines, domestic or family concerns—reappear, but war prompts melancholy, sorrow, echoes of conflict, and desire for peace, solitude, and tranquility. War's uncertainties, misfortunes, and death intrude, without fully disrupting the poet's psychic equilibrium. Her distilled, direct lyricism and simple, harmonious discourse intimately depict a happy home and family. Riba's most significant impact was as teacher, not poetic model. He encouraged and criticized without directly influencing her lyric expression, and Arderiu insists that their poetry differs so that parallels cannot be drawn. Nevertheless, others insisted that Riba had written her books, allegedly "too good for a woman." Riba was imbued with Greek ideals of harmony, measure, and order, whereas Arderiu was deeply rooted in Catalan culture and tradition—although her emphatically urban, realistic poetry focuses upon the here and now. Both had contacts with the *noucentisme* movement, but this proved far more decisive for Riba than Arderiu,[2] who remained closer to anonymous song and other oral genres.

Another hiatus ensued before Arderiu's next collection appeared. In postwar Catalunya few incentives existed to write in Catalan (publicly outlawed by Franco for association with separatist and independence movements). Economically, times were difficult: shortages, restrictions, and suffering postwar Barcelona appear between the lines of *Es a dir* (1959; That Is to Say), which won the 1958 Ossa Menor Prize in manuscript and the Lletra d'Or Prize in 1960. It appeared the year of Riba's sudden death. Arderiu, physically and spiritually devastated, spent two years in depression. Essential continuity informs Arderiu's thematics and style: her colloquialism, simple and direct, becomes almost laconic; limited thematic novelty inheres in reflections of changing history and circumstances. Major themes include nature, Catalan geography, towns, landscapes, and villages and seascapes, plus increasing preoccupation with time's passing and times past.

Arderiu published her last book, *L'Esperança encara* (1969; Hope, Still), during her seventieth year. Reflecting 10 years of widowhood, this collection exhibits more maturity and less joy, but her thematic continuity and stylistic consistency render further evolution nearly imperceptible. Delicate, luminous poems treat childhood and adolescence, looking backward to her "crazy" youthful vitality and rebellion, unconventional attitudes and pure joy of living. Arderiu's continuity originates in her immutable gender role, the wellspring of poetic inspiration and the bulwark of her constant internal identity, notwithstanding vicissitudes. Modifications in attitude appear—for example, death (fearful in her youth) becomes a friend in old age. The central section of *L'Esperança encara,* "The King's Table," consists of short religious and Eucharistic poems, while "Afterward" paints the void left by her husband's death. Happier memories lighten the gloom: days spent in Mallorca, Ithaca, Delphi, and the picturesque Catalan fishing village of Cadaqués (scene of García Lorca's summers with the family of Salvador Dalí). Arderiu recalls in "La Meva Cambra a Cadaqués" (My Room in Cadaqués) that for her husband's sixtieth birthday, numerous Barcelona writers, artists, and artisans contributed to purchasing and refurnishing a fisherman's cottage for the couple, complete with paintings and books donated by their creators. Arderiu also pays homage to Catalan lyricists: Ausías March, Sant Jordi, Montserrat, Josep Carner, Blai Bonet, Roselló. This final, elegiac collection also depicts widowhood after long, fruitful companionship suddenly changed to living in the past. She recalls years as adolescent, wife, mother, and grandmother, when she wrote her poems above all for Carles. Resisting sorrow and despair, she turns increasingly to faith and religious traditions.

Obvious differences notwithstanding, Arderiu's poetry and poetic persona bear comparison with Jorge Guillén: both proclaim profound general acceptance of life, where things are deeply positive, a world essentially *bien hecho* (well made). The poetic persona exudes joy and hope, exulting in humble objects, thoughts, and happenings, the distilled alchemy of sensations and living matter. Arderiu writes from an irrepressible urge: "If I did not write / I would be sad / for me the poet's work / is like my daily bread." Her poetry proves less abstract than that of better-known contemporaries, more personal but only in comparison with "pure" poets: she should not be termed autobiographical. Her depiction of minute, daily objects serve as springboards to more abstract, eternal themes: love, time's fleetingness, death, joy, dreams, mother-hood, rebellion, and plenitude. Certain constant motifs occur through-out, especially the wind (symbolizing danger, threat, change, or unidentified sinister forces and sometimes death); trees (always positive elements but never abundant); and the house, often representing the poet's own internal subjectivity. The house constitutes escape from the real, objective world "outside," but this enclosure can become the scene for solitary struggles with herself. Various critics note that Arderiu iden-tifies herself with the house, but not as simple domesticity or acceptance of feminine cloistering; rather, the house intervenes between herself and others, defending the poetic ego and zealously preserving its intimacy.

Arderiu's early poems aspire to fullness of life, conveying undefined longings, yearning toward love, contemplation of golden dawns and starry nights, discoveries in reading and childhood epiphanies. Her poet-ry falls short of feminist but is unmistakably feminine, with such themes as giving birth and maternal and conjugal love. Occasional lines reveal wider gender preoccupations: "L'Humil Heroisme" (Humble Heroism) celebrates women's work and loyalty, their unassuming, unquestioning risk-taking to care for children and husband. Other poems beg domestic protection, treat waiting as women's lot, and depict fear, ambivalent emotions, and the sadness of farewell. Faces become motifs of anguish; war and exile appear via motifs of storm, shipwreck, fog, battle, ruins, and truce. Images of wilted flowers and truncated springtime convey reactions to war with elegies for lost relatives, the war dead, the wrench-ing grief of exile, memories of the house and garden left behind. The title poem, "L'Esperança encara," recapitulates reactions to Carles's death: initial rejection, denial, resignation, acceptance of solitude, and discovery that not all is lost: "he lives in my [heart and] soul." Arderiu's characteristic concision, directness, telling details, and verbal economy achieve unmediated impact as she depicts widowhood's darker nights, eerily silent without the other's breathing at her side.

Arderiu produced five books containing slightly more than 200 poems bringing her recognition as accomplished and significant; admired within the Catalan cultural ambient, she was deemed the out-standing woman poet of Catalunya during her final decade. In com-menting upon her own poetry, she repeatedly, unassumingly used the words "intuitive, intimate, and very Catalan." Her circumstantial but personal poetry of hope, faith, and love—always serene, transparent, fluid, and coherent—is devoid of affectation and pretense. Important collections include *Poesies completes* (1952); the bilingual (Catalan/

Castilian) *Antologia poètica* (1961, 1982); *Obra poètica* (1973), the most definitive edition of her work; and the critical anthology *Contraclaror* (1985; Against the Light), with a sensitive Introduction by Catalan poet Maria-Mercè Marçal. Arderiu links Maria Antònia Salvà, Rosa Leveroni, and Cèlia Viñas Olivella,[3] a succession of worthy Catalan women poets excluded from the canon and allowed to lapse into oblivion.

Concha Méndez

Concha Méndez, born in 1898 (some sources say in Madrid; others San Sebastián), gained recognition in Spain before the Civil War, having published four collections, one of which, *Vida a vida* (1932; From Life to Life), was reprinted in 1979 with her last book, *Vida o río* (Life, or the River). Early collections include *Inquietudes* (1926; Worries) and *Surtidor* (1928; Fountainhead), wherein critics detected echoes of Alberti and Cernuda. *Canciones de mar y tierra* (1930; Songs of Sea and Land) appeared in Buenos Aires. In 1928 García Lorca introduced her to poet Manuel Altolaguirre (some seven years her junior), whom she married in 1929, with numerous figures of the Generation of 1927 in attendance. Méndez helped in Altolaguirre's publishing enterprises (he and Emilio Prados founded *Litoral* in 1926, and the couple cofounded a press whose products included Pablo Neruda's *Caballo verde para la poesía, Héroe,* and *Hora de España*—the first two being significant vanguard reviews and the last the major Republican cultural organ during the Civil War). Living in a small hotel, Méndez dressed in overalls, serving as typesetter. Although she apparently had more books of poetry than Altolaguirre, she has been relegated to critical oblivion, "virtually erased" from literary annals after the Civil War (Bellver, 28).[4] In 1937 she fled the war, taking her two-year-old daughter to France, where French poet Paul Eluard gave them refuge. There she lost her newborn son, lamented in the elegiac *Niño y sombra* (1936; Boy and Shade). After Altolaguirre joined them in Paris in 1939, they moved first to Cuba, living there until 1943, then settled in Mexico. In Havana, Méndez published *Lluvias enlazadas* (1940; Interlaced Rains), pessimistic war poems reacting to bloodshed, violence, and the horrors of civil conflict, articulating her tensions, anguish, uncertainty, and pain. She also published such dramatic works as *El Solitario* (1940; The Lonely One). *Poemas, sombras y sueños* (1944; Poems, Shadows, and Dreams) and *Villancicos de Navidad* (1944; Christmas Carols) both appeared in Mexico.[5] As do many Spanish women's writings on the Civil War, Méndez's works express concern with war's impact on families rather than an interest in combat, battle-field heroics, and machismo.

Méndez draws upon Spanish lyric traditions and popular metrics, especially in her *canciones* (songs) with the neopopular air characterizing works of Lorca and Alberti. Her prewar poetry (according to Francisco Ayala's 1928 review) exuded vitality, enthusiasm, strength, decisiveness, and youthful optimism. By contrast, her poetry of war and exile exhibits a "preoccupation with the horrors of war, articulation of loss, pain, and despair, expressions of ambiguity, a somber tonality, and images of darkness and negativity" (Bellver, 27)—reactions characterizing exiles. Preoccupied by war's separation of families and resulting emotional problems, Méndez highlights women's culture, psychological survival and family well-being rather than ideology. Having lost her son and her country, Méndez lost her husband when he abandoned her and their daughter in exile. Negation, absence, emptiness, and irreparable separation between past and present destroy her personal and literary continuity. She depicts her inner trauma, struggles with nostalgia, homesickness, and identity crises. Her marriage's disintegration approximately coincided with her mother's death, and Méndez turned inward, becoming introspective and withdrawn, producing self-referential works while despairing, then recovering to affirm her own strength. Motherhood and her daughter's presence proved crucial: subsequent poems reiterate the strength of mother-daughter bonds. Méndez established an intertextual "sisterhood" with Rosalía de Castro, a kindred soul with whom she shared her grief.

Separated by exile from the poetic center, Méndez was marginalized (as characterizes much exile experience), obliging her to draw more heavily on personal circumstances. Language and the act of writing contribute to her eventual reaffirmation, as does her "cathartic dialogue" (Bellver) with Rosalía and her recovery of feminine roots. Apparently Méndez ceased publishing until *Vida o río* appeared in 1979. Despite relegation to critical oblivion for half a century, Méndez produced nine books of poetry and three plays, figuring among Spain's more significant women poets of exile. She died in Mexico in 1986.

Minor Figures

Herminia Fariña e Cobián (1904–66) wrote primarily in Galician, producing plays and poetry during the 1920s. *Seara: Poesías gallegas* (1924; Grain field: Galician Poems), 34 poems exhibiting lingering influences of *modernismo* upon metrics and structure (otherwise typifying nineteenth-century Galician verse), follows Rosalía de Castro's thematics. Marked by orality and using colloquial and conversational language, Fariña's poetry celebrates Galician landscapes, their beauty and tranquility, voicing sadness, longing, and nostalgia for the homeland. Folk themes and sentimentality abound.

Josefina de la Torre (b. 1910), an accomplished musician, like García Lorca, studied violin, piano, and guitar, playing in concert orchestras, and participated in theatrical productions in her native Canary Islands and Madrid. The erstwhile leading actress of the National Theatre, she also played major roles in radio dramas and wrote short fiction. Composed early in life, her poems appeared in the periodicals *Alfar, Azor,* and *Gaceta literaria* and the collections *Verso y prosa* and *Versos y estampas* (1927; Verses and Vignettes), with a Prologue by Pedro Salinas. *Poemas de la Isla* (1930; Island Poems) use free verse and rely heavily on marine imagery and thematics, reflecting the island ambient typically painted by Canary poets: water, shore, light, sand, storm, sun, sea, and foam. Spontaneous, filled with youthful vigor and vitality, this collection combines light tones with free verse—the most significant lyric device being abundant and carefully wrought metaphors. With *Marzo incompleto* (1968; Unfinished March), originally published in *Fantasía,* the poet looks backward in longing for an "incomplete springtime" as maturity gives way to old age. Retrospective contemplation reveals her alienation, frustrated maternal urges, unhappiness in love, sense of being-toward-death, and awareness of physical aging. The vivid nature motifs characterizing earlier works yield to confessional and cathartic baring of emotions, appropriately expressed without technical adornment.

Pilar de Valderrama

Pilar de Valderrama (1894–1979) relates in her memoirs, *Sí, soy Guiomar* (1981; Yes, I'm Guiomar), that her father became governor of Zaragoza shortly before her birth (the name Pilar honors the city's patron saint). Her father suffered an undisclosed malady, becoming catatonic and demented before dying when Pilar was barely six. Interned in a Catholic boarding school for a decade, she returned home after her mother's remarriage. Insistent courtship by a middle-aged stepbrother drove her in 1913 to hasty marriage at age 19 to Rafael Martínez Romarate, a handsome, intelligent, and socially prominent compulsive womanizer. Given her strict Catholic upbringing, Valderrama tolerated his affairs while suffering psychologically because of his coldness and the deaths of her first daughter and beloved younger brother. Melancholy and frustrated, she turned to poetry; many poems exhibit autobiographical and personal substrata. Chronologically, Valderrama belongs with "elders" of the Generation of 1927 (e.g., Salinas), but artistically she resembles the Generation of 1898.

Valderrama had borne two daughters and a son and published her second book of poetry before March 1928, when her husband hysterically confessed that his longtime mistress had just committed suicide. Valderrama, who had coped with briefer affairs, was stunned; she left home, escaping to Segovia, where intense cold drove her back to Madrid. Depressed and under medical care, she returned to Segovia in June with an introduction to Antonio Machado. They first met on 26 June 1928, and Valderrama took refuge in their friendship; the nationally renowned but timid and lonely poet, instantly smitten, made her "muse, queen, goddess" of his final years. Valderrama, known primarily as Machado's secret, platonic love rather than for her writing, attained modest renown and wrote, albeit sporadically, throughout her life. Their surreptitious meetings during six or seven years were usually in public places: Moncloa Gardens, quiet neighborhood cafés, occasional train rides, memorialized in poems by one or both.

Valderrama's first collection, *Las Piedras de Horeb* (1923; The Stones of Horeb), moderately well received, was subsequently excluded from her *Obra poética* (1958; [Selected] Poetic Works). *Huerto cerrado* (1928; Closed Garden), reflecting readings of Saint John of the Cross and Fray Luis de León, Jorge Manrique, and Bécquer, also echoes Machado, to whom she sent this volume prior to their meeting. Critic Rafael Cansinos Asséns praised *Huerto cerrado* enthusiastically; even more significant praise was accorded her third collection, *Esencias* (1930), by Machado. Several poems bear witness to their love, incorporating verses by Machado, his manner or vocabulary. *Un Tercer mundo* (1934; A Third World), subtitled "A Dramatic Poem," strikes autobiographical resonances with its love triangle. The married heroine, unhappy with her cold, inattentive husband, takes refuge in books and prescription drugs, leaves home and meets a melancholy poet who immediately falls in love with her. The play's dénouement takes place in a platonic, metaphysical "third world" of illusion. The title also evokes the "private place" Valderrama shared with Machado, an imaginary space of spiritual encounter where they "met" in thought an hour before midnight.[6]

In 1935 Valderrama wrote "Testamento de un amor imposible" (Testament of an Impossible Love), whose first five strophes begin, "If I die first"; final verses imagine her immaculate spiritual encounter with Machado after death. Their meetings were suspended by civil strife and terrorism before the Civil War. Valderrama's husband had advance notice of the uprising. In May 1936 the estranged couple moved to protect their children, renting a villa in Estoril, Portugal. Literary historians have blamed Valderrama for ending the relationship with Machado, but her autobiography indicates this was involuntary. With their correspondence interrupted by the conflict (Machado was in the Republican zone, Valderrama in the Nationalist), Machado's "Canciones a Guiomar" (Poems to Guiomar) turned bitter, reflecting sad belief that his beloved's silence meant rejection. His last poem to her, a 1938 sonnet beginning, "De mar a mar entre los dos la guerra / más profunda que la mar" ("From sea to sea the war between us / deeper than the sea"), describes his situation on the Mediterranean coast with her on the Atlantic and Spain divided between them. Valderrama later adopted the opening words, "De mar a mar," to entitle her final collection, a homage to Machado unpublished until after her death. Following the war, Valderrama published *Holocausto* (1943; Sacrifice), prefaced with a sonnet by Machado's brother, Manuel.[7] *Holocausto* expresses her reaction to wartime deaths and losses: her therapeutic relationship with Machado and then his death; the death of her son, a young artist; and the deaths of many relatives and friends. Valderrama's home in Madrid was also badly damaged. Her memoirs indicate she spent three years in almost constant depression. *Holocausto* attempts to exorcise her grief.

Freed by widowhood, Valderrama published *Obra poética* (1958), including *Espacio* (Space), which begins with an "Amorous Dedication" to Machado, evoking their spiritual fusion. Other poems recall their silent walks and psychic togetherness transcending time, space, and even death. Incorporating lines from Machado's *Campos de Castilla,* Valderrama evokes his soul in the landscape he loved, experiencing his proximity through their mutual devotion to Castile. She paints the Castilian landscape as viewed from Madrid, looking northward to the distant Sierra de Guadarrama. From 1958 to 1979 Valderrama abstained from publishing, but not from writing. Unpublished works, collected under the title *De mar a mar* (1984; From Sea to Sea), were entrusted by Valderrama's daughter Alicia after her mother's death to Carlos Murciano, who edited and published 52 poems. Letters from Machado

and conversations between the two inspire several poems; others commemorate their encounters, recall little-frequented neighborhood cafés
where they met, or paint mutual discovery and intellectual collaboration
(Machado would read Valderrama his work-in-progress, incorporating
her suggestions). Other poems allude to the deaths of Valderrama's son,
mother, and lover; the deaths of the three important men in her life and
her own death are variously anticipated, described, and reconciled.

Marina Romero

On 5 February 1908 Marina Romero Serrano was born in Madrid. Her
liberal, enlightened family sent her to the International Institute for
Girls, an education unusual for its early beginnings and international
focus. Romero completed her *bachillerato* (high school equivalency
degree) at the Instituto Escuela, guided by progressive principles inform-
ing the Intitución Libre de Enseñanza, which formed much of Spain's
emergent twentieth-century intelligentsia. Romero studied philosophy
and literature at the University of Madrid, and in about 1930 began
writing poetry; her slim first collection, *Poemas "A"* (Poems "To"),
appeared in 1935. With Spanish government grants, she completed an
M.A. (1937) at Mills College in Oakland, California. She taught Spanish
literature (1938–70) at Douglass College (the women's college of
Rutgers University) and also taught at Middlebury College in Vermont.
In 1970 she returned to Spain. As a Republican sympathizer, her prolonged expatriation had aspects of self-exile, conditioning her poetry
written outside Spain with longing that displaces her earlier lighthearted
ludic stance in books written (according to Noël Valis) under the
"influence of the Generation of 1927, especially Pedro Salinas, in its
rhetorical and lyrical playfulness and neopopular strains."[8] Romero's first
poems, conceived in the era of "pure poetry" or "dehumanized" art,
avoid the confessional mode. Reticence concerning autobiographical and
anecdotal materials persists throughout her published verse. In *An
Encyclopedia of Continental Women Writers,* Valis notes Romero's "pleasure
in wordplay and verbal virtuosity . . . offset by exploitation of the simple
rhythms and imagery of popular poetry," underscoring her "tendency to
. . . merge refined and popular strains of writing into one."

Nostalgia de mañana (1943; Nostalgia for Tomorrow) incorporates
poems written between 1930 and 1935. Many are neopopular songs,
then in vogue. In the second half Romero initiates the personal thematics
predominant in her mature works, anticipating the gravity characterizing

exile themes. *Presencia del recuerdo* (1952; Presence of Memory), 53 poems dedicated to the memory of exiled poet Pedro Salinas, evokes the mentor whose work Romero admired while still in Spain. Word play and rhetorical games do not disappear completely, but love and sorrow; the universal, eternal theme of time and its passing; the radical solitude of poets; and themes of death, loss, and memory acquire heightened visibility. In "Desde esta lejanía" (From This Distance)[9] the poet reads beside a river, but instead of the page before her, she sees "villages and seas / castles and byways / of my homeland" and feels a sharp stab of nostalgia (63). The exile dreams of return, realizing that the idealized landscape of her personal springtime cannot be relived. In *Midas: poema de amor* (1954; Midas: A Love Poem) the exemplary myth of the king with the "golden touch" provides an extended metaphor for the treasure of love, emotional "gold" possessed and lost; initially it signifies amourous plenitude, which slips progressively away. This motif unites the 53 compositions, which may be read as a single unit. *Paisaje y literature de España: Antología de la Generación de 1898* (1957), part of Romero's professional activity, received the Istituto Nacional del Libro Español Prize from Spain's National Institute of Books.

Love, time, solitude, and loss and memory, present throughout Romero's poetry, intensify with succeeding works. *Sin agua, el mar* (1961; Without Water, the Sea) melds and fuses these themes with awareness of aging, personal mortality, and the existential sense of life as being-toward-death. Greater depth and simplicity accompany heightened intimacy. Loneliness, loss of human love, and resultant radical solitude lead the poet to seek other relationships, human and divine, enunciating social preoccupations. Valis reads the poems of *Sin agua, el mar* (numbered from last to first, in descending order) as diminishment (259), ending in dispossession, bleakness, and nothingness, as only memory remains. Vocabulary, syntax, and rhetoric are similarly reduced to the bare minimum.

After returning to Spain in 1970, Romero wrote numerous books for children, including *Alegrías: Poemas para niños* (1973; Happiness: Poems for Children), *Campanillas del aire* (1980; Bells in the Air), *Churrupeta va a la luna* (1985; Churrupeta Goes to the Moon), and *Disparatillos con Masacha* (1985; Silliness with Masacha). *Honda raíz* (1989; Deep Root), subtitled "Variations on a [Single] Theme," consists of 47 sonnets and one final poem of four quatrains treating lost love remembered. These sonnets evoke unconditional surrender, joyous carnal encounter, infinite desire for the lover's presence, togetherness, followed by "Cinderella's" return to reality at midnight, separation and longing, pain and bitter-sweet remembrance. The final epigraph, from Pablo Neruda ("Love is so brief, forgetfulness so long"), characterizes the love affair reconstructed retrospectively throughout. The first-person poetic consciousness recalls her life of daydream and memory devoted to reinventing brief moments of pleasure. One sonnet concludes that it was "better to have loved and lost / and be able to claim as food / the scant grains of cracked wheat / than to pass through life without a friend / raising walls against the wind / in a display of feigned valor."[10]

The poetic persona recalls the lover's taking her gift of self as his due, leaving her behind when he moved on; she relives the pain of returning to a formal relationship—communicated briefly, indirectly, without reproach. The poems abound in carnal imagery, metaphors of the body: lips, hands, hair, mouth, chest, skin, blood, pulse, heart, veins, flesh and bones. Binary oppositions provide a central structuring device: day/night, joy/sorrow, presence/absence, light/shadow, empty/full, chill/warm, truth/deception, living/dying, thirst/satiation, yesterday/today; the pain of recall repeatedly clashes with the desire to remember. Ultimate ability to recall without pain (Sonnet 44) accompanies redis-covery of the world's beauty and joy of living. Sonnet 47 exults, "My heart is now autonomous" (57); the last poem describes a twilight exis-tence wherein enjoyment of a belated "liberation" (from the lover's power) remains overshadowed by love lost, time invested for naught. The collection depicts paradigmatic feminine fidelity, devotion, and chastity for a probably married lover. Romero, not aggressively feminist, never invokes women's rights or mentions abuse of women, nor does she allude to other women across the centuries who shared heartbreak and humiliation as the "Other Woman," waiting in the background and ulti-mately relegated to oblivion. The feminist content of her poetry inheres in the understated confidence in her own worth, the autonomy of her voice, and the full sense of liberty and responsibility assumed in her exis-tential posture.

Ernestina de Champourcín

Ernestina de Champourcín (b. 10 July 1905 in Vitoria) is termed a Basque poet by Otxoa,[11] who considers Concha Méndez another Basque of the Generation of 1927. Champourcín never wrote in Basque, but Basques' writing in Castilian is not peculiar to women (Pío Baroja and Miguel de Unamuno used the dominant official language, as have many

Catalans and Galicians). Champourcín received a trilingual education (English, French, and Spanish) at home with private teachers up to age 10. During her adolescence the family moved to Madrid, where she obtained her *bachillerato* at the Instituto Cisneros, whose atmosphere of misogyny she recalled years later with distaste.[12] University study was frustrated by her father's demand that her mother accompany her and her own stubborn rejection of his conditions. Without formal preparation in poetics, her early poetry exhibits influences of Romanticism, modernism (symbolist backgrounds, readings of Verlaine and Lamartine), and Juan Ramón Jiménez. Her outspoken admiration for Jiménez and his work probably contributed to critics' identifying her with an outmoded paradigm.

Champourcín's poetry, remote from theoretical preoccupations and experimental innovations but imbued by enduring religious preoccupations, is very personal, defying simplistic categorization. Accquaintance with coeval male poets brought her closer to "pure poetry." In Gerardo Diego's 1962 anthology, *Poesía española contemporánea, 1901–1934,* Champourcín states rather flippantly that the only "real and essential fact" of her biography is her birth date, that childhood and adolescence were her life's only "truly intellectual cycle," when she read and wrote in utter seriousness. Disdaining the "horrible epithet of poetess," she proclaims her "absolute lack of poetics, guiding concepts and principles" save for an affinity to vagueness and wandering (460). Elsewhere she explains that she writes "because God wills it." Four collections published during her first decade of writing—*En silencio* (1926; In Silence), *Ahora* (1928; Now), *La Voz en el viento* (1931; Voice in the Wind), and *Cántico inútil* (1936; Futile Canticle)—brought her moderate respect. José Angel Asunce mentions pressures on Diego to exclude her from the second edition (1934), citing a 1990 interview with Champourcín (xii) without explanation; Andrew Debicki notes commentaries by Guillermo de Torre and Díaz Plaja reflecting traditional views of woman as emotional, irrational, and intellectually inferior.[13]

Observers consider Champourcín's first four collections (published prior to her marriage and exile) a discrete division, termed "poetry of human love," in contrast with exile works dubbed "poetry of divine love." *Ahora* and *La Voz en el viento* exhibit sensibility and intimate simplicity, invoking underlying Romantic reminiscences. In the latter and *Cántico inútil* Champourcín refines and pares her language, moving closer to "pure poetry." Youthful works with their enormous spiritual energy exalt love, earthly and divine, viewing life as hope and solitude. *Cántico* (sonnets and ballads written between 1932 and 1935) figures among her most significant works. Champourcín was no militant feminist, but she defended women's rights to "dignity" and helped found Madrid's Liceo Femenino, together with María de Maeztu, María Baeza, Pilar Zubiaurre, and Concha Méndez (Asunce, xvi), serving as secretary until this organization was closed by hostilities. Intellectual friendships in Madrid included Juan José Domenchina, another budding poet, active in leftist Republican politics. Following war's outbreak in July 1936, Champourcín worked as a nurse and hospital auxiliary until marrying Juan José Domenchina in November 1936. Shortly afterward, they accompanied the Republican government to provisional capitals and exile in France, spending three months in Toulouse. Champourcín published in Republican periodicals, including *El Sol, La Gaceta Literaria, Mujer, La Estafeta Literaria,* and *Blanco y Negro.*

Living as refugees in France, the couple accepted Alfonso Reyes's invitation to teach in Mexico. Champourcín adapted well to life in exile, unlike Domenchina, who soon quit teaching, alleging lack of training and vocation. Domenchina—cerebral, polemical, dogmatic, and caustic—exalted his own creativity, suffering from his "personal tragedy." His melodramatic depression left Champourcín to fend for them both. The Fondo de Cultura Económica offered translation work that became Champourcín's major activity for years. She translated history, philosophy, sociology, anthropology, literature, biographies, and great works of poetry, rendering Elizabeth Barrett Browning's *Sonnets from the Portuguese* to Castilian. Eventually translating some 50 titles for Revista de Occidente, Rialp, and other publishers, she abandoned poetry for some 15 years. Champoururcín retrospectively re-created these years in *Primer Exilio* (First Exile), written after returning to Spain.

Presencia a oscuras (1952; Presence in Darkness), the fruit of years of intensifying introspection, depicts Champourcín's quest for her own truth(s) and path in life. God assumes the guise of reason; mistico-religious values accompany the poet's vision of the deity as friend, refuge, presence, answer to ultimate questions. The theme of "divine love" intensifies after Domenchina's death (1957), as Champourcín summons her religious faith, especially in *Cárcel de los sentidos* (1964; Prison of the Senses), *El Nombre que me diste* (1966; The Name You Gave Me), *Hai-kais espirituales* (1967 Spiritual Hai-kais [the Spanish approximation of haiku]), *Cartas cerradas* (1968; Closed Letters), and *Poemas del ser y del estar* (1974; Poems of Being and Existence). Champourcín's change parallels the shift from carnal passions and corporal preoccupations to seeking spiritual freedom and truth characterizing Domenchina's final collection, *El Extrañado* (1958; The Lost), which returns to extreme traditionalism after early experimentalism. The *Hai-kais* seek the pure, secret Word (*Verbum*) via anguished prayers, insistent pleas for mystic integration in the Godhead, classic references to life as death, blindness, and solitude. In *Cartas cerradas* Champourcín celebrates others longing for mystical union with God, as in her "Letter to Thomas Merton." This series expresses her struggle to adapt to widowhood, coping with grief and sublimating human urges.

Champourcín returned to Spain in 1972 in Franco's twilight years, establishing herself in Madrid. Familiar landmarks revived memories of the 1930s, yet she encountered a vastly different city, "enclosed" behind walls, covered with asphalt. Obsessed with salvaging Domenchina's work and rehabilitating his literary reputation, Champourcín found the environment still unreceptive. The "walled," closed city, a metaphor of solitude, existential alienation and incommunication, underscores urban dehumanization. Champourcín apparently felt more "exiled" in Francoist Madrid than in Mexico. These sentiments imbue *La Pared transparente* (1984; The Transparent Wall), critiquing the "foreign" homeland. In 1988 octogenarian Champourcín published *Huyeron todas las islas* (All the Islands Have Fled), an introspective, pensive leave-taking of life, things, and persons she once loved.

Asunce proposes four divisions or periods for Champourcín's works: the first two collections, "early poetic exercises" (up to 1928); the next two collections, or "poetry of maturity" (1928–40), both subsumed by "human love" characterizing the prewar works; poetry of "divine love" (1940–72), whose terminal boundary is return from exile; and "poetry of love via evocation and desire" (1972–91). This scheme expands upon without contradicting that proposed in Joy Landeira's annotations of Champourcín's works in Carolyn Galerstein.[14] Debicki correctly notes the early works' superior imaginative quality vis-à-vis the "didactic message" of later ones (58). *En silencio,* focusing on the poetic ego and internal rhyme play, seems profoundly and unabashedly emotional, Romantic, and intimate. Countervaling modernist motifs—music, poetry, colors, melancholy, sadness—and modernist intertexts echoing Juan Ramón Jiménez attenuate Romantic effects. In *Ahora* poetic sensualism produces heightened visibility of sensorial data as contemplation of the external world diminishes the ego-centered emphasis. Whereas *En silencio* had focused on the heart, *Ahora* presents both heart and sense perceptions. Debicki emphasizes important, transforming, visionary imagery and the creation of objective correlatives for her emotions (49).

La Voz en el viento synthesizes emotion and sensuality: poems become more precise, formally closer to the spirit and techniques of the Generation of 1927. Critics generally recognize significant qualitative differences between the first two collections and the next two, with clear superiority accorded the latter for increased technical versatility and control, better integration of form and content, lessened anecdotal or biographical material. Between her second and third collections, Champourcín became a defender of "pure poetry," refining and purging sentiment and striving for atemporal effects via more objective focus, reducing conjugated verb forms (and subject pronouns). The individual ego is further effaced by the abstract sentiments evoked (plenitude, eternity, divinity, beauty, totality, infinity, essence, liberty, originality, and transformation). Symbols replace emotion, with the road image representing change through love's transforming power, identified with underlying subjective passion.[15] Debicki identifies visionary metaphors, prosopopoeia, and humanization and depersonalization, plus traces of surrealist imagery.

Champourcín's abstraction increases in *Cántico inútil,* and love becomes less personal, more universal, although frequent references to human anatomy (hands, face, fingers, lips, and chest) and senses (touch, sound, and sight) characterize this "poetry of human love." Asunce terms these motifs "symbology of the human body" (xlii); despite abstract presentation, they allude to real persons and the chemistry of their encounters. Asunce asserts that God symbolizes or personifies all human amorous striving (xliii), while Debicki observes the fusion of human and divine planes in a mythic vision of union (59).

The next six books, which Asunce considers especially important (xliv), use "divine love" to externalize the poet's suffering, loss, desires, and frustrations and the emotional upheaval of exile and death. Existential alienation, Domenchina's definitive absence, and intensified solitude underlie this lyric outpouring. But *Cartas cerradas* expresses more mundane concerns, including "existential" or protest poetry in Spain, incorporating "unpoetic" ingredients. Champourcín considers lyricism undermined and attenuated by "garbage in the corners, dog vomit, and stench in the doorways . . . of run-down hotels and taverns" (285);[16] she inquires how poetry can be possible without mystery. Her "Sealed Letters" to God present half a dialogue (God does not reply). The implied dialogue is not new for Champourcín, but the interlocutor is no longer the human "tú" (thou). Despite rejecting "social poetry," Champourcín's language becomes more colloquial and conversational, more direct, with less ornamentation and fewer rhetorical devices. Collections composed after exile contain generally brief pieces in *arte menor* (eight or fewer syllables), using assonance. Ascetic in spirit and form, dominated by obsession with the search (symbolized by the road), these poems advance the quest for spiritual goals via renunciation and transcendence. The wall symbol appears, signifying separation in space and time: the wall symbolizes exilic separation, separation from her husband by death, and separation from spiritual goals. Asunce notes Platonic substrata, comparing the symbolic wall with Plato's allegory of the cave (xlix). Platonic intertexts are more apparent in *El Nombre que me diste,* whose title emphasizes the name's transcendent nature. Essence— pure, immaterial, and incorporeal—now dominates the spiritual quest.

Strong, overriding ascetic preoccupations in *Cárcel de los sentidos* and *El Nombre que me diste* reflect the widowed poet's struggle against her own sexuality, indirectly confessed in lines such as these: "prison of the senses / . . . put sentries at all the exits / to patrol against my weakness" (239); "I'm still besieged by fragrances / from the road I've left behind" (240); "dry lips burning with unhealthy desire" (240); "cleanse this unquiet flesh" (225); and "Help me to carry / the burden of my body / . . . poor, exhausted flesh which knows not how to fly" (225). Champourcín's repeated references to imperious bodily demands and her loneliness and emptiness produce prayers for strength to "will not to go / where easy acts call / to avoid the shore where senses suffice" (231). Restraining laments, she nonetheless protests, "I can't accustom myself / to this total vacuum / this not having anything / or anyone: this path / without trees or fountains" (262). Tree and fountain, transparent Freudian images of human sexuality, connect to the *Hai-kais espirituales,* where the tree symbolizes divinity, humanity its shadow (cf. Asunce, li). Asceticism implies continued vigilance against bodily appetites, and the Eucharist, the body of Christ, becomes the poet's defense against her own body. She builds upon traditional models of classic Spanish poetry, most importantly Saint John of the Cross, the source of several epigrams. The Divine Mother, absent from "classic" mystical writings, frequently serves as interlocutor.

Compositions following Champourcín's return to Spain—her "poetry of evocation and desire" written between 1973 and 1991 (cf. Asunce)— reflect renewed contacts with her native soil, producing less joy than sorrow. In *Primer Exilio* she records her recollections of war, the couple's itinerary from Madrid to exile, the refugees' path to Vera Cruz and

Mexico City. After leaving, she writes movingly of the Caribbean and the tropical refuge where she spent more than three decades. Positive New World portraits contrast with Old World dehumanization, cruelty, materialism, heartlessness and spiritual desolation in *La Pared transparente*. Pervasive surrealistic/expressionistic atmosphere and frenetic movement underscore loss of human communication and warmth (cf. *Poet in New York*). The bridge motif connecting these works to Champourcín's earlier poetry is love, humanity's hope of salvation from existential solitude, incommunication, and alienation. Jiménez Faro affirms that Champourcín's six decades of poetic evolution constitute a single search for truth and light (15), citing Arturo del Villar, who considers *La Pared transparente* stylistically and thematically linked to *Primer Exilio* (14). Champourcín's progressively more naked poetry, concentrating upon ultimate meaning, seeks distilled intensity. Poetic devices are reduced to the barest minimum, rhetorically and metrically; once-favored Alexandrines and hendecasyllables disappear, underscoring a world of nothingness, peopled by palpable nonentities or nonbeings—nonpersons incapable of communication.

Huyeron todas las islas, a senescent, scant 32 pages, reveals Champourcín's fatigue, awareness of approaching death, and readiness to quit the fray. The title, drawn from Apocalypse 16:20, evokes the concept of human beings as "islands" of existential solitude; their "flight" or deaths leave other islands (including the poet) isolated. The sense of life as being-toward-death and time's fleetingness informs this farewell work. *Los Encuentros frustrados* (1991; Frustrated Encounters), 10 brief poems occupying only five pages, appeared separately and suggest definitive leave-taking. Roses and other flowers, twilight, and the road—persistent symbols from Champourcín's earlier works—now presage the final journey. Autumnal chill, fatigue, and a confused jumble of shining memories frame the affirmation that "The truth is that nothing / can ever completely end / and sometimes we forget it / in our anxiety" (442). Docilely she awaits "an hour always unknown" (444), desiring to know nothing, "neither know nor dream / but invent it all" (446). Fitting final words for a poet, these lines reaffirm poetry's transcendent worth, recalling its etymological meaning—"creation."

Jiménez Faro's introduction mentions two other women who published their first collections the same year (1926) as Champourcín: María Teresa Roca de Togores (*Poesías*), and Cristina de Arteaga (*Sembrad* [Sow the Seed]). While suggesting that women poets were more numerous in the 1920s than usually recognized, Jiménez Faro deems Champourcín the "only feminine representative of the Generation of 1927" (11), omitting Chacel, de la Torre, Arderiu, and others.

The foregoing group of women poets cannot be absolutely separated from others of similar birth dates treated later; nor is it merely a question of exile. Divisional critieria consider time of first publication, whether the poet was known in Spain before the Civil War, and esthetic differences (i.e., whether individuals write "social poetry"). Many factors unite these women, including intergenerational friendships underscoring the ultimately arbitrary nature of divisional schemes, whether based upon "generations," politics, place of residence, or other criteria. While striving for a more unitary vision (downplaying time in exile and linguistic factors, for example), organization according to criteria other than the "generation" will, it is hoped, better communicate the development of women's lyrics within the overall history of Spanish poetry on the Peninsula.

Chapter Five
Carmen Conde

In justifying the label Generation of 1927, some argue that most "members" published their first works in 1927; but Dámaso Alonso (1921), Pedro Salinas (1923), García Lorca (1923), Rafael Alberti (1924), and Vicente Aleixandre (1928) did not. Not all who attended the "generational" homage to Góngora exhibit similar esthetic evolution, nor did all "members" of the generation attend that ceremony. Nor do the nuclear members (most cited by critics) share identical esthetics: *ultraísmo,* futurism, neo-Gongorism, and surrealism each influence some, and the surrealism of Alberti, Aleixandre, Cernuda, and Lorca differs.

Carmen Conde, whose *Brocal* (Well Rim) appeared in 1929, was fully involved in vanguard experimentation by 1931 (ultraist and surrealist echoes sound in *Júbilos* [1934; Jubilation]), yet she rarely appears in studies of the Generation of 1927—typifying omission of women by those involved in canon-making. Her birth date qualifies her for this illustrious company: Conde (1907) precedes Miguel Hernández (1910) and is two years younger than Altolaguirre (1905) and three years younger than Alberti and Cernuda. Her social preoccupations have served to exclude her, but that argument is fallacious: Alberti and Hernández evinced *engagement* before the Civil War, and critics now recognize social content in Lorca's poetry and theater. "Social poetry" by survivors of the generation appears in the mid-1940s and early 1950s, which should make Conde a precursor, rather than exclude her.[1] As to personal contacts with "official" members of the Generation of 1927, she met Alberti and Lorca once each;[2] friendships with Aleixandre and Alonso began in the mid-1930s. Conde considers herself a writer "without a generation" (Galerstein, 77) but mentions belonging to the "Generation of 1930"—apparently her invention.[3] She feels no kinship with the so-called Generation of 1936 (emerging writers killed in the war or exiled). Almost 100 books[4] (some 40 collections of poetry, including anthologies and editions of collected works, plus nine novels, several plays, approximately 20 volumes of children's literature, and 20-odd collections of criticism, memoirs, and miscellany) published under her own name and a pair of pseudonyms entitle her to separate consideration.

Early Life and Autobiographical Sources

Conde has written repeatedly about her early years, from her anecdotal lyric memoir, *Empezando la vida* (1955; Beginning Life, subtitled "Recollections of a Childhood in Morocco"), to the 1986 three-volume memoir series, *Por el camino, viendo sus orillas* (1986; Along the Road, Seeing the Shoulder). Poems in *Cita con la vida* (1976; Date with Life), "almost an autobiography" (*Voz,* 75), are not anecdotal but convey emotions of birth, life, and being-toward-death (*Voz,* 95). Biographical data appear in *En la tierra de nadie* (1960; No Man's Land), and José María Rubio Paredes in *La Obra juvenil de Carmen Conde* (1990) makes available previously unpublished juvenilia (1920–30) and autobiographical gleanings. *Carmen Conde, de viva voz* (1992; Carmen Conde, Live) presents wide-ranging interviews, with abundant autobiographical insights and trivia. The poet's prologues frequently provide autobiographical and anecdotal information. Conde's memoirs and prologues recall that her father, of Galician ancestry, was orphaned at 13. Raised by a guardian, he learned the goldsmith's trade, practicing as a jeweler after the family business was lost owing to what Conde terms his generosity and naive trust of relatives and administrators. Comforts of infancy (cook, chauffer, nanny, and laundress, plus various cars and her own horse-carriage) vanished when Conde was six, and her privileged existence turned difficult and insecure.

Carmen Conde Abellán was born 15 August 1907 in the Mediterranean port of Cartagena (Murcia).[5] Maritime motifs are pervasive in her poetry, and her love of the sea prompted her adoption of the pseudonym Florentina del Mar ("of the sea"; Florentina is patron saint of Cartagena).[6] Conde relates in *Empezando la vida* that her father was 19 when he married her mother, then 15 (*OP,* 163). Facing bankruptcy, he emigrated to Barcelona at age 39, when Carmen was six (123), placing her birth during the marriage's fourteenth year. This plus lack of siblings explains paternal indulgence pervading her memoirs. Conde, significantly, never suffered treatment as inferior to her brother(s). Especially close to her father, who believed unreservedly in her talent, she terms her mother very disciplined, practical, and realistic, a profoundly religious woman who encouraged repression in her daughter (*Voz,* 13) and who had little faith in her daughter's literary abilities (14–15). Nevertheless, Conde emphasizes their close relationship, stating, "Mother loved me too much, almost insanely" (*Voz,* 104). This devout Catholic inculcated her faith in Conde; the adult poet exhibits profoundly Christian attitudes, consistently chaste expression, and enduring altruism and idealism. She told interviewers that Pope Paul VI blessed her right hand so her writing would never depart from her Christian beliefs (*Voz,* 69). Conde paints her youthful self as uninterested in material possessions but fascinated by literature, rejecting typical gender stereotypes, restless, pensive, independent, studious, and imaginative (13).

Following catastrophic business losses, Conde's father emigrated to Melilla (another port) in Spanish Morocco, where Carmen and her mother joined him in 1914, remaining until 1920. Conde loved the Arab market, the multi-ethnic atmosphere, the sea and desert. She attended the Colegio Inglés (British School), where favorite classmates included Muslim and Hebrew girls, some of them lifelong friends. Recalling this magical awakening, Conde's second book, *Júbilos* (1934), subtitled "Poems of Children, Roses, Animals, Machines, and Winds," re-creates these years. *Empezando la vida* evokes childhood in Cartagena and life in Spain's Moroccan "protectorate," often visited in later years. In 1920 the family returned to Cartagena for what Conde considers her definitive formation. "Confidencia literaria," from *Entregas de poesía* (1944), reproduced as the Prologue to *Ansia de la gracia* (1945; Anxiety of Grace), depicts the years 1920 to 1930 with Conde's "first love," the boy's sudden death, and her own grief, sparking her first impulse to poetry; her subsequent literary-mystic fervor produced a durable devotion to Santa Teresa.

Young Adulthood, Early Works, and Marriage

Financial exigency led to Conde's seeking work, which few young ladies then did. Wishing to escape housework and her mother's implacable insistence on domestic skills (*Voz,* 15), she worked sketching ship parts in a British firm in Cartagena (1923–28). Juvenilia rescued by Rubio Paredes depict office companions, construction workers, English managers, office bosses, shipyard supervisors, working conditions, and her own efforts to write on the job. From 1925 onward she published stories and poems in the local press, finishing a first novel (apparently never published), which years later won a prize from the *Diario español* of Buenos Aires.[7] In 1927 Conde began work toward certification in pedagogy, obtaining a degree in primary education (January 1930); in 1936 she passed the *oposiciones* (government examinations) for would-be teachers. The year 1927 was important not only for poetry but Conde's life: she met Antonio Oliver Belmás, a young poet whose first book, *Mástil*

(Mast), had appeared in 1925. Four years later they were married. Through Oliver she read works of Gabriel Miró and Juan Ramón Jiménez, who significantly influenced her writing. She also met Gabriela Mistral, later a beloved friend. After exposure to modernism, Conde perceived her prior writings as sadly anachronistic.

Preceding *Brocal* (in the *Obra poética, 1929–1966* are the words "Poemas en Prosa" (Prose Poems); portions appeared in *Ley* and *Diario poético,* sponsored by Juan Ramón Jiménez, whose support helped Conde begin publishing. Perhaps "lyric prose" better describes these 49 brief, untitled compositions whose format is prose, not verse. Often fewer than five lines, some recall Ramón Gómez de la Serna's *greguerías* (autonomous pieces based upon original metaphors and humor). Passion for nature and life accompanies joyful, newfound mutual love in Conde's lyric sketches of sunsets; open, moonlit windows; southern breezes and emerging stars; crystalline darkness or luminous morning; sails in the port; horizons beyond the water; and almond blossoms in spring. Sensorial and chromatic elements predominate, with inanimate objects personified (the church bells "kiss each other good-night" [32], and evening stars appear "well-bathed and coiffed, wearing a big smile" [35]; another star is barefoot, and night enjoys "a huge bed of sun in the furrowed fields" [34]).[8]

Conde uses transformation or transubstantiation: as evening stars emerge, the terrace becomes a boat, carrying her to the sea (37); the poetic consciousness is alternately sky (36), wind (36), tower (38), light (37, 41), and motionless traveler on the rivers of love (40). Occasionally indirect, metaphorical celebrations of erotic joy assume cosmic proportions: "I grew taller, taller . . . and from my heart flowed the candid barks of daybreak" (34). This larger-than-life aspect, combined with the transformational techniques, resembles Vicente Aleixandre's metaphors, which Carlos Bousoño terms "visionary." Candelas Newton explains the title of *Brocal* thus: "[The poet's] skin is the well-rim or mouth through which the exterior is internalized in the roundness of the feminine womb, thereby acquiring its identity."[9] The lyric speaker, cosmic woman, occupies the four points of the compass, holding handfuls of stars. Her exuberant vitalism, communicated in images of wind, flowing hair, body parts, and verbs of motion, expresses ontological plenitude and expanding consciousness of the poet's greater being. This sensuous dynamism contrasts with immobility and petrification in postwar works such as *Mi libro de El Escorial* (My Book of Escorial [the monastery-palace of Phillip II]).

Conde first visited Madrid in 1929, making personal contact with Jiménez and meeting Ernestina de Champourcín. She published an essay on educational reform (1931), lectured on pedagogical topics (1927–29), and wrote a few poems grouped under the rubric "1930," but illness forced her to rest (*OP,* 246). After recuperating, Conde married Antonio Oliver in 1931. They originally lived with her parents; following her father's death (except during the war) they resided with her mother. Oliver's health was delicate (he died in 1968). Oliver became Conde's most trusted critic, reading her works and destroying those he found inferior (Martín, 91). Conde indicates their literary connections were broken during the war (*Voz* 22–23). She terms Oliver's poetry much more "classical" than hers (27). Their adult extension school, or "People's University of Cartagena," dates from the year of their marriage (1931), and both worked there as teachers. Closed at the war's outbreak (1936), it reopened in 1981, in the post-Franco era, with Conde as honorary president (Martín, 92). During the war (1936–39) Conde studied at the University of Valencia (the Franco regime did not recognize her degrees).

The young poet suffered two painful blows in 1934: her only daughter was born dead due to inadequate obstetric care, and her beloved father died soon afterward. Conde moved to Madrid, observing, "Never have I been more alone or more unhappy" (*OP,* 246–47). Personal tragedies do not darken *Júbilos,* completed earlier, but Conde changes direction from lyric prose toward the verse medium. Gabriela Mistral, then the Spanish-speaking world's foremost woman poet, provided the Prologue to *Júbilos,* which contains several sections: "Children," "Roses," "Animals," "Machines," and "Winds." The first group contains lyric portraits of childhood friends, girls from Cartagena and Melilla (often Moorish and Jewish), impoverished children, dead children, children of fear and suffering. "Insomnio" presents a little boy, kept awake by monsters. Conde focuses on beggars, pariahs, and single mothers with their children, shunned by "morally superior" segments of society. "Animals" evokes childhood pets, her mare Golondrina, the burro Polvorilla (Powder Box), the vagabond white and brown dog Sultana. "Machines" include airplanes, talking typewriters, a locomotive whose life story spans years. Gabriela Mistral has noted the wind's importance for Conde, its personification as "spirit of the Earth" and practical joker (51), to which should be added its usefulness (several pieces treat the wind's helpfulness to mankind—running windmills and pushing sailboats). Wind symbolically connects to the past, as evinced by depictions of the wind in cemeteries, abandoned houses, and the historic castle of Bellver (ancient royal residence of Mallorcan kings). Frequently personified ("The Wind in the Schoolhouse" and "The Wind Seeks His Love"), wind—the creative element—becomes the breath of life in "Creation"; its absence produces immobility in "The Windless Landscape."

While residing in Madrid in 1934, Conde finished a collection identified as *Días por la tierra* (Days on Earth). Her "personal anthology," *Memoria puesta en olvido* (1987; Memory in Oblivion), lists *Días por la tierra* as published in 1977. Conde often changed titles, making it unclear whether the manuscript of 1934 coincides with the title published 43 years later. Back in Cartagena (1935–36), she penned her *Cartas a Katherine Mansfield* (Letters to Katherine Mansfield), monodialogues with the deceased novelist discussing poetics and art, the relationship of inspiration and technique (Letter 4), literary genres (Letter 1), and other women writers including Gómez de Avellaneda and Carolina Coronado (Letter 5). Intuitive, autodidactic, and independent, Conde has limited knowledge of poetics and rhetoric. *Cartas* provides some orientation to her poetics.

The War Years and Early Postwar Period

Conde was no political activist, but her social concerns placed her in the Republican camp. Oliver volunteered for the Loyalist army but (given his health) never served in the trenches. Conde mentions his radio work for the Republican command in Murcia, among Spain's most tranquil wartime cities (she moved her mother there during bombardments of Cartagena [*Voz,* 33]). A recent history of wartime culture in Murcia mentions Oliver as war correspondent for *Nuestra Lucha* (a Socialist daily); he compared the struggle with the medieval Reconquest, lyrically exalting the Popular Front.[10] Neither Conde nor Oliver wanted exile, though he faced imprisonment or worse for his wartime activities. Politically unable to obtain work, Conde lived with relatives and friends in Madrid while Oliver awaited trial (he was freed in 1945).

Conde and Republican intellectuals were chastised by decrees restricting publication under their own names (they could not exploit or enhance prewar literary reputations or receive critical notice). She did translations, bibliographic work, and various archival jobs (having studied library science during the war). Fear of incarceration probably explains Conde's low profile during these years. Her *Obra poética, 1929–1966* contains four manuscripts from 1938 to 1941: *Sostenido ensueño* (1938; Sustained Daydream), *Mientras los hombres mueren*

(1938–39; While Men Are Dying), *El Arcángel* (1939; The Archangel), and *Mío* (1941; Mine), all contrasting markedly with the upbeat air of prior publications. *Sostenido ensueño,* lyric prose without narrative content, consists of 35 brief, meditative, melancholy, abstract compositions avoiding reference to the conflict. Titles suggest Conde's anguish: "Fate," "Destiny," "From the Darkness," "Solitude," "Hope," "Rage," "Discouragement," "On Death," "Power," "Desire." The rhetoric often evokes violence, with metaphors of knives, swords, cutting, pain, blood, desolation, screams, burning, fear, and futility. *Mientras los hombres mueren* mourns war's destruction: the poet grieves for all men, all of war's victims, while the 1940s and 1950s regime permitted mentioning the war only in the context of Falangist self-glorification and Fascist exaltation of violence. This collection contains 33 mostly untitled poetic prose pieces headed by Roman numerals, then three titled compositions—"War in the Port," "It Was Only a Word" (on the death of liberty), and "The War's Over," which ends, "Peace has fallen" (*OP,* 206), where the verb selected connotes collapse more than fall. Conde's rhetoric of body parts powerfully describes the bombed, scorched earth: "barbed wire strung with dried hearts, vessels of virgin adolescent genitalia, land flowering with blood, pierced eyes, shrunken breasts; land stabbed by shouts, froth, sobs and death-rattles" (189).

Poetic references to motherhood and children, to empty cradles and young mothers in mourning, combine with images of grieving maternity turned to sterility, communicating war's destruction with chilling images of bombings: "the street bent over with fear, split into visceral peels of stone beneath pieces of exploded children" (208). All mothers (including animals) suffer, sharing symbolic barrenness. Conde, who lost her only child at birth, identifies with all mothers whose children died in the war. Among 21 numbered compositions entitled "To the Children Killed in the War" appears the exhortation (found in postwar women poets, including Figuera and Fuertes) that women refuse to gestate cannon fodder: "Women in mourning . . . refuse to conceive children until men erase war from the earth!" (210).

Themes in *El Arcángel* (reprinted in *Memoria* [1987]) suggest composition after cessation of hostilities: violence no longer pervades the rhetoric; mystic impulses accompany resignation, aspirations to faith, ambition, and desires to see dreams become reality. The archangel motif (here and in *Derribado arcángel* [1960; Fallen Archangel]) introduces metaphysical meditations. *Mío,* 24 numbered prose poems, contemplates the solidity of earth and monuments such as Phillip II's royal monastery of El Escorial, stones of the Castilian landscape. The permanence of things beyond war's destructive power reassures. Conde's *Obra poética* contains no more prose poems; the next section, subtitled "Poems in Verse" (free verse and unrhymed lines in traditional meters), uses a poetic format. Assonance and consonant rhymes are used inconsistently, within single compositions; later Conde experiments with blank verse. Major lyric devices are repetition, cadence, parallelistic structures, metaphors, condensation, and ellipses.

Unemployable in Spanish-run institutions given official refusal to recognize her degree, Conde taught contemporary Spanish novel and poetry to foreign students at the Instituto de Estudios Europeos. Meanwhile, using the pseudonym "Florentina del Mar," she published children's books, juvenile fiction, biographies, and historical works; two titles under the pseudonym "Magdalena Noguera" treat religious monuments. Two brief, enigmatic poetry collections belonging to 1944 were privately published: 500 copies of *Pasión del Verbo* (Passion of the Word) and a deluxe collectors' edition of *Honda memoria de mí* (Deep Memory of Myself). Although listed in *Obra poética, 1929–1966,* neither appears in the most complete edition to date of Conde's poetry. *Honda memoria* became publicly available when included in *Memoria* (1987). Conde mentions *Pasión del Verbo* as the only published evidence of her "transformation" from 1930 to 1942—years when she wrote a great deal but only for herself (*OP,* 247). She omits *Honda memoria de mí,* which also represents change.

Honda memoria lacks internal subdivisions, titles, or numbers, but larger print for first words signals new compositions. The verse format distinguishes these from earlier prose poems. Simple and quasi-conversational, these 13 unrhymed pieces lack sustained metric patterns and regular stanzas. Their common denominator is memory, although Conde interpolates present-tense reflections on herself, her body, her zest for living, her personality and habits. Tenuous cadence and assorted metaphors constitute the primary poetic devices of these pieces, which—format notwithstanding—wax more prosaic than earlier lyric prose. Conde comes to terms with her own survival, her guilty sense of joy at being still young and intact after so much suffering and death. She rejects old age, wishing to avoid shriveled breasts, swollen belly, inflexible waistline, and flaccid legs, reveling instead in colors, sounds, laughter, and song, nature's beauty and the pleasure of being. Senectitude is negative for Conde; physical aging connotes erosion of plenitude, diminishing the persona (cf. *Corrosión* [1975]).

Identification with nature informs *Mi fin en el viento* (1947; My End in the Wind), consisting of parts of ten, seven and six poems, respectively. "Lluvia en mayo" (Rain in May) varies the pathetic fallacy: the poet makes the rain a metaphor for her melancholy (war's residue); fields of poppies and spring's reawakening inspire dreams of fields "without a single man buried therein" (*OP,* 295).

Conde's voice becomes that of the earth, thirsting for ancient waters buried beneath burning sands—one of several dichotomies (life/death, past/present, light/darkness, body/soul, joy/sorrow) representing the difficult balancing act required to live under Franco. Lacking overt political statements, "Canto funeral por mi época" (Funeral Chant for My Epoch) constitutes an elegiac lament in blank hendecasyllables for lost vitalism and freedom, followed by a single Alexandrine quatrain entitled "Conformity," thanking God for the times He might have sent suffering but did not, and concluding, "In hours of grief, time passes so slowly / that one ages not from years but from sorrow" (322). Postwar poets commonly used a divine interlocutor to circumvent censorship; complaints impossible to express otherwise sometimes passed when cast as prayers. Scriptural references functioned similarly (cf. *Pasión del Verbo, Ansia de la gracia, Mujer sin Edén*). Like such Generation of 1936 authors as Luis Rosales, Leopoldo Panero, and Luis Felipe Vivanco, Conde attempted to avoid censorial attention, emphasizing the intimate and emotional. *Pasión del Verbo,* unpublished for a long time, is termed "brevísimo" (extremely brief). Conde cites part of one poem identified as coming from *Pasión del Verbo,* "Conocimiento" (Knowledge). The entire poem, title unchanged, appears in the second part of *Ansia;* evincing love of life, restlessness, and the poet's inability to limit her creativity despite desiring perfection, it suggests that *Pasión del Verbo* resembled "pure poetry": elliptical, sometimes telegraphic and cryptic. Like Juan Ramón Jiménez, Conde endlessly examines her esthetic sensibilities, desires, and perceptions.

Few postwar Spanish writers lived by the pen, even novelists and dramatists (the exception was newspaper writing). Teaching offered more reliable income, so Conde produced scholarly anthologies and critical works to strengthen her academic credentials: *Dios en la poesía española* (1944; God in Spanish Poetry) and *La Poesía ante la eternidad* (1944; Poetry Faces Eternity). *La Amistad en la literatura española* (1944; Friendship in Spanish Literature) appeared under the pseudonym "Florentina del Mar." Conde's later introductory essay on the Brontë sisters' lives prefaced an edition of their selected works in translation. She produced anthologies of women poets: *Poesía femenina viviente* (1955; Living Feminine Poetry), *Once grandes poetisas americohispanas* (1967; Eleven Great Spanish American Women Poets), and *Poesía femenina española* (Spanish Women's Poetry) in two volumes (1939–50 in 1967 and 1950–60 in 1971). No comparably inclusive source exists for the years thereafter. "Why shouldn't I help other women?" Conde asked interviewers, noting that men have had advantages throughout history (*Voz,* 122). *Poesía amorosa contemporánea* (1969; Contemporary Love Poetry) is the latest of Conde's panoramic anthologies; *Acompañando a Francisca Sánchez* (1964; Accompanying Francisca) incorporates papers of the common-law wife of Rubén Darío (Conde's husband specialized in Darío, providing impetus for her investigation). In 1963 she published a specialized esoteric anthology, *Viejo venís y florido . . . ,* medieval Spanish ballads (preserved in the oral tradition of Sephardic Jews and Muslims expelled from Spain)—songs she learned from Moorish friends in Melilla.

Mature Poetic Works

Ansia de la gracia portrays poetic fusion with the sea, although Conde also identifies with the earth—the soil, but not the stones, which represent pain, trials, and anguish. Trees, flowers, fountains, and birds constitute positive symbols of vitality and hope. Dámaso Alonso, in "Pasión de Carmen Conde" (*Poetas españoles contemporáneos,* 1958), mentions impassioned sensibility and intense human ardor, terming *Ansia* an investigation into mankind's destiny, aff•ming life forces against death, exploring the meaning of existence, and motivated by a terrible, frenzied love of all creation. Contrasting with static contemplation in *Mío* and *Mi libro de El Escorial,*[11] which emphasize the eternal paradigm of being, *Ansia* seeks earlier exuberance and plenitude. Conde's response to Oliver's long-awaited return provides stimulus. "Love" contains 12 poems, beginning with "Offering": the poet identifies with water (deep fountains, puddles, ice), inviting her implied interlocutor to "Come swim in me" (*OP,* 251), echoing earlier cosmic eroticism. "Springtime," "Garden," "Restlessness," "Surrender," "Meeting," "Possession," and "Discovery" celebrate felicitous conjugal love. Water metaphors predominate in "Discovery," where the poet affirms, "My rivers will be tributaries of your rivers / We will navigate together; you will be my sailboat / and I will guide you through hidden seas" (256). Critics during the puritanical Franco era especially lauded Conde's capacity for "chaste" metaphorical communication of sexuality.

In "Destiny" visions of Castile and intertextual echoes of earlier works (in mentions of archangels and the Escorial gardens) yield to more subjective themes (e.g., "Fatigue," "Intuition," "Continuity," "Assurance," "Presentiment," and "Conscience"). "Origin" evokes creation myths, an ongoing process repeated whenever meditative spirits seek silence to hear God's voice in nature. "In the Beginning" suggests that each soul contains worlds, each poet or dreamer becomes a new Adam, naming the universe. But metaphysical motifs number fewer than the physical: "First Love," for example, celebrates the lover's body—shoulders, head, arms, chest, and locks of hair. Refusal to accept death—a constant in Conde's work, like the rejection of aging—leads her to deny that the beloved will someday turn to dust: "Ashes, this madness / which you bring with life still new in the world? / You will never die, never be extinguished!" These potentially blasphemous sentiments escaped the censors, perhaps distracted by the conventional topos of carpe diem and tempus fugit in "Cementerio Romántico," which recasts the conventional Dance of Death as the cemetery's monologue. Two of three poems subtitled "Mother" concentrate on the aging mother's physical decadence; the third contemplates distance and silence between Conde and her mother. *Ansia de la gracia,* among the poet's most varied collections, evinces her artistic maturation.

Sea la luz (1947; Let There Be Light) first evokes the seeds of death that each person carries inside, against which Conde rebels, describing death as revolting and rigid in contrast to life's flexibility and freedom. Vitally and esthetically, she rejects the "odious dark puddle" and degrading process of decomposition: filthy liquid, hairy worms, putrefaction of the flesh, disgusting fluid, and unrecognizable bones that convert the deceased into something unfamiliar. The body loses its being—not only its identity but its ontological status, existentially speaking—when no longer perceived by the living. In the second canto, the poetic voice dialogues with God, demands explanations, becomes an enormous sword, acquires eyes, cries out at the injustice of being born "for so much nothingness." Facing the existential limit-situation, the poet admits, "This thing which ends is myself. I can't get beyond me" (348). Struggling to affirm herself, she proclaims woman's worth, with metaphors of maternity on a cosmic scale. Humble things—the odor of fresh thyme, Mediterranean light, a bite of fruit—symbolize life's value.

Woman without Eden

Mujer sin Edén (1947; trans. *Woman without Eden,* 1986) is considered Conde's most significant collection: poet-critic Leopoldo de Luis terms it "the most significant book of poetry written by a woman in the Spanish language."[12] Citing artistic quality, coherence, and Weltanschauung, Luis places *Woman* in the "first line" of the general panorama, "without distinctions of gender . . . in which woman—half of humanity—investigates her stock and, without pathos, sings its praises" (13). *Woman*'s boldness for Franco Spain in the mid-1940s inhered less in protesting traditional Judeo-Christian treatment of women than its unorthodox premises and implications. Nevertheless, biblical intertexts often helped to array protest works in the guise of religious meditations: Vicente Aleixandre's *Sombra del paraíso* (1944) and Dámaso Alonso's *Hijos de la ira* share *Woman*'s motifs of expulsion from Paradise and God's wrath. Probable subtexts equate the Republic's fall with the fall from grace, the Civil War's horrors with divine retribution. Critics of the 1940s perhaps overlooked these implications; most opt for vagueness, mentioning "mysticism" or "scriptural symbolism." Angel Valbuena Prat's *Historia de la Literatura Española* (1950) identifies echoes of Santa Teresa and theological intuitions, terming *Woman* a kind of *auto sacramental* (mystery play).

More perspicaciously, Vicente Aleixandre (in an unpublished letter [cited by Luis, 12]) noted the book's rebellious bent and stressed its subversion of traditional concepts of guilt and Original Sin, arguing that if Eve's union with Adam in Eden was her destiny, she was innocent, together with all who followed. Concha Zardoya considers Woman the work's poetic essence, no mere motif, but its ultimate raison d'être.[13] For Víctor García de la Concha, *Woman* seems at first glance biblical allegory that provides its narrative substratum; but polarization of Eve and Mary converts the work to allegorical discourse on woman's painful condition throughout history.[14] *Woman without Eden* consists of five unequal cantos: (1) the Garden, three poems; (2) early generations after expulsion, 15 poems; (3) the Flood and its aftermath, four poems; (4) New Testament incidents, 12 poems; and (5) vaguely present-day, two poems. Woman (identifiable with Eve, Sarah, Hagar, the wife and daughters of Lot, the Virgin Mother Mary) represents *all* women; the only significant poetic persona, she is the speaking consciousness and supratemporal voice of her gender.

Canto 1 recounts expulsion from Eden; Woman wrestles with her conscience and burden of guilt, arguing that Original Sin was predestined

(Conde later suggests that Cain—"wrongly" conceived in the Garden—
drew God's wrath, suffering discrimination). Imbued with love and sensuality, sharing Man's solitude, Woman desires mutual love. Aware that
humanity is now mortal, she prefers mortality. Conde postulates the
original notion that the Creator wanted Man for Himself, and because of
Woman, He lost Man; hence His wrath against her (Luis, 15). In Canto
2 the primal pair admires their earthly domain, savoring the first fruits
and flowers. Conde's early sensuality reappears in Woman's rebellious
rejection of modesty (she prefers nudity's naturalness to the skins they
donned upon expulsion from Eden). In "Nostalgia de mujer" (Woman's
Nostalgia) she addresses God using the familiar "tú" (thou): "You don't
love me." Because of her transgression, neither does He love her son, she
argues, terming Cain "hijo de la ira" (60; "child of wrath"). Conde's technique is intertextually complex: biblical resonances camouflage intent,
while Cain and Abel motifs and the myth of fraternal hate and murder
suggest an emblem of Spain's Civil War. In "Habla de sus hijos a Dios"
(Woman Talks to God about Her Children) divine preference for Abel
and condemnation of Cain create injustice, arbitrary discrimination, and
hate among humankind; divine favoritism produces war, exodus, invasion, genocide, pestilence, famine, racial differences and uprisings.

In Canto 3 Woman contemplates the world newly emerged from the
Flood, celebrating Noah's salvation of innumerable species from the
waters. Anticipating new beginnings, Woman dares not affirm life's
newness but limits herself to rhetorical questions. Her discovery of the
ocean, "Junto al mar" (Beside the Sea), recalls Conde's love of the
Mediterranean. "Imprecación a la vejez" (Indictment of Old Age) reiterates rejection of biological evidence of mortality. Canto 4 re-creates
major events of the four synoptic Gospels, alluding to the Apocalypse of
John. Mary's role, central to Conde's thesis, apotheosizes Woman as the
mother of God (cf. "La Mujer divinizada"), logically implying pardon for
all women; this canto presents Woman's struggle with the Beast and
rejection of evil (Woman previously defended certain pleasures of "sin").
Final placement accords the two poems of the fifth canto special significance. In "Súplica final de la mujer" (Woman's Final Plea) Woman
inquires whether God never pardons, the real question being whether
men will ever stop insisting on Woman's "guilt."

Judith Richards's study of revisionism in *Mujer sin Edén* combines
mythic criticism, semiotics, and Lacanian and feminist theories, analyz-
ing the poem in light of Woman's search for identity and autonomy
through rewriting patriarchal myths of creation.[15] Richards compares

Woman with Emily Dickinson's retelling the same story with a subversive slant, undermining reader expectations and displacing original authority. Conde alters chronology, abandoning the Bible's male narrator for feminine voice, making Eve (and Woman) the narrator and displacing Adam. As narrative, the Fall was a linguistic event and thus open to reinterpretation. Conde empowers Eve, making her the sustaining strength of her offspring; by not presenting Eve's death, the poet can rework her as quasi-immortal embodiment of all women. Through discourse analysis, Richards demonstrates revision of the male authoritarian Logos (71–74), identifying the most aggressive subversion as replacing Adam with God himself as Other in Eve's dialogue.

Proclaiming her refusal to bear the blame for things gone awry in the Garden, Woman suggests that God is also to blame: He allowed the serpent to exist; the result evinces weakness on His part as much as hers. Conde has often described *Woman* as protest, affirming "that business of Adam's rib and all the rest is drivel. God made two human beings, two persons with the same rights and duties toward each other. . . . Woman has her own life, apart from her companion's . . . her own thoughts . . . [even though] before she was only an echo of man" (*Voz,* 83). "It seems like God didn't care for woman; although He created her so that man would not be alone, the one He really loved was man. . . . He must have made man [in His image] in order to see Himself" (*Voz,* 95). *Woman* suggests the divinity's anthropocentric narcissism, bitterly protesting society's enormous, millennial gender inequality. Conde's feminine protagonist has evolved notably since *Brocal.* The early persona—cosmic woman holding handfuls of stars—was female but more than human; in *Woman* the protagonist's initial specific identity (Eve) incorporates additional identities, becoming eternal, generic Woman in the process, concerned with women's suprahistoric problem (alleged responsibility for Original Sin, "justifying" the inferior feminine social condition).

Varied Themes

In *Iluminada tierra* (1951; Illuminated Earth) Conde views poetry as mysterious and marvelous, a "state of grace" isolating the poet from all contact or sharing with others. *La Enamorada* (The Lover) paints the enamored female persona instinctively seeking her lover. An unbridled pagan spirit, symbols of fecundity, corporal beauty, desire and powerful erotic passion surge through the verses, limited by absence, sorrow, pain, and incommunication. Sensuality looms large: flower fragrances, the taste of wine, tactile perceptions. *Tiempo en ser* (Time in Being) laments woman's fatigue, solitude, and suffering at the death of her child. *Del andar y sentir* (Of Walking and Feeling) recalls places visited, memories relived poetically, along with sorrow for war's chaos and destruction. In *Se hicieron país las sombras* (The Shadows Became a Country) characteristic optimism reappears with light's symbolic victory over darkness.

Vivientes de los siglos (1957; Living Ones of the Centuries) consists of 10 poems, with the first section, "Homelands," being positive and the second, "Places of Exile," negative in tone. Poems treating the classic elements—water, fire, air, and earth—are followed by the cryptic "Origin." The second half presents life's downside—desperation, oblivion, and anguish. *Los Monólogos de la hija* (1959; The Daughter's Monologues), Conde's tribute to her mother, consists of short, simple verses almost without verbal adornment (alive when Conde wrote, her mother died in 1960). Frustrated maternal urges produce motifs of suffering, pain, anxiety, disenchantment, fatigue, disillusionment, unfulfilled dreams, and futile desire. In *Derribado Arcángel* (1960; Fallen Archangel) Conde expresses world-weariness, fatigue, and debilitation, crying for strength to combat evil while longing for the "light of childhood." *En un mundo de fugitivos* (1960; In a World of Fugitives) seeks strength and purity in past youth, regressing to the womb. Anguished and accusatory, Conde denounces hate, anger, and death and affirms love for life.

Los Poemas de mar menor (1962; Poems of the Lesser Sea) recalls youth on Spain's Levantine coast, the clear Mediterranean light, almond trees, palms and figs, the fish of these waters and the fishermen. Also written but unpublished at this time were *Devorante arcilla* (1962; Devouring Clay) and *Enajenado mirar* (1962–64; Alienated Gaze), included in the *Obra poética,* along with *Humanas Escrituras* (1945–66; Human Scriptures). *En la tierra de nadie* (No Man's Land), dated "Castilla 1959," consists of 15 numbered compositions using four-line strophes with assonance in even-numbered lines, unlike Conde's usually unstructured pieces. No-man's-land, the poet's own subjective space, the goal of her personal search for self-realization, eludes her; she finds only solitude, which becomes her land alone.

Su voz le doy a la noche (1962; Its Voice I Give the Night) contains 10 tormented poems despairing of abandonment and solitude, the terrible silence left by the deaths of father, daughter, and mother. She expresses hatred of death, venting desolate feelings of irrevocable orphanhood. *Jaguar puro inmarchito* (1963; Pure, Unwilted Jaguar), dedicated to Nicaragua, was inspired by a trip when Oliver's work on Rubén Darío was recognized by the Nicaraguan government. Conde's affirmations of love for humanity and the need to defend human dignity echo "social" poetry. Appealing to fraternity, generosity, and humanitarianism, she reaffirms poetry's testimonial mission. Conde wonders at the New World's tropical lushness, immense jungles, seething wildlife, and savage youth, contrasting nature's cosmic forces with civilization.

Minor and Later Works

Canto a Amanda (1951; Song to Amanda) conveys gratitude to the friend with whom Conde lived following the war. *Réquiem por Cayetano* (1958) and *Réquiem por el Dr. Calandre* (1961) are elegies. Other collections repeat constants of Conde's work without major variations: *A este lado de la eternidad* (1970; This Side of Eternity); *Cancionero de la enamorada* (1971; The Lover's Songbook); *Cita con la vida* (1976; Date with Life), in which the poet evokes her birth and childhood, the distances traveled down life's road; and *El Tiempo es un río lentísimo de fuego* (1978; Time Is a Slow River of Fire). *Días por la tierra* (1977; Days on Earth), subtitled "Incomplete Anthology," contains a Prologue by Miguel Dolç; *Carmen Conde: Antología* (1982), edited by Leopoldo de Luis, includes a biography. Both texts provide good introductory overviews. Rosario Hiriart edited *Antología* (1985) and, in collaboration with the poet, *Brocal y Poemas a María* (1984), reprinting Conde's "most loved" book 55 years later. In 1988 the Torremozas collection of women's poetry published *Ansia de la gracia* with *Una Palabra tuya,* 21 poems dated "Cartagena 1930" to "Madrid 1982." Religious motifs include angelic musicians, the Virgin and Child, the Lord of Hosts, Assumption of Mary, Saint John the Baptist and two other Saint Johns, the Last Supper, Holy Week, Easter, and Santa Teresa.

In 1940 Conde had read Thomas Carlyle's "On Heroes, Hero Worship and the Heroic in History," six lectures explaining the hero as living on the plane of truth, beauty, and the eternal, perceiving inward, primal reality and the true nature of things. The hero motif reappears sporadically in her work, symbolizing vitalism and optimism. *Corrosión* (1975) treats hero motifs, but time has dimmed Conde's youthful spirit, and life's beauty—adolescence—is remembered nostalgically, with notes of anguish. Composed after the death of Conde's husband in 1968, absence of the other creates an ontological vacuum in which being is eroded by nothingness. Newton terms *Corrosión* Conde's most important mature work, embodying her most significant constant themes: the poet meditates on life's fugacity and futility, lamenting her solitude with the tag line "No te tengo conmigo ya" ("I no longer have you with me"). Rejecting physical evidence of aging, she condemns her mirror image as duplicitous and "corroded" (hence the title). Bitter images abound: darkness, viscosity, venom, destruction, burning, and death—a rhetoric of dejection. But Conde combats despair and time's corrosion with heroic discourse (Newton, 69), denying change.

La Noche oscura del cuerpo (1980; Dark Night of the Body) evokes Renaissance intertexts by the sixteenth-century mystic Saint John of the Cross in "Dark Night of the Soul" (1582–85), but it is neither metaphysical nor does it revive medieval disputes of body and soul. "Se empieza por el presentimiento" (One Begins with Presentiment) contains varied themes: awareness, conscience, dreams, hope, memory, and vocation—abstract and subjective—and objective motifs (birds, Castile's fields, and the sea). "Generations or Mother of Peoples" consists of 16 numbered meditations inspired by a stay in Toledo. Seven untitled compositions forming "Dark Night of the Body" dialogue with death as life faces physical extinction. *Desde nunca* (1982; From Never) looks backward and forward (serenely), moving toward accepting death; fatigue, discouragement, and solitude diminish life's hold, yet springtime still strikes responsive chords. *Hermosos días en China* (1985; Beautiful Days in China) commemorates visiting there (1976), with compositions devoted to Peking, the Great Wall, the Nanking Museum, Shanghai children, the "Forbidden City," and Kwanchow. In *Cráter* (1985) Conde reflects upon love, loneliness, companionship, solitude, and innumerable "others" of the poetic consciousness.

Myths acquire special significance: Orpheus and Euridice, Narcissus and Echo, Tantalus and Theseus, Sappho and Antigone (symbolizing love) are discussed by Manuel Alvar.[16] *Una Palabra tuya* groups poems written over several decades, while *La Noche oscura del cuerpo* contains largely miscellany; collections with a unifying theme (*Hermosos días en China* and *Cráter*) add little to Conde's stature but may offer another dimension. With almost 100 titles published, Conde is easily the most prolific of Spain's women poets, even after subtracting approximately half as prose. Although quality is uneven and later works suffer from repetitiveness, Conde at her best is powerfully personal and feminine. Rather than expecting major works of an octogenarian, critics must admire the energy that keeps Conde producing. Winner of Spain's Premio Nacional de Literatura (1967; National Prize for Literature) and the first woman elected to Spain's Royal Academy (1979), Conde has garnered more significant honors to date than any other Spanish woman poet.

Chapter Six
Major Postwar Poets

If generational concepts prove inapplicable to women poets of the years between the wars, such traditional critical tools apply still less to younger counterparts. Ortega y Gasset defined chronological lapses between generations as 30 years; the period separating Spanish postwar writers from the previous recognized "generation" (i.e., 1927) is 10 to 15 years. Postwar evolution of survivors of 1927 toward "social poetry" ("committed" or impure art), initiated before the war by Alberti, Miguel Hernández, and others, increases the confusion. While modernists and poets of 1927 responded to powerful international esthetic impulses, social literature's motives spring from Spain's local sociopolitical problems.

Geographically dispersed as refugees or living in "internal exile," these writers seldom enjoy generational associations. Scholars disagree as to which labels should apply, and the major factor uniting these writers—the war—also divides them: whether termed the Generation of 1936, the War Generation, the Exile Generation, or *generación escindida* (splintered generation), their joint existence has been debated. Concha Zardoya provides an example: for Gullón and Conde, she belongs to the Generation of 1936; for Del Río, she is part of the postwar generation, while Cano considers her "contemporary"; an Editorial Coculsa anthology includes her with the "Mid-Century Generation" (consisting of writers who were children during the war, largely "social" poets, novelists, and playwrights).[1]

Despite my original plan to treat all exiles together, to categorize the era's women poets by transitory political status would be arbitrary: exile and expatriation overlap, and distinctions between internal and external exile may mean little more than geographic location. Nor was exile a single, clear, definable period. Geographic exile—a major literary theme for poets unable to return home—affords no basis for uniform classifications. Literary historians should question the reasonableness of still classing as exiles those whose exile lasted 10 or 20 years but ended decades ago.

No women poets were significant in the transitory postwar manifestations of *triunfalismo* (Falangist self-exaltation), the neo-traditional

Garcilasismo (an antivanguardist resurgence of the sonnet), and similarly reactionary revivals of classical rhetoric and lexicon. Renewed formal emphasis, anachronistically retreating into traditional metrics and themes, accompanied patriarchal and phallocentric values. During the late 1940s poets associated with the review *Espadaña* advocated collective and individual involvement with contemporary problems, the expression of emotions and angst, testimonial content and colloquial expression, plus the treatment of religious themes. The mid-1940s "Cántico" group in Sevilla opposed the "monotony" of *Garcilasismo* plus its opponents' existentialist and anti-estheticist rhetoric, preferring a return to "pure poetry," art, musicality, and creation of idealized beauty. "Cántico" advocated reconnecting with symbolist currents. No major woman poet belongs to either group, but these currents and an accompanying tendency to free verse—as already seen in Conde—appear in Zardoya, Figuera, and Fuertes.

Concha Zardoya

María Concepción Zardoya González was born to Spanish parents on 14 November 1914 in Valparaíso, Chile. Her father, from Tudela (Navarra), and mother, born in Santander, lived 20 years in Chile but maintained strong emotional ties to Spain, nurturing their children on stories of their Spanish forebears. Zardoya's mother, educated in Barcelona, spoke Catalan to her daughter: "It was our 'secret' language," the poet reminisced.[2] Zardoya's association with Spanish poets and the publication of most of her work in Spain, plus the years she lived there and her becoming a Spanish citizen, dictate considering her as Spanish.

Zardoya's father struggled against financial straits obliging her mother to work as a seamstress. Zardoya, who helped her mother upon finishing her homework, became especially close to her younger brother, Alfonso Juan, her playmate and best friend, killed at 20 in Spain's Civil War. Discovering Spanish literature during her *bachillerato* in Chile, she conceived a lifelong love for Spanish classics. When the Second Republic was proclaimed Zardoya's parents returned in June 1932; they resided briefly in Zaragoza and Barcelona, where the future poet worked painting antique furniture, fostering solidarity with the proletariat (evoked in *Diotima*). Zardoya's brother became a bricklayer, furthering her working-class identification. Moving to Madrid, she attended the university there (1934–36) while teaching kindergarten and tutoring high school students. Sometimes lacking food and heat, she did secretarial work for Gabriela Mistral (the Nobel prize–winning poet, then Chilean consul in Madrid). Despite scarcity, Zardoya's university studies were intellectually stimulating; illustrious professors included Américo Castro, Pedro Salinas, José Ortega y Gasset, and Manuel García Morente, and she also met Pablo Neruda and Miguel Hernández.

Considered a "Christian Communist" by friends before the war, Zardoya distanced herself from both communism and Catholicism (not without religiosity, she disliked organized religion). Employed by the Ministry of Public Instruction, Zardoya performed cultural functions and supervised wartime library installations. Grief for her brother's death, along with her first love and other friends, imbues Zardoya's earliest poems, published in *Hora de España* (1938). Five early collections composed during the war remain unpublished.[3] *Violencia del duelo* (1937–38; Violence of Bereavement), her first wartime book, unpublished except for poems cited above, was partially included in *Ritos, cifras y evasiones* (1985; Rites, Figures, and Evasions). No other works written before *Pájaros del nuevo mundo* (1946; New World Birds) were published. During the war Zardoya developed lasting friendships with Dámaso Alonso, Rafael Alberti, and Vicente Aleixandre.

In May 1939 Zardoya returned to Madrid, working as seamstress, typist, and teacher at the private Colegio Athenea (1943–48). Studying independently, she completed her modern philology degree by examination at the University of Madrid in 1947. From 1942 to 1946 she used the pseudonym "Concha de Salamanca," given the regime's hostility to Republican sympathizers (the name Salamanca reflects admiration for Unamuno, whose adult life was spent there). Compiling data for Aguilar, she published 12 volumes of history and legends and rendered into Spanish poems of Walt Whitman (1945–46), on whom she lectured, receiving an invitation to the United States.

Pájaros del nuevo mundo incorporates South American (Chilean) flora and fauna as background but treats neither the New World nor birds. Chilean settings—symbolic, cosmic, larger-than-life—project her terrifying vision of war in Spain; birds represent the fallen. Primary themes are liberty and death. A comparable emotional climate characterizes *Dominio del llanto* (1947; Domain of Weeping), the poet's personal and collective painting of pain and death in unrhymed poems of 11-syllable lines suffused with mystic love for creation. Against the surreal, deathlike landscape littered with dead children and disinterred corpses, the poet enunciates a future major theme, the beauty of the world. Without ever naming Spain, *Dominio* depicts the despair of the vanquished. The somber, negative shadow of Franco darkens the collection.

With her Republican background blocking advancement in Spain, Zardoya went tearfully into exile in 1948, moving to the University of Illinois, where she completed her doctorate in Spanish literature in 1951. Her dissertation, "Spain in American Poetry (1607–1950)," she later expanded into a history of North American literature. *Los Signos* (1954; Signs), runner-up for the 1952 Ifach Prize, represents lyric intuitions of profound and mysterious symbolism, initiating Zardoya's ontological and metaphysical themes. Less somber and tragic than earlier works scarred by the psychic violence of war, *Los Signos* repeats the positive vision of *La Hermosura sencilla* (1953; Simple Beauty).

Zardoya taught at Tulane University until 1963, returning briefly to Spain in 1953 to research *Miguel Hernández (1910–1942)* (1955). While writing *Desterrado ensueño* (1955; Expatriate Daydream) she learned of her father's death. Dedicated to Spanish political refugees, that collection's 119 pages invoke the remembered homeland. Allusions to injustice and suffering alternate with evocations of beloved cities, rivers, buildings, plants, and people—teachers, poets, artists, and musicians. *Debajo de la luz* (1959; Beneath the Light) received the Boscán Prize for 1955. Characterized as metaphysical love poetry, this scant 57-page volume probes beneath appearances (cf. *Los Engaños de Tremont* [1971]), seeking a platonic essence. Somewhat like Pedro Salinas, whose poems sought to penetrate the soul, Zardoya seeks to project light upon things to discover their spirits, thereby contributing to spiritualizing the material world. The poet humanizes, personalizes, and attributes emotion to objects: the window gazes compassionately on an injured horse fallen on the ice, on birds, insects seeking refuge, and children playing nearby. Nature emanates light and wholeness, while man, equated with stone, does not absorb light. But sleeping men are good, as are the dead; death returns mankind to wholeness and unity, oneness with nature. Zardoya crisscrosses boundaries between life and death, past and present, memory and reality.

For the next 22 years Zardoya alternated poetry with teaching and literary criticism (of twentieth-century Spanish poets). She published a dozen poetry collections and nearly as many volumes of literary history, biography, and criticism. Retiring at 62, she returned permanently to Spain but has remained active, publishing another dozen poetry collections, lecturing, and participating in cultural events. Rodríguez Pequeño lists 26 poetry collections and 10 volumes of criticism by Zardoya;[4] additional poetry volumes have appeared since his 1987 cut-off date. Like many exiles, Zardoya has remained relatively unknown to Spanish readers, despite prizes and modest critical successes.

La Hermosura sencilla attempts to overcome war's trauma, expressing anew life's joys. Clearly and with simple delicacy, Zardoya conveys visual and sonorous impressions of nature's beauty, divided in four sections: "Things," "Animals," "Mountains and Woods," and "Souls" (the difference between the three material categories and the spiritual quality of the fourth suggests soulfulness by association in the others). "Basket of White Clothing" evokes other white shapes and snow-covered wintry landscapes. Noteworthy among "Animals" is the cat: elegant, artful hunter, sleek and graceful. Some critics note influences of Jorge Guillén, to whom Zardoya dedicates the collection (Rodríguez Pequeño, 47). Zardoya's gallery displays stylized sketches of simple things, magnified and contemplated in unaccustomed aspects. Things, animals, landscapes, and the soul are painted with love of detail (Zardoya's passion for minutiae recalls the art of Azorín). The communication between human souls and animals and inanimate objects and the poet's respect and love of all living creatures prompt comparisons with Saint Francis of Assisi. Loving respect for insignificant things also characterizes *Ritos, cifras y evasiones,* whose 25 poems celebrate the classic elements (earth, air, fire, and water—plus light), bread, wine, meat, wood, birds, and snow, clouds and the "faces" of objects.

Autobiographical and emotional resonances abound in *Desterrado ensueño,* which is filled with nostalgia, homesickness, grief for dead friends and relatives, and the pain of expatriation. Interrogatory and exclamatory constructions, styled in free verse, evoke Spain's towns and cities. Zardoya's books typically revolve around specific themes: her Prologue to *Retorno a Magerit* explains that she visualizes the entire work with its unifying theme(s) and sentiment, its dominant philosophy or motifs; each poem contributes to the whole. Major themes include death, the war, nature, exile, salvation, love, Spain, dreams, memory, solitude, art, travel, music, poetry, or time, among Zardoya's obsessive concerns. Certain insistent themes (death, grief, time) appear in several works with numerous variations—for instance, travel may include towns and villages, geographical features of Iberia, mountains and forests, various countries of Europe, regions of the United States, specific sites such as cemeteries or architectural monuments, and so on. Gender issues, however, scarcely appear, and Zardoya's poetic personas are vaguely androgynous or asexual.

In the 65 poems of *La Casa deshabitada* (1959; The Abandoned House), as in *Desterrado ensueño,* exile as primary unifying theme subsumes the poet's "half-life," with her body in America and her soul in Spain. The empty house—the leitmotiv of loneliness—symbolizes solitude overcome momentarily through imagination. Sometimes Zardoya suggests emptiness metrically, using brief lines (three or four words) that, without becoming telegraphically staccato, emphasize separateness.

Mirar al cielo es tu condena (1957; Your Sentence Is to Look at the Sky), subtitled "Sonnets to Michelangelo," reflects Zardoya's deep love of art. Art, one form of salvation visualized by the poet (together with memories, dreams, and love), allows humanity to transcend daily existence and earthly life. Michelangelo's painting and sculpture inspire 12 compositions. Man's insignificance in total creation and the existential anguish resulting from sentience and awareness of human limitations are themes suggested by Michelangelo's masterful sculptures. Art appears repeatedly in Zardoya's works, including *Corral de vivos y muertos,* with homages to El Greco, Velázquez, Goya, Solana, and Picasso, seeking to capture lyrically the spirit of each. Zardoya's admiration for Miró produces *Poemas a Joan Miró* (1984); Cézanne, Kandinsky, and Eva Lloréns also have poems dedicated to them. Goya, another favorite, inspires poems in *Los Engaños de Tremont* and *Retorno a Magerit:* "La quinta del sordo" (The Deaf Painter's Estate) contains 18 pieces responding to individual Goya paintings, especially of monsters and atrocities. Various poems celebrate the Louvre, jazz, Debussy, Bartók, Vivaldi, de Falla, Tomás de Vitoria, and Pablo Casals.

Art reappears in *Los Perplejos Hallazgos* (1986; Perplexed Discoveries), the poet's responses to masterpieces of painting and sculpture by famous contemporary artists whose expositions she visited in Madrid in 1984–85. "Homage to Paul Cézanne" contains 33 pieces in varied metrical forms (sonnet, tercets, and quatrains of blank verse). "Interludes," written largely in free verse, responds to works of Antoni Tàpies, Fernando Zóbel, Giorgio Morandi and Jean Arp; "Homage to Juan Gris" consists of 27 compositions in unrhymed heptasyllables. Names of masterpieces become titles for the corresponding poems. *Los Ríos caudales* (1982; Mighty Rivers), subtitled "Apology for [the Generation of] 1927," emphasizes creative process, poetry, and the poet's mission. Zardoya celebrates the Generation of 1927, romantically painting poets as seers capable of describing metaphysical realities and eternal truths.

She also depicts, however, the poet-creator as laborer, investigator, and tireless worker, a "seismograph registering changes in the human spirit." While produced after the vogue of social poetry, this collection's attitude contrasts with Figuera and Fuertes in their disparaging allusions to "pure poetry." Zardoya's use of intertexts, however, coincides with Fuertes.

Zardoya relies little on traditional rhyme, exhibiting metric independence and exploiting heptasyllables and other *arte menor* lines, hendecasyllables, Alexandrines, and forms as varied as sonnets and free verse. Major poetic devices include repetition, prosopopeia, alliteration, interrogation (rhetorical questions), exclamation, apostrophe (invoking God, Spain, family), anaphora, assonance, reiteration, *enjambement,* ellipses, enumeration, and antithesis. Zardoya admits variation in modes of poetic expression but separates these passing fashions from the essence of poetry, as seen in "A Few True Words" from *El Corazón y la sombra.*

Elegías (1961) features subjects from the writer's past and present; Spanish, foreign, and personal history; literature and art; and painting an elegiac landscape peopled by souls of Spain's greatest poets, Zardoya's own deceased family and relatives, and various foreign writers. Evoking writers' biographical and social circumstances and the spirit of their epochs, she seeks stylistic essentials: Antonio Machado, García Lorca, Garcilaso, Bécquer, San Juan de la Cruz, Quevedo, Unamuno, Juan Ramón Jiménez, and contemporary José Luis Hidalgo figure among shades summoned by Zardoya. Elegies to family members constitute the book's final section, with her dead brother inspiring passionate, brutal, morbid and tender lines.

In *La Estación del silencio* (1989; Season of Silence), a Spanish edition of *Elegías,* Zardoya adds new elegiac poems but essentially repeats and expands the earlier volume. This text has four parts: "Spanish Elegies," "Foreign Elegies," "Family Elegies," and "Imaginary Elegies." Often addressing poet subjects in the intimate second person, Zardoya displays ample acquaintance with their writings through paraphrase, intertextual allusions and citations, sometimes ironically modified. She underscores the theme of death in Quevedo; mystical ascension in San Juan, and Antonio Machado's images of voyage. Lexically rich yet unencumbered by obscure vocabulary or complex rhetorical figures, her elegies convey her vision of life: "Vivir es ver morir" ("To live is to see death"). Usually avoiding rhyme and using panegyrical or measured, reflective tones, Zardoya here prefers traditional meters: the heavy Alexandrine and nimbler hendecasyllable. Thoughts on death include reasons for life, joy, and hope; the elegies express grief but also affirmation.

Altamor (1986) reiterates earlier themes: life and death, nature, time, ontological preoccupations, joy and suffering. The first section honors the sun, intoning four exalted hymns; remaining parts, more somber and less grandiloquent, include elegies with a positive note, viewing death as "new life" and reconfirming bonds between living and dead. Nature at its most grandiose and spectacular, humanized and consoling, constitutes a significant presence. Life overshadows death, surrounds and shrouds it, attenuating bereavement. *Corral de vivos y muertos* (1965; Pen of the Living and Dead), Zardoya's tenth collection and among her most significant, substantial, and characteristic, repeats the title of one of its 13 divisions, alluding intertextually to Unamuno's "En un cementerio de lugar castellano" (In a Castilian Village Cemetery), which describes the neglected, weed-infested, fenced enclosure filled with graves as a "corral" for the dead. Zardoya abolishes the boundary between life and death, implicitly transferring the metaphor to all of Spain, with living and dead alike enclosed in Franco's prisons.

Several poems in this collection express preoccupations with exile, the search for peace, longing for the Spanish homeland, and tender remembrance of compatriots, living and dead. Landscapes and objects are endowed with souls and emotion, ancient castles and rocky shores with thoughts, rebellion, and hopes of freedom. The poet weeps for the orphaned, the dead, Spain's dying and dusty villages, war's ruins, weary peasants, the heartless sky and wind, and those hungering for bread and freedom. Looking backward in sorrow, she recalls brooks and streams; geraniums and poplars; fish and shadows; fishermen, woodcutters, and shepherds; fields of wheat and rye; olives and wine; cities and lullabies. She personifies the countryside—the Cantabrian coast and misty hills— with its half-starved burros and scarred hands of child workers, evoking Unamuno and Antonio Machado (whose austere yet tender visions of Castile resemble her own) in epigraphs and intertexts. Her dedication, "With the Hope of Winning a Painful Citizenship which Some Would Deny Me," reaffirms love for Spain's spiritual connotations. One observer—noting the poet's lucid style and sensorial, figurative language, the absence of artificial constructions, obscured meanings, and ornamental imagery—termed her a "Hispanic Robert Graves."[5]

Donde el tiempo resbala (1966; Where Time Slips), subtitled "Belgian Ballad Collection," contains reactions to Belgian landscapes (identified with vitality and life). Notes of sadness continue, but pain and death matter less than the enchantment emanating from timeless landscapes, like the sleepy canals where time "slips" past. Probing beneath superficial appearances, Zardoya seeks love, enduring ideals and dreams. Contemplating the historic medieval guild town of Ghent, she regrets Spain's sixteenth-century dominance of the Low Countries. Color and painting acquire heightened visibility, with Flemish tapestries inspiring several pieces, including one on the unicorn.

In *Hondo Sur* (1968; Deep South) the poet looks to America and backward to New Orleans, painting critical vignettes of social problems against the background tapestry of southern geography: swamps, bayous, cotton fields, and decaying plantations. Basic concerns include time, death, suffering, human prejudices, imperfections, recollections evoked by the landscapes painted. The major link to Zardoya's other books is her concern for victims of injustice. Alluding to contemporary social history, she evokes racial prejudice, Bull Connor, Martin Luther King, Jr., and the songs of Marian Anderson, inserting bits of Negro spirituals, lullabies, and dances, references to African-American customs and oral traditions. Symbolic southern mountains highlight oppositions between an idyllic nature and the mechanized metropolis. In *Forma de esperanza* (1985; A Form of Hope) the poet laments multiple injustices, hungry children, and the pain of the lonely.

Los Engaños de Tremont (1971; Deceits of Tremont) refers not only to Boston (Tremont-on-the-Green) but to Spain. Zardoya's negative vision of Franco, characterized as a "black swan" for his "deceits," indicts persecution of the defeated by his regime. Deceit consists of cowardice, lies, and false purity, implicitly denounced in 114 blank sonnets. Other "deceits" include the portrait of the poet's mother (a simulacrum), "deceptions" of music and art, civic deceits, deceits of the written word plus deceitful perspectives for viewing reality. Internal realities—love, hate, communication or the lack thereof, authenticity, immortality, the essence of life—may be buried beneath surface appearances; the poet examines simple daily objects (broom, chair, table, kitchen utensils) in search of their "trans-reality." Poet Isabel Paraíso sees the work as synthesizing all Zardoya had done previously, with "perfect order" in metrics (all blank sonnets), distribution (24 groups of four sonnets each), and thematic graduation (from objects, to nature, human life, art, the poet's life, and spiritual life).[6]

Las Hiedras del tiempo (1972; Ivy of Time) paints landscapes where the poet has lived or roads traveled from Chartres to Manhattan, Fiésole to Canada. Varied skyscapes and interiors project lights and shadows through 28 poems, repeating sections 1 and 3 of *Debajo de la luz* (1955; Beneath the Light) and incorporating earlier compositions whose common denominator is light. *El Corazón y la sombra* (1977; Heart and Shadow), chronicling the quest for self-realization, uses heart and shadow to symbolize personal existence and collective, anonymous history or "intrahistory" (Unamuno's term for quotidian reality, scorned by historians). Opposing perspectives characterize the intimate, soulful ego; past and present, memory and continuity, vary the contrasting perspectives. In this dense, seven-part volume, themes of beauty and poetry's importance rank beside awareness of life's originality and uniqueness. Zardoya judges her own poetry (in the Prologue), mentioning free verse, abundant rhetorical questions, and dialogue techniques among major stylistic devices. Constant themes include time's passing, being-toward-death, the past, and memory's positive value (cf. Antonio Machado). For poet-critic Ana María Fagundo, Zardoya comes "close to her much-admired Miguel de Unamuno in her constant concern for the metaphysical."[7]

Diotima y sus edades (1981; Diotima and Her Ages), more experimental in form and structure, is subtitled "Autobiography in Four Times (Infancy, Adolescence/Young Adulthood, Maturity, and Old Age)." Diotima, a symbolic quest figure with universal and eternal attributes, facilitates dialogue with a double of the poet, who insists that her Diotima differs from Plato's and Hölderlin's. The poetic persona—direct and austere—retraces Zardoya's past, varying pronouns (you, I, we), which reduces differences between speaker, author, reader, poet and persona. Chronicling her intellectual history, the poet uses Diotima as interlocutor, fusing history and continuity, past and present facets of the poetic self (*you* representing past, *I* the present), juxtaposing critical judgments with lyric inspiration. Solitude is a leitmotiv in poems closing the four parts (or "times"). Seldom using rhyme, Zardoya incorporates many traditional meters, from quasi-popular lullabies to love sonnets, exploiting colloquial registers with minimal imagery and verbal economy.

Retorno a Magerit (1983; Return to Magerit [i.e., Madrid]), Zardoya's nineteenth poetry collection, contains an authorial Prologue identifying her central themes as death, love (including empathy and pity), consciousness of tragic destiny, Spain present and distant, dreams (as recollection, salvation, and refuge), light (representing humanity's supreme aspirations), and temporality. *Retorno a Magerit* (employing a putative ancient form of the city's name) lyrically expresses the poet's emotional traumas after 30 years in exile—her reencounter with the Madrid she had frequented and the realization that "you can't go home again." "Por las calles se fueron" (They Went through the Streets), containing 11 poems, depicts street vendors, beggars, gardens, and ghosts encountered while wandering through Madrid, the "final" city, where Zardoya intends to die when exile and loss will fuse with dreams of eternity. The central third part dominates this Goyaesque collection of 48 poems—appropriately, a homage to Goya, 18 verbal pictures of famed works. Another implicit intertext, the *esperpentos* of Valle-Inclán (another distorted, grotesque vision), reinforces Goya's "dark paintings." Statues, the second section, celebrates works gracing major streets and plazas of Madrid. *Retorno a Magerit,* with *Corral de vivos y muertos* and *Diotima,* figures among Zardoya's most moving works.

Manhattan y otras latitudes (Manhattan and Other Latitudes) describes arrival at Kennedy Airport, still mentally aloft, unsure of her bearings. Contrasting the stars' serenity with the city's corruption, she questions the metropolis and civilization that constructed it. Fifteen poems depict Manhattan and its materialism, excoriating the city's dehumanizing crowding and indifference to individual suffering. Six poems celebrate art in New York, including Picasso's Spanish Civil War masterpiece, *Guernica.* Ten poems, subtitled "Other Latitudes," re-create places the poet has lived (including Indiana and Boston), expressing more affection. Calm views of nature inspire *No llega a ser ceniza lo que arde* (1985; Not All that Burns Is Ashes). Serene reflections on life's enigmas—contemplations of dawn, sunset, rain, and gardens—lead to meditations on life, time, choice, and existential process. Images of fire, water, light, and shadow underlie this essentially affirmative collection. Fire, associated more with light than destruction, and water—traditional symbol of life, continuity, and creative force—are not opposite but complementary images of vitality. Like Don Quixote, Zardoya cares more for the road than the inn.

Somewhat nondescript books of the 1980s and 1990s include *Patrimonio de ciegos* (1992; Patrimony of the Blind), wherein art and imagination reappear (modern expositions, music, such mythical figures as Persephone, Medusa, and the Minotaur), together with travel, landscapes, and motifs of violence (a mutilated statue, a machine gun, cancer). Thirty-seven poems comprise four unequal parts entitled "Festival of the Imagination," "The Inclined Tower (Homage to René Magritte)," "The Triumph of Persephone," and "If You Didn't Love Life." *Grádiva y un extraño héroe* (1987; Gradiva and a Strange Hero) collects 15 poems, including "The Door," "The Remote Eagle," "Identities," "We're All Philosophers," "The Mask," and "Alabaster Desert." Gradiva, a beautiful dream figure, resembles a classical nymph or statue of Venus, while the "Strange Hero" appears amid

crowds and traffic, scaling a skyscraper and suffering arrest for his feat.
"Poet in Harlem" might have been subtitled Homage to García Lorca,
given pervasive allusions to *Poet in New York*.

In 1993 Zardoya published *El Don de la simiente* (The Gift of the
Seed), celebrating "seeds" sown by women poets and gathered from
Zardoya's readings. The first of 21 poems indicts the silence to which
women poets are relegated: "Our verses are hidden. Were they born /
to die in unknown holes?" (9). Part 1 begins with Rosalía de Castro, continuing with Delmira Agustini, Gabriela Mistral, Alfonsina Storni, and
Juana de Ibarbarou. Part 2 celebrates twentieth-century Peninsular
women poets: Rosa Chacel, Ernestina de Champourcín, Carmen Conde,
Concha Lagos, Cristina Lacasa, Acacia Uceta, Elena Andrés, Luzmaría
Jiménez Faro, Ana María Fagundo, Amparo Amorós, Isabel Paraíso,
Fanny Rubio, and young Acacia Domínguez (daughter of Acacia Uceta
and her poet-husband, Enrique Domínguez Millán). Zardoya's sketches
probe each woman's lyric spirit, revealing the author as connoisseur and
sensitive reader of women's poetry.

Angela Figuera

Born in the Basque city of Bilbao 30 October 1902, Angela Figuera
Aymerich was the eldest of nine children of an industrial engineer and a
teacher. Her mother's delicate health required Angela's caring for
younger siblings, probably fostering her strong maternal instincts; special significance is accorded themes of motherhood and love for children
in her poetry. Figuera began writing poems and children's stories in adolescence, usually destroying them. One 200-page notebook of unpublished juvenilia was saved by her cousin and future husband, Julio
Figuera. After her father's death in 1927, Figuera lived with an uncle in
Madrid, attending the university. In severe economic straits (dependent
upon Angela and her grandmother), the family moved to Madrid in
1930, where Figuera taught in private schools and tutored children of
the wealthy. Lacking official certification, she prepared herself for public
examinations as a secondary school teacher, obtaining a job in Huelva in
1933. She married her cousin Julio and they moved to Andalusia, living
uneventfully until the outbreak of the Civil War, save for the death during labor of her first child in 1935. The war separated them before
Figuera's son Juan Ramón was born in December 1936 (her husband
served in the Republican army). When her husband was transferred to a

village near Murcia, Figuera taught there; subsequently she and her husband (like many Republicans) lost their jobs.

While devoting herself to her home and child, Figuera found time for writing. *Mujer de barro* (1948; Woman of Clay), published when she was 46, consists of poems written over more than a decade: "Muerto al nacer" (Born Dead), concerning her first son's death, is among the earliest. The poetic voice, clearly feminine, re-creates a domestic universe, primarily the nuclear family, depicting her son's infancy, childhood, and developmental discoveries and offering intimate insights into the mother-child relationship. "Poems of My Son and Myself" celebrates his third and fifth birthdays, first day at school, games, childhood disguises, and nonstop questions. "El Fruto redondo" (The Round Fruit), featuring more philosophical or introspective poems, reflects on the poet's esthetics. *Mujer de barro* joyfully affirms maternity as the vehicle for perpetuating the species, positively embracing womanhood as defined by patriarchal Spanish society. Reflecting the intimacy of a happy marriage, these poems convey the poet's private subjectivity. Some sensual, erotic lyrics (daring for the puritanical postwar years) blend traditional themes with popular forms.

John C. Wilcox perceives in Figuera "an occluded feminist vein, the evidence of which [she] denied"[8] in her using the female figure "as no other Spanish 'Social Poets' had done" (68). While lauded for maternal themes, Figuera went to "great lengths in a few strong poems to completely demystify the condition of motherhood" (68). Wilcox believes that Figuera subtly critiques the phallocentric canon and was "developing her own poetics, one that was woman-centered, gynocentric not androcentric, in which metaphors of procreation and genesis are described from a woman's point of view and experience" (70). As Figuera's feminism has not been recognized, "her poetry has been depreciated and the uniqueness of her vision obscured" (89).

Soria pura (1949; Pure Soria) depicts summer vacations in the Sorian village of Burgo de Osma and bicycling in the surrounding countryside. The title, an intertextual allusion to Antonio Machado's "Soria fría" in *Campos de Castilla,* confirms Figuera's devotion to Machado, important for her mature poetics. Although her first two collections exhibit personal concerns rather than collective ones, they owe less to the Generation of 1927 (to which Figuera belongs chronologically) or vanguard influences than proletarian attitudes and social protest of the "mid-century generation." Figuera usually eschewed literary "isms," cherishing her independence. The 48 poems of *Soria pura* are divided into six sections: one is a homage to Antonio Machado; others describe humble flora and fauna (much loved by Machado), small streams and rocky outcroppings, forays into hidden nooks and quiet glades. The poetic persona delights in discovering nature, not romanticized but humanized—realistic and concrete. Earth, trees, summer storms, and somber peasants foreshadowing later social emphases predominate in the bleak Sorian plateau. *Soria pura* expresses the relief of war's survivors, who cautiously face the uncertain future. The poet dwells not upon wartime trials nor current hardships but centuries of human history imposed upon timeless nature.

Most observers identify Figuera with Spain's "social literature," a neorealist protest movement affecting all genres, characterized by veiled political criticism and dissent and concentrating on economic problems. Social poets express solidarity with victims of social injustice (especially the class structure). Most social literature covertly opposed the Franco regime, depicting the working class and peasants as victims, while wealthier citizens (mostly Franco supporters) emerged as parasites. Poetry became an arm for changing society (in the words of Gabriel Celaya), adopting aggressively utilitarian style and lexicon. While Figuera's Republican background made such writing risky, her growing awareness of political reprisals, social injustice, and economic stagnation moved her poetry away from personal concerns toward socially critical themes. The seven of her eleven titles considered most typical (or most "social") appeared during social literature's heyday (1950–62): *Vencida por el ángel* (1950; Overcome by the Angel), *El Grito inútil* (1952; Futile Cry), *Víspera de la vida* (1953; Vespers of Life), *Los Días duros* (1953; Hard Times), and *Belleza cruel* (1958; Cruel Beauty). Figuera completed her last major collection, *Toco la tierra* (1962; I Touch the Earth) during 1959–61, before moving to Avilés where her husband was working.

During a decade in provincial isolation from literary circles, loss of contact with other writers and advancing age slowed Figuera's activity. She spent her final years in Madrid, suffering from heart and lung disease, dying in 1984. Her last books were narrative poems invented for her granddaughter, *Cuentos tontos para niños listos* (1979; Stupid Tales for Clever Children) and *Canciones para todo el año* (1985; Year-Round Songs), published posthumously. Secondary bibliography is sparse—largely posthumous tributes or brief mentions in anthologies or panoramic works. Discounting these and prologues to certain editions of Figuera's works, critical notices include reviews, interviews, and half a dozen scholarly essays.[9] Rather than feminist, Figuera's poetry is feminine;

early books celebrate motherhood, marriage, conjugal love and domestic life. Maternity has been termed the axis of her poetry (Quance, 13); identifying fully with the traditional roles of wife and mother, Figuera would probably have protested categorization as feminist.

Figuera's reading of Gabriel Celaya's *Las Cosas como son* (1950; The Way Things Are) brought realization of the inadequacy of traditional lyrics (Saladrigas, 48). Turning self-critical in *Vencida por el ángel,* Figuera denounces the "old Angela" for selfishly sequestering herself in domestic bliss while ignoring the world's problems. Biblical accounts of Jacob's wrestling with the angel are metaphorically equated with her avoiding humanity's suffering and being overcome. The first poem of *El Grito inútil* looks backward at "pure poetry," uncommitted poetry for art's sake or for pleasure, concluding that there can be no turning back. Figuera progressively abandons traditional poetic forms and themes, sounding more aggressive notes, becoming less personal and affirmative, more denunciatory and critical.

As her activism grows, Figuera identifies with other mothers in their problems and suffering: her pro-maternal politics denounces poverty, violence, war, and oppression. Turning from private, personal concerns toward public, collective problems, the poet rejects traditional metrics, approaching free verse and adopting a less lyrical, more prosaic and direct style. Rhyme seldom appears in Figuera's works. Repetition, acquiring ironic undertones from elements introduced in the interim, figures among her most significant poetic devices; metonymy, metaphor, rhetorical questions, litotes (understatement), prosopopeia, and dehumanization likewise appear frequently.

Personal concerns do not disappear entirely from Figuera's social poems, nor do collective and political concerns completely displace universal poetic themes—love of parents, the search for ultimate answers, abiding existential and metaphysical issues—but these recede from the forefront. Figuera progressively simplifies expression, most notably in *Belleza cruel,* becoming increasingly protest-oriented. In *El Grito inútil* and *Víspera de la vida* the historical present—with its political problems and economic injustice—joins real, human concerns more specifically relevant to woman's condition: a major difference between Figuera's work and that of Gabriel Celaya or Blas de Otero (or Dámaso Alonso's *Hijos de la ira*) is her frequent focus upon women. The first poem of *El Grito inútil* asks whether the poet as woman can succeed in a sociopolitical endeavor if men have failed. Her leitmotiv questions poetry's usefulness, voicing caveats that male poets did not formulate; she wonders if social literature has any political impact, whether the pen is equal to the sword, whether the social poets' altruistic devotion to victims of injustice is futile.

Utilitarian poetry—renouncing beauty and "artistic" goals—deprived poets of creative satisfaction; readers found such pedestrian, limited, and sociological themes boring, which contributed to the movement's demise. Although Figuera continued to write social poetry, she suspected it was a "futile cry," protesting from conviction that it was the poet's duty. "Unity," one of her frequently anthologized poems, appeals to universal human brotherhood as the way to a better world; "Postwar" calls upon war's survivors to rejoice in living yet recognizes their psychic wounds. "Mujeres del mercado" (Women in the Market), one of Figuera's most feminist pieces, depicts working-class women in the city market: prematurely aged, ragged, and dirty, they hunt the cheapest produce and meat to feed drunken husbands in fetid rooms, with little to anticipate except perhaps another unwanted pregnancy.

The title poem of *Víspera* juxtaposes labor and cries of childbirth with the death throes of a bit of human flotsam that was once a man. Reiterating motifs of maternity, another poem treats blood; another addresses the mother of a young poet recently drowned. Flora and fauna, no longer objects of delight, become images of frustration. Notes of solitude and alienation reinforce protests against the unknown and unknowable. More personal material appears in memories of childhood Christmases, a tribute to the poet's father ("Cuando mi padre pintaba" [When My Father Painted]), an elegy to a dead sister and another on her mother's death. *Los Días duros* consists of Figuera's first three "social" books (*Vencida por el ángel, Víspera,* and *El Grito*), plus previously unpublished poems; it was combined in 1954 with her first two books as *Obra completa* (Complete Works). The 11 previously unpublished poems (*Los Días duros*), more aggressive and strident, proclaim solidarity with mothers of the world, denouncing contradictions between Spanish society's cult of the Virgin with its idealization of mothers and patriarchal disempowerment of women. Explicitly renouncing passivity and her earlier life-style, Figuera again condemns placing her individual concerns (whether as wife, mother, or lover) before collective struggles and sorrows. Tears and images of violence abound, as do existential themes, questioning the purpose of human existence and reiterating the poet's obligation to protest.

Figuera withheld other poems, knowing they risked censorship, endangering her long-awaited job at the National Library, begun in

1954 and continued until leaving Madrid in 1962 (interestingly, Fuertes, Conde, and Zardoya all worked as librarians or archivists). A library grant for study in Paris in 1957 permitted smuggling her more overtly critical, perilous compositions out of Spain. She mailed the most aggressive poems from France to a friend in Mexico, where they were entered in prize competition, resulting in Mexican publication of *Belleza cruel* (1958; Cruel Beauty), unpublished in Spain until 1978, three years after Franco's death. Exiled poet León Felipe's polemical Prologue to *Belleza cruel* details how Figuera revolutionized his opinion of poetry in Franco's Spain, revealing her own work plus that of Celaya, Otero, José Hierro, and Victoriano Crémer. Other observers saw nothing new in *Belleza cruel*. J. P. González Martín deems the maternal her dominant sentiment and manner overall, whether expressing her own motherhood or her feelings as "collective mother of the 'forgotten' [of society]."[10]

Belleza cruel embodies Figuera's sharpest reactions to misery and injustice in postwar Spain. The first of 19 poems contemplates the paradox of creating art and beauty amid injustice and ugliness, pointedly alluding to "esthetic" poetry or selfish "cruel beauty" (echoing title poems of *Los Días duros* and *Vencida por el ángel*). This theme reappears in "El Cielo" (The Sky) and "La Rosa incómoda" (The Uncomfortable Rose), evoking the esthetics of Juan Ramón Jiménez. "Cruel beauty" is the egotism of poets' cultivating art rather than championing humanity. Figuera's brief three-part collection reiterates the poet's duty to protest injustice, stressing the need for peace and freedom. The Cain and Abel motif in *Belleza cruel* reiterates that of *Víspera de la vida,* symbolizing violence between brothers (i.e., civil war). "Guerra" (War) adopts the maternal perspective of Eve to lament having given birth to war. Testimonial themes and denunciations acquire greater anger and directness, hostility and sarcasm; Figuera calls the powerful and privileged to account in "Balance," which targets not traditional social inequities but the Franco regime. She subverts Falangist myths—traditional gender roles, idealized motherhood, and "untouchable" religious dogma. Via a poor laborer's letter to God, she invokes Christ as carpenter, inviting Him in colloquial, cliché-laced language to join the workers' struggle.

Social poetry's limited thematics ultimately brought the movement's demise, and perhaps Figuera perceived sooner than male "social" poets the futility of their altruistic endeavor. While some writers continued to cultivate the social vein throughout the decade, poetic changes appeared by the mid-1960s. Figuera published only one more social collection, *Toco la tierra* (1962; I Touch the Earth), subtitled "Litanies," before

lapsing into prolonged silence. Her Prologue insinuates fears of repeating herself—perhaps motivating increased formal diversity, ranging from
unaccustomed sonnets to long poems in free verse, with abundant parallelistic devices. Although less forceful than *Belleza cruel, Toco la tierra*
recapitulates her most characteristic vein. Images of the soil in Figuera's
first and last titles (*Mujer de barro* and *Toco la tierra*) evoke the Great
Mother, source of all life, providing a sense of having come full circle.
Figuera's *Obra completa,* with her husband's biographical essay and critical introduction by Roberta Quance, contain 30 poems not previously
published in books. "Poeta puro" (The Pure Poet) echoes one leitmotiv of
Figuera's mature poetry—the collective social duty of poets—expressed
in an atypical sonnet. "Romance de puebloespaña" (Ballad of Spain's
People) commemorates the Asturian miners' strike of May 1962, grimly
repressed by the Franco regime. Figuera considered the strike proof that
the spirit of liberty still lives.

Figuera's children's books contain her only extant examples of conso-
nantal rhyme. Her *Cuentos tontos* resemble works by Spain's eighteenth-
century "fabulists" (variants of Aesop's fables), although the tone is more
playful. Like Mother Goose rhymes, her children's verse has political
undertones: the satiric "Tale of the Silly Little Witch Who Couldn't Get
Her Identity Card" details misadventures when attempting to fly without
the government's required identity papers. Characteristic themes such as
motherhood also appear in the children's books. In "La Mosca" (The Fly),
for instance, the poet imagines the mother fly's fate if the thousands of
eggs she lays had to be individually nursed, bathed, put to bed, and taken
to school. Figuera's children's books reveal that she possessed more extensive command of poetic technique than she normally used, plus a rich,
festive, satiric potential not developed in her writings for adults.

Gloria Fuertes

Born in Madrid in 1918, Gloria Fuertes was the daughter of working-
class parents. She describes the family's neighborhood as having "many
needy, many whores, and some convent or other."[11] Her mother was a
seamstress; her father worked as a doorman and usher. The autobiographical poem "Poeta de seis años" (Six-Year-Old Poet) indicates that by
her first communion, she considered herself not a girl or boy but a poet.
Fuertes's adolescence was saddened by the Civil War, a profoundly
painful first love at age 15, and her mother's death when she "most
needed her."[12] Fuertes states that her parents neither loved her nor each

other (*HG*, 148). She studied practical skills: cooking, embroidery, child care, tailoring, and a smattering of grammar and literature; her interest in poetry disconcerted rather than pleased her mother. Fuertes noted satirically, "en mi pueblo / no dejan escribir a las mujeres" ("in my village / they don't let women write" [*OI*, 72]). Her father, however, "always had a book in his hand; he knew the classics very well."[13] Fuertes worked as a stenographer, kept books during the war, and wrote poetry daily (*OI*, 27). Following the war, she sent some children's stories to the weekly *Maravillas,* received a job offer, and moved to a boarding house (her father had remarried). She continued writing poetry, plays, and stories for children and producing children's records for some three decades, along with writing poems for adults, whom she often treated as children.

Fuertes's first poetry collection, *Isla ignorada* (1950; Unknown Island), shows little social preoccupation. Love looms large—love reciprocated and love lost, and especially the motif of *entrega* (self-abnegating surrender). Fuertes indicates that these poems were written during the Civil War (Villar, 13). Despite some colloquialisms and popular language, Fuertes's influences were surrealism and *postismo,* an ephemeral neovanguardist movement headed by Carlos Edmundo de Ory (an intimate friend whom she met in 1942), and including—besides Fuertes— Eduardo Chicharro and Silvano Sernesi. *Postismo,* an estheticist tendency seeking audacity, freshness of expression, linguistic rigor, and adventure, constituted the postwar derivation of prewar surrealism. Fuertes indicates that the first poet she met "in the flesh" was Gabriel Celaya (*OI,* 29), a prewar surrealist.

Fuertes is not known for works written under the aegis of surrealism and *postismo* (present in declining proportion in early collections) but for her social poetry; she abandoned *postismo* because it "didn't reach the people" (working class) and, like Figuera, expressed distaste for "pure poetry." Fuertes proclaims her literary independence and total lack of influences, but Brenda Cappuccio mentions that critics detected influences from medieval ballads to Quevedo, Unamuno, Antonio Machado, Gómez de la Serna's *greguerías,* Miguel Hernández, *postismo,* and the "mid-Century Generation."[14] Cappuccio quotes Carmen Conde's *Poesía femenina española viviente,* terming Fuertes "madrileña barojiana y goyesca, de los *Caprichos* menos virulentos pero más populares" (91; "a Madrid denizen a la Baroja and Goya, from the least virulent, most popular *Caprices* [of Goya]").

In *Una Nueva poesía española (1950–55)* Max Aub detected echoes in Fuertes of the *sainetes* (traditional satiric farce) and zarzuela (Spanish musical comedy), also mentioned by Cappuccio, who cites Rubén Benítez's dictum that Fuertes's worldview resembles not only Goya's but that of Hieronymous Bosch, Albrecht Dürer, and Rafael Solana, who coincide in dark, infernal, grotesque portrayals, expressionistic *avant le mot*. Fuertes stresses communicating what she feels and consistently uses direct, colloquial language with large doses of oralism. Santiago Daydí-Tolson observed Fuertes's directness, dramatic qualities, popularity, and orality but also her "defiant and boorish language" (99) and "rebelliousness" sometimes "mistaken as social commitment" (not mutually exclusive; Fuertes exhibits both). Fernando Quiñones in *Ultimos rumbos de la poesía española* (1966) cites "popular" traits, occasional "crudeness" and a "whiff of the *esperpento*" (grotesque distortions in expressionist works of Valle-Inclán). Quiñones notes excessive assonance—syntactic and morphological misfits suggesting carelessness—but also enormous variety and popular wisdom, a mixture of innocence, intuition, and absurdity, amusing and hair-raising by turns.

The title of *Antología y poemas del suburbio* (1954; Anthology and Suburban Poems) evokes urban social problems; *suburbio* in Spain denotes a no-man's-land where squatters, drifters, and street people construct makeshift shelters and eke out a living—a movable slum occupying areas of future urban expansion. Stylistically gray and prosaic, Fuertes's predominantly pedestrian and roundly antirhetorical language avoids pretentiousness and solemnity. Despite nonconforming protest poems, the volume enunciates themes of love and loss, autobiographical anecdotes, God's presence in the city, poetics, war memories, losses of friends and loved ones, and the poet's solitude. Throughout her early years Fuertes emphasizes her proletarian origins. Declaring her independence of middle-class morality and bourgeois convention, she adopted a bohemian lifestyle when few Spanish women dared defy patriarchal mores openly. Anthologists refer obliquely to her fondness for taverns and her series of lovers. Fuertes neither repressed nor concealed her sexuality—shocking conduct in the Franco era.

In 1955 Fuertes began taking courses in library science and English at the Instituto Internacional; she worked intermittently as librarian and archivist after completing her degree in 1960. While co-director of the poetry review *Arquero,* she published *Aconsejo beber hilo* (1954; I Advise Drinking a Trickle), containing surrealist poems, some with feminist themes, and neorealist, sociopolitically critical protest poetry. María Stycos includes Fuertes in her analysis of "Intertextuality in Selected Spanish Poets since 1939," noting her disparagement of Juan Ramón

Jiménez while affirming her own preference for reality.[15] Fuertes comments on problems for women writers in Spain's traditional, phallocentric society, plaintively admitting (in "I Confess") that being strong can be an onerous obligation for the woman alone. Daily life in Madrid's streets, public transportation, and intimate glimpses of the poet's solitude figure among recurring themes. *Todo asusta* (1958; Everything Is Frightening) depicts quotidian fears, irrational frights, anxieties, unlikely monsters, aspects of social life, personal relationships, feelings and memories, plus simply being alone. This collection defines the poet's mission as testimonial documentation of life but also treats more universal themes: love, death, hope, family, memories, and diverse emotions. Critic-poet José Luis Cano dates Fuertes's poetic reputation from 1962, when fellow poet Jaime Gil de Biedma published selected poems as *Que estás en la tierra* (Who Art on Earth).[16] This intertextual reference to the Lord's Prayer alludes not only to God's frequent presence in Fuertes's poetry but to the human guise in which she portrays the divinity, plus her abiding concern for those of this world. Fuertes published several children's books, obtaining a Fulbright grant in 1961, and taught Spanish poetry at Bucknell University in Pennsylvania; homesick for her beloved Madrid, she returned in 1964 and resumed teaching at the Instituto Internacional. In 1972 she received a March Foundation fellowship for creative writing. During the 1970s she collaborated with Spanish television, producing enormously popular programs aimed at younger audiences.

Like her 15 or more books for children, Fuertes's dozen collections of poetry for adults are often deceptively playful or childlike in style, suffused with irony or apparent sarcasm. Her poetry tends to witticisms, using graphic, colloquial, clever, and deliberately prosaic language, sometimes daring and cynical, intentionally shocking or incongruent, incorporating surprise endings or twists. Her highly subversive poetry derives much of its impact from reversing reader expectations.[17] Her popular, quotidian, and occasionally vulgar vocabulary (workers' expressions, slang, and dialectic forms) partly explains her success; she plays with words and sounds, achieving effects comparable to baroque *conceptismo* (conceits). Because language per se is crucial, with its original sounds (assonance, alliteration, aspects lost in translation), her poems have not been widely translated. One anthology exists in English, *Off the Map: Selected Poems by Gloria Fuertes,* translated by Philip Levine and Ada Long (1984).

Fuertes's style reflects her concept of poetry as direct communication with humanity; like many social poets, she sees poetry as an instrument for improving the world, an arm for changing society for the better. *Ni tiro, ni veneno, ni navaja* (Neither Gunshot, nor Poison, nor Knife) alternates hope and hopelessness, sadness and humor, anguish and surprise. Fuertes treats varied themes in *Cómo atar los bigotes del tigre* (1969; How to Tie the Tiger's Whiskers), defending "open poetry," a naked lyric devoid of rhetorical adornments, accessible to all. She expresses desire to serve as "a giant aspirin for the world's aches and pains; whoever tries me will find relief." Her dialogue with Poetry, admonishing her reluctant interlocutor not to hide from her, discusses beliefs in Christ and humanity, confessing the autobiographical origins of her "best" poems—"love letters" over which she has wept. Her "Poética" lists pain, anger, and humor as primary ingredients, avoidance of traditional meters and rhyme, except for humorous effect. Of technique, she says, "what a bore!" and "Never count syllables." She concentrates on content rather than precepts and form, relying on repetition—lines, phrases, words, or sounds—enumeration and exaggeration. Condensation—telegraphic at times—irony, playfulness, false naïveté, and surprising imagery also abound.

Like Unamuno, Fuertes maintains that she never corrects or rewrites anything (Villar, 13). *Poeta de guardia* (1968; Poet on Duty) significantly elaborates her concept of poetry and the poet's mission, viewing poets as sentries or doctors on call, awake while others sleep. In her longest collection (146 poems) poetry emerges as all-consuming activity for Fuertes, obliged to remain alert, battling life's trials. Suicide presents a constant temptation amid love's disappointments, existential solitude, and sadness. She portrays life as a lottery (a recurring theme). Various love poems reveal that she has loved not too wisely but too well—again and again. Punning on her name, she plays with its correspondence to "glory," penning "Gloria to God" poems, depicting God the Father as worker—for instance, a plumber urgently summoned to repair her "leaking faucet" of tears.

Sola en la sala (1973; Alone in the Parlor) contains Fuertes's most pathetic expressions of loneliness, sorrow, grief, and pain, exorcising anguish during an especially difficult period of struggle with humiliation, frustration, disappointment in love, and abandonment. No longer protest poetry, the collection is primarily subjective (one distinguishing feature of social poetry involved abandoning *yo* [first-person singular] for *nosotros* [first-person plural], or collective preoccupation). Obsessively using *yo,* Fuertes employs highly visible autobiographical and anecdotal elements, considered the basis for identification with her readers or listeners (she frequently visits provincial towns and villages giving public recitations of her poetry). This enhances orality in her work but has little thematic impact: Fuertes seldom portrays village ambients, favored by several social poets (and members of the Generation of 1898). Her poems, consistently brief, were termed "Moments" in her first book, while the central section of *Poeta de guardia* (1968; Poet on Duty) consists of "mini-poems." Major themes include suffering, loneliness, love or the illusion thereof, loss of love, lack of communication, existential solitude, poverty, injustice, pain, frustration, penury, exploitation, war, and misery.

Fuertes treats the seamy, painful side of reality, using settings avoided by elitist poets (taverns, slums, and bordellos) and people omitted in "pure poetry" (drunks, confidence men, hustlers, beggars, and transvestites). While Fuertes cannot be termed naturalistic because of her humor, irony, and "unscientific" compassion, her topics typify naturalism. Cataloguing themes, techniques and poetics, Fuertes simplifies the critic's task (and therefore figures among the best-studied of contemporary women poets). "Poética" (*Poeta de guardia*) prefers life over literature (i.e., wine and love over the dubious satisfactions of writing about them: "He cambiado / de técnica y de estilo / ¡Y manos a la obra! / Escribir sobre tu cuerpo / con los dedos mojados en el vino" ["I've changed / my technique and my style / So let's get to work! / Writing on your body / with my fingers wet with wine"]). Notwithstanding her erstwhile commitment to social poetry, Fuertes rejects narrow circumscription of the lyric for utilitarian and political ends, reflecting that "poetry shouldn't be an arm / it should be an embrace / an invention / a discovery of the Others" (*HG,* 313). This attitude, plus her neobaroque word play, intertextuality, and self-reflexive moments, anticipate poetics of the next wave of lyricists.

Fuertes expresses closeness to an omnipresent God, with whom she maintains a wide-ranging dialogue, sometimes calling the divinity to account for life's misfortunes. Her profoundly human vision of God borders the sacrilegious for traditionalists: one poem in *Poeta de guardia* compares God with a bullfighter and humanity with the bull; another inquires, "What would God be without us?" Elsewhere, God the Father chats with a plumber called to repair the leaky pipes of an aging, run-down Heaven. Establishing the interdependence of God and humanity, Fuertes concludes that mankind benefits from faith's consolations, while "the saddest thing about God / is that He can't believe in God" (*HG,* 43).

Although Fuertes maintains her faith, doubt invades *Sola en la sala* (1973; Alone in the Parlor) as she thinks that religion may be humanity's invention to face anguish and death. *Historia de Gloria,* however, transcends doubt, as Fuertes affirms her personal relationship with God the Father and with Christ, whom she considers a fellow poet.

Death, an insistent motif, appears as return to origins, rest for the world-weary, sometimes an unexpectedly comic figure whom the poet ridicules. Fuertes humorously reflects upon death's "inconveniences" (one cannot wind the clock, for example), burlesquing the Romantic gesture of suicide by jumping out the window (which is in the basement). Frequent jokes, often at her own expense, distinguish Fuertes from other Spanish poets of either gender, as does her self-deprecating humor (the exception is Jesús Munárriz, an esthetic fellow traveler of the *novísimos*).[18] José Luis Cano rightly notes that humor does not equal joy for Fuertes; anger and pain outweigh levity. And death is very much part of existence; a final "thunderous silence" underscores life's brevity and the absurdity of wasting it in war and stupidity.

Cano mentions that Fuertes's urban world retains little of the original natural landscape; this aspect characterizes the next wave of poets, whose omnipresent mass media, urbanization, and pop culture require cityscapes rather than rural ambients. Fuertes paints Madrid's traffic and noise, its place names, buildings, businesses and street corners, machines, asphalt and cement, plus occasional trees, dogs and cats, varied hominid fauna, and sky. She depicts more interiors than exteriors, with closed spaces including the kitchen where she writes and other familiar domestic surroundings. Her autobiographical anecdotes and self-portraits reflect on being misunderstood or unloved, on solitude, "illness, self-loathing, madness, and suicide."[19] Her solitude spawns nocturnal terrors, visions of phantasmagoric creatures (Cano emphasizes the phantom in *Ni tiro ni veneno* and *Poeta de guardia*). She depicts malaise and surreal, infernal scenes engendered by darkness and her overactive imagination. Silvia R. Sherno streses miniaturization and gigantism (92–93) and metamorphoses (94), transformations of self into eagle, dove, ostrich, elephant, walrus, hedgehog, goat ("cabra sola"), lamb and lion, and, most often, a tree. The poetic persona also becomes a mollusk, a mule, a sea urchin, and a quill-less porcupine (Sherno 1989, 249). Fuertes frequently mentions her body, usually self-deprecatingly, offering intimate details of daily toilette, feminine physiology, and physical aging.

Fuertes, like Figuera, often treats childbirth and maternity; considerably more feminist than Figuera, she demythologizes romance (cf. "Algo más que unos cuerpos juntos es el amor" [*HG,* 191; "Love is something more than joined bodies"]), spoofing and punning in "El Amor es una función que no funciona" (Love Is a Play that Doesn't Work). Fuertes laughs at her own rejection in "Penitis tengo doctora" (Madame Doctor, I Have Penitis), an "inflamed pain of loving and not being loved in return." She ridicules matrimony in "Legalmente soltera" (Legally a Spinster), affirming, "It isn't worth investing everything / to give warmth to somebody / who's only interested in you / sometimes, on impulse, some days." As Sherno notes, Fuertes depicts herself as powerful (92) but often does so tongue-in-cheek. Celebrating her autonomy in "Poeta independiente" (Independent Poet), she reflects that while "not a mother, nor a wife, nor a widow, nor a nun," she is nevertheless, thanks to her poetic achievements, all of these and more. Fuertes rejects gender stereotypes, including the anthropomorphic concept of God as male. See, for instance, "El lo sabe" (He Knows All), which begins, "Because He knows everything beforehand—HE or SHE or whoever" (*OI,* 207). Fuertes compassionately and affectionately depicts transvestites and sex-change operations in "Mis amigas los hombres" (My Girlfriends the Gays). Citing archetypal bent, black-shrouded female figures dotting rural Spanish landscapes, Fuertes affirms in "Apunte" (Sketch) that "village women / dress in mourning for themselves" (*HG,* 365). From a poem to her sick dog to playful word games and meditations on suicide and old age, she ranges across topics transcending sociopolitical protest (with which most anthologies and literary histories include her). González Martín stresses differences between Fuertes and Figuera, although literary historians generally underscore social poetry's sameness. Her uniqueness results from her rare irony and humor, innovative language, and "more profound emotion" (González Martín, 95–97).

Canonical studies of the period mention Figuera and Fuertes but not Zardoya. Curiously, critical studies of Figuera refer to Celaya, Hierro, and Blas de Otero, but not to Fuertes, while those of Fuertes (for example, the González Rodas Introduction to *Historia de Gloria*) fail to mention Figuera but cite some dozen male poets. Without coinciding, anthologists occasionally include other women with less poetic output (María Elvira Lacaci, Concha Lagos, Susana March, and others). No canonical works have attempted more representative coverage of women

poets in the period, of the more prolific ones, or all the women significant as social poets. Fuertes is younger than Figuera (as is Zardoya—not
considered "social"), but all three write of the war, deal critically with the
Franco regime, and publish their major works in the same period. Each
is very much an individual, and their works reflect their personalities,
but together with Conde they are the most prolific and important
women poets of the first three postwar decades.

Chapter Seven
Postwar Poets in Castilian

Nobody questions when Spain's postwar era begins, but little agreement exists as to the end point. During the first quarter-century following Spain's Civil War (1939–60s), the crisis mentality was prolonged by economic stagnation, monolithic political ideology, continued stifling of opposition (unacknowledged censorship and political imprisonment), and legislated Victorian morality. After treaties for U.S. bases in Spain were signed (1957–58) and the country was opened to tourism, economic recovery began, along with foreign influences and incipient diversity. The 1960s Press Law reforming censorial practice plus national education reforms in the 1970s and accelerating economic expansion initiated Spain's transition to democracy and consumerism before Franco's death in 1975, seemingly ending the postwar period.

Powerful esthetic considerations exist for arguing that "postwar" poetry ends during the 1960s. Social poetry (identified with the postwar period) flourished in the 1950s, declining in the 1960s (although social collections appeared until decade's end). Meanwhile, poetic changes emerge, including "poetry of discovery" (Debicki) and the younger *novísimos,* launched by José María de Castellet's anthology in 1970.[1] Differences notwithstanding, both groups are post-neorealist, rejecting pedestrian "social" thematics, politicoeconomic criticism, and anti-esthetic attitudes. The late 1960s evolution in esthetics and political climate creates a natural cut-off point between still-ongoing contemporary poetry and that belonging to an era now past—the postwar period.

Most twentieth-century literary panoramas include several overlapping age groups or "generations" producing simultaneously, and women poets are no exception. Because women often begin publishing late, grouping by birth dates alone may prove unsatisfactory; war's disruption of normal chronologies increases the difficulties of grouping by ages. Phallocentric mores and personal lifestyles (including maternity) have traditionally excluded women from literary circles or schools so that dates of publication and their writings themselves provide the most reliable bases for categorization. Some women who flourished during the postwar period are still productive, but most have slowed or suspended publication; others have died. Because of age, affinity to postwar esthetics or because they wrote preponderantly during the Franco years, the women treated in this chapter differ from those still producing (younger, postmodern, experimental or more linguistically oriented writers whose production belongs mainly to the post-Franco era).

Minor Poets

María Alfaro was born in 1900 in Gijón (Asturias). In 1934, during the Republic, she began publishing literary criticism in the major Madrid daily, *El Sol*. Her travels include France, the United States, and Latin America; apparently she resided for a time in Paris, directing a literary segment for *Radio Mundial;* following return to Spain, she served as correspondent for *Les Nouvelles Litteraires*. Alfaro enjoyed modest success as poet and novelist, and besides her critical essays, she published translations from the French and English (Corneille plays, Mark Twain novels). Among her poetry collections are *Poemas líricos: Selección, versión, y prólogo* (1945), *Poemas del recuerdo* (1951; Poems of Recollection) and—apparently—*Memorias de una muerte* (n.d.; Memoirs of a Death).

Asunción Madera (b. 1901 in Las Palmas, Gran Canaria) writes under her nickname "Chona" Madera. She began writing in the mid-1940s; themes include island geography and the sea, poetry and aspects of language, and love. Among her works are *El Volcano silencio* (1944; Volcanic Silence), *Mi presencia más clara* (1956; My Clearest Presence), *Las Estancias vacías* (1961; Empty Rooms), *La Voz que me desvela* (1965; The Voice that Keeps Me Awake), *Los Contados instantes* (1967; Counted Minutes), *Continuada señal* (1970; Continuing Signal), and *Mi otra palabra* (1977; My Other Word).

Josefina Romo Arregui (b. Madrid circa 1910) began publishing poetry during the Republic, including *La Peregrinación inmóvil* (1934; Motionless Pilgrimage), *Romancero triste* (1935; Sad Ballad Collection), and *Acuarelas* (1936; Water Colors). She obtained her doctorate in philosophy and literature from the University of Madrid in 1944, teaching world literature there and at City College (City University of New York) from 1960 to 1963. Thereafter until her death in 1979, she was at the University of Connecticut, meanwhile traveling over much of Europe, Africa, and America. Romo's enduring literary interests led to her founding the review *Alma,* directing *Cuadernos literarios* (1942–52) and the "Poetry Collection for Bibliophiles" initiated by Carmen Conde in 1946.

Solitude is among Romo's major poetic preoccupations, a solitude combatted with words—for silence only compounds solitude. Death is the definitive response to solitude, life only the prelude.

Romo's postwar poetry collections include *Aguafuertes y otros poemas* (1940; Engravings and Other Poems), *Cántico de María Sola* (1950; Canticle of María Alone), *Isla sin tierra* (1955; Island without Soil), *Elegías desde la orilla del triunfo* (1964; Elegies from the Shore of Triumph), *Poemas de América* (1967; Poems of America), *Autoantología* (1968; Self-Anthology), and *Poesía Ucrónica* (1972; Uchronic Poems). Academic essays include studies of Lope de Vega, Romanticism, and Gaspar Núñez de Arce; volumes related to poetry include one on Gabriela Mistral, plus *Máscara y rostro de la poesía* (1946; Face and Mask of Poetry), *El Romanticismo en la vida de los poetas románticos* (1950; Romanticism in the Lives of Romantic Poets), and *Concepción Estevarena, poetisa romántica* (1965; Concepción Estevarena, Romantic Poetess). Besides solitude, silence, travel, and memory, Romo's poetry treats alienation, the dehumanization of contemporary metropolitan civilization (contrasted with nature, symbolized by simple plants or insects), existential freedom, independence, death and the unknown. Several of the *Poemas de América* are elegies dedicated to modernist poets (e.g., Rubén Darío and José Asunción Silva). *Canticle de María Sola*—of which Romo herself is the protagonist—celebrates her self-sufficiency and liberation.

Clemencia Laborda Medir (1908–80) was born in the Catalan province of Lérida but spent her early years in Avila, later moving to Madrid. Largely self-taught, she read widely from poets of the Generations of 1898 and 1927, especially Juan Ramón Jiménez and García Lorca. Machado, Dámaso Alonso, and Carmen Conde praised her "impeccable mastery of form." Laborda treated traditional themes (religion, love, family), wrote civil and occasional poetry, and lived long enough to treat space-age exploits and man's landing on the moon. Her first religiously inspired collection, using classical forms, was *Jardines bajo la lluvia* (1943; Gardens in the Rain), which was well-received by critics. Other poetic works include *Caudal* (n.d.; Treasure), *Ciudad de soledades* (1948; City of Solitudes), *Retorno a la provincia* (1961; Return to the Province), *Niños y jardines* (n.d.; Children and Gardens), *Poesías religiosas* (n.d.; Religious Poems), and *Tiempo del hombre, tiempo de Dios* (1972; Man's Time, God's Time). Laborda achieved modest renown as a playwright, with at least half a dozen domestic and moral dramas, and published two novels. Admiration for Lorca did not include experimentalism or vanguardist influences; Laborda cultivated classic metrical forms (tercets, eight-line *octavas reales,* 10-line *décimas,* especially sonnets and traditional ballads). Prayers, glosses, homages to friends and relatives, spiritual meditations, love poetry, landscapes, memories of distant places, nostalgia, dreams, childhood, time, and intimate commitment figure among Laborda's most frequent themes. Galerstein lists two collections reportedly unpublished at Laborda's death—*Vacaciones bajo los árboles* (Vacation beneath the Trees) and *En busca de los recuerdos perdidos* (In Search of Lost Memories).

Pino Ojeda (b. 1916 in El Palmar de Teror, Gran Canaria) belongs to the Canary Islands school of poets. She began publishing her poetry in the periodical *Mensaje* and founded and directed *Alisio,* a poetry review. Her first collection, the postsymbolist *Niebla del sueño* (1947; Mist of Dreams), was followed by *Como el fruto en el árbol* (1954; Like Fruit on the Tree), containing subjective, introspective and intimate free-verse compositions filled with serenity, dreams, gentle melancholy, love of simple living and acceptance of life's complexity. Ojeda, also a painter, has had successful individual and collective expositions. After *La Piedra sobre la colina* (1964; The Stone on the Hill), which treats themes of time, flux, life, and poetic expression, some two decades of silence ensued, although she reportedly wrote numerous unpublished theatrical works, short stories, and books of poetry. Her most recent collection, *El Alba en la espalda* (1987; Dawn on my Shoulder), treats universal poetic constants including death and its presence in daily life; time's destructive aspects; absence and memory.

Trina Mercader (b. 1919 in Alicante) lived some 20 years in Morocco, founding and directing the review *Al-Motamid* and the "Intimad" poetry series. While admiring Vicente Aleixandre, she wrote independently. The autobiographical *Tiempo a salvo* (1956; Time Saved) recounts her life up to the time of writing. *Sonetos ascéticos* (1971; Ascetic Sonnets) contains 39 poems in three parts, respectively entitled "Life," "Death," and "God." The first treats nature's perennial sadness (continuing the Romantic fallacy, rain symbolizes weeping); the second treats transcendence of affliction via poverty; and the last expresses hope for eternal life.

Carmen Barbera (b. Cuevas de Vinromá circa 1920), both novelist and poet, has several novels and four books of poetry. Her lyric collections include *Despedida al recuerdo* (1955; Farewell to Memory), *Tiempo interior* (n.d.; Internal Time), and *Cartas a un amigo* (1965; Letters to a Friend); *La Colina perdida* (1961; Lost Hillside) appears from bibliographical citations to be poetry as well. Other works are *Adolescente* (1957); *Al final de la ría* (1958; At the End of the Fjord), and *Debajo de la piel* (1959; Beneath the Skin). One brief notice indicates that five of her seven novels received literary prizes.

María Eugenia Rincón was born in 1926 in San Esteban de Gormaz (Soria). Shortly after mid-century she began writing poetry dominated primarily by the theme of love, whether for lover, parent, or child. Strong autobiographical substrata combine with controlled emotion and verbal directness. Works include *Tierra secreta* (1962; Secret Land), treating maternity as a liberating and profoundly joyful experience (as opposed to passionate love, which brings both joy and sorrow); *Frontera de la sombra* (1973; Border of Shadow), offering meditations on death—especially the death of the poet's father—and on time's passing, including memories of her childhood; and *Boca sin tiempo* (1974; Mouth without Time), which recounts a love story from meeting to separation and death. The feminine perspective portrays the lover as a sometimes child, needing woman's nurturing.

María de los Reyes Fuentes Blanco (b. 1927) has spent most of her life in her native city of Seville, where she has served as head of its social welfare agency. She began writing in the late 1950s, and has won several regional and metropolitan poetry prizes for her free-verse collections plus special mention for the 1961 national literary prize. Fuentes founded the periodical *Ixbiliah* and during four years directed the poetry segment for Spain's Radio Nacional. Her major themes include love and the Andalusian past, especially Seville's classical (Roman) and Arabic periods, and regional folklore or oral traditions. Works include *Actitudes* (1957; Attitudes), *De mí hasta el hombre* (1958; From Me to Man), *Sonetos del corazón adelante* (1960; Sonnets from the Heart Forward), *Elegías del Uad-el-Kebir* (1961; Elegies of the Guadalquivir), *Romances de la miel en los labios* (1962; Ballads of Honey on My Lips), *Elegías Tartessias* (1964; Tartessian Elegies), *Oración de la verdad* (1965; Prayer for Truth), *Concierto para la Sierra de Ronda* (1966; Concert for the Ronda Mountains), *Acrópolis del testimonio* (1966; Acropolis of Testimony), *Pozo de Jacob* (1967; Jacob's Well), and *Aire de amor* (1977; Love Air). Other titles attributed to her are *Fabulilla del diamante salvado* (1967; Fable of the Saved Diamond), *Motivos para un anfiteatro* (1970; Motifs for an Amphitheater), *Misión de la palabra* (1973; Mission of the Word), *Apuntes para la composición de un drama* (1975; Notes for Composing a Drama), *Elegie Andaluse* (1985; Andalusian Elegy), and *Jardín de las revelaciones* (1985; Garden of Revelations).

Martín Vivaldi

Elena Martín Vivaldi (b. 1906 or 1907) studied philosophy and humanities at the university in Granada, becoming a librarian in 1942, about when she began writing poetry. She worked in Huelva and Seville, returning to Granada in 1948. *Primeros poemas* (First Poems; written 1942–44) remained unpublished until 1977. Coeval with Carmen Conde, she matured during the heyday of the Generation of 1927, whose works echo in her lyrics. Her first published book, *Escalera de luna* (1945; Moon Ladder), appeared during postwar *tremendismo,* with which she shares little save anguish. José Ortega (*Dictionary of Literature of the Iberian Peninsula*) detects influences of Garcilaso.[2] Elegiac tones and themes of impossible love (echoing courtly traditions) provide similarities; Martín Vivaldi's preference for free verse distances her from postwar *garcilasismo,* although she writes occasional sonnets. Affinities with Bécquer and traces of Juan Ramón Jiménez and fellow Granadan García Lorca outnumber influences of Salinas and Guillén.[3]

   Martín Vivaldi's confessional poetry, intimate and confidential, stresses sentiment and psychic states, more individual than collective (and thus unrelated to postwar social poetry, save for plain, simple language). Lucid and precise, she prefers concrete realities objectively described. While sometimes deliberately prosaic, Martín Vivaldi generally avoids colloquial registers. Themes of love (love past or lost) and poems of pain, nostalgia, suffering, and oblivion predominate; the poet strives to synthesize contemplation and passion with intellect. Her collections appeared mostly during the 1970s: *Diario incompleto de abril* (1971; Incomplete April Diary, written 1947), subtitled "Homage to Bécquer," remained unpublished over two decades. Written while residing in Seville (where Bécquer lived), these free-verse compositions address April with dramatic monologues celebrating nature and springtime. More rain than sunshine and more darkness than light makes a somber, melancholoy spring.

   Martín Vivaldi's most significant theme—unrequited love—emphasizes the beloved's cold disdain. A tragic affair (ended when the love of her life terminated their relationship) produced enduring aloneness, seen in First Poems and *El Alma desvelada* (1953; Sleepless Soul; written 1942–43). The poet bares her soul metaphorically: dry lemon trees symbolize dead love, killed by the "hard freeze of life" (Asís, 139). Darkness, death, and night provide metaphors of solitude, unmistakably connoting rejection. Fading flowers evoke remembered youth, with loneliness—the poet's destiny—being grayness. The multivalent sea variously symbolizes life, death, and human absence.

Cumplida soledad, 1958–1976 (1976; Fulfilled Solitude), *Arco en desenlace* (1963; Bow Unlaced; written 1953–62), and *Materia de esperanza* (1968; A Matter of Hope; written 1958–66) elaborate the theme of intense love become solitary suffering. *Cumplida soledad* enunciates progress toward inner peace and self-sufficiency: the poetic persona accepts loneliness, the impossibility of another love, death's inevitability. Nocturnes in this collection have drawn high praise. *Durante este tiempo* (1972; During This Time), dedicated to the Generation of 1927, one of her most thematically varied collections, ranks among the most technically accomplished. Three subdivisions correspond to major preoccupations: "Día a día" (Day by Day) meditates upon quotidian existence; "Paisajes" (Landscapes) abounds in seascapes and rainy nocturnes reflecting internal landscapes; and "Las Ventanas iluminadas" (Lighted Windows) depicts an urban environment both modern and timeless, populous yet lonely. Clearly preferring lived experiences and situations to imagination, the poet evokes time's passing, mourns the loss of friends (including an elegy on the death of Celia Viñas), and voices her lasting existential solitude. Later collections include *Nocturnos* (1981; Nocturnes; written 1974–81) and *Y será su nombre mar* (1981; And His Name Was Sea, written 1974–81). *Los Arboles presento* (1977; I Present the Trees) is an anthology, while *Tiempo a la orilla* (1985; Time on the Shore) reprints 10 books published bewteen 1942 and 1984, unpublished works, and poems previously published in newspapers and periodicals.

"Concha Lagos"

Concepción Gutierrez Torrero (b. 1909 or 1913 in Córdoba) uses the pseudonym "Concha Lagos" and represents the Andalusian School of "personal poetry." Since 1956 she has resided in Madrid, founding and directing *Cuadernos de Agora* and the homonymous publishing enterprise until 1964 (thereafter continuing with the publishing house). Her associates have been such well-known poets and critics as Gerardo Diego, José Hierro, Jorge Campos, and José García Nieto. Lagos lived in France, traveled widely in Europe, and was elected to the Royal Academy of Córdoba; selected poems have been translated into English, French, Portuguese, and Italian.

Balcón (1954; Balcony) contains 59 brief poems on traditional themes—love, nature, the search for answers to ultimate questions. *El*

Pantano (1956; Swamp), subtitled "From a Woman's Diary," consists of 49 lyric fragments recounting life on Spain's boggy northern coast from the feminine perspective of an Andalusian woman (mask of the author). Disillusionment expressed in *Los Obstáculos* (1955; Obstacles) counterbalances greater optimism in *Al sur del recuerdo* (1955; South of Recollection), a fragmentary lyric novelette recalling youth in Andalusia. Greater despair appears in *El Corazón cansado* (1957; The Weary Heart): Lagos sees life confined to daily routines, her hopes and plans reduced to naught. Existential notes, enunciated here, combine with later metaphysical concerns. Hoping to eternalize each day, the poet laments her impossible maternity, now seeking (like Unamuno) compensatory literary survival.

Lagos uses predominantly traditional or classical themes and meters, drawing occasionally upon popular metrics and free verse. Her unpretentious style and quotidian vocabulary, characterizing "social poetry," commemorate women's roles and special perceptions, subtly underscoring the feminine. *La Soledad de siempre* (1958; Everlasting Solitude) develops religious and existential themes in 27 poems: being-toward-death, mortality, hope, and despair. In a trilogy whose titles use water imagery (symbolizing purification and transformation), Lagos contemplates life, childhood, and youth. *Agua de Dios* (1958; Water of God), containing 13 somber, bitter poems, depicts childhood. *Arroyo claro* (1958; Clear Stream) paints the sea and Spain's brooks, rivers, and landscapes in 51 poems haunted by solitude and temporal preoccupations. The extensive ballad collection *Canciones desde la barca* (1962; Songs from the Boat) uses aspects of sailing as metaphors for life's journey.

Campo abierto (1962; Open Field), dedicated to 11 "social" poets, approaches social commitment via an exploration of poetics. *Luna de enero* (1960; January Moon) uses mid-winter to re-create emotional desolation after renouncing passionate love. *Golpeando el silencio* (1961; Striking the Silence) consists of elegies to several exiled poets and to Gabriel Celaya, leader of poetic opposition inside Spain. Although not protest poetry, these poems (like *Campo abierto*) implicitly support "social poetry"; while somewhat atypical of Lagos, *Golpeando el silencio* contains a useful introduction by Manuel Mantero. *Tema fundamental* (1961; Fundamental Theme) traces spiritual growth through mystical meditations to religious plenitude. *Para empezar* (1963; To Begin) reprints *Campo abierto* plus miscellany. Lagos's religious vein reappears in *Los Anales* (1966; Annals), treating the Christian mysteries; the virtues of faith, hope, and charity; and the existential motifs despair, anguish, and

mortality. This collection's philosophical maturity and seriousness anticipate melancholy reflections and questioning of human shortcomings in
Diario de un hombre (1970; Diary of a Man), themes reiterated in *El Cerco*
(1971; The Fence), which portrays the poet as prophet or seer. Lagos's
convincing personal vision of human spiritual life blends resigned fatal-
ism with pessimism concerning past and present plus anxiety for the
future. Her most mature and emotionally charged pieces manipulate
structure and perspective. The book's three parts—"Around the Earth,"
"Chronicles," and "Return to Paradise"—evoke transit. Unlike earlier
compositions, these are long, essaylike, and discursive; interior organization proceeds chronologically from youth through maturity to near
death. *El Cerco* initiates another trilogy continued with *La Aventura*
(1973; The Adventure), wherein quasi-mystical time-space frames life as
serial transformations, and *Fragmentos en espiral desde el pozo* (1974; Spiral
Fragments from the Wellspring), developing themes of human limitations, religious quest, and search for metaphysical knowledge.

The title of *Gótico florido* (1976; Flowering Gothic) evokes architecture, as do some subtitles (e.g., "Porch" and "Cornerstone"). Stones,
columns, towers, obelisks, bridges, altar pieces, galleries, arches, tombs,
gargoyles, and colonnade inspire existential meditations. Human fugacity contrasts with tenacity; man carves in stone (symbolizing life) the
signs of fleeting existence, attempting to mark life's trail on earth. The
conflict between affirming life and human being-toward-death produces
struggle between light and darkness, hope and despair, but Lagos does
not surrender easily. Many meditations from her best works—*El Cerco,*
and *Fragmentos en espiral desde el pozo*—reappear. *Antología 1954–1976/*
Concha Lagos (1976; Anthology) includes representative selections from
collections up to and including *Gótico florido,* plus Emilio Miró's
Prologue.

Teoría de la inseguridad (1980; Theory of Insecurity) and *Por las ramas*
(1980; Along the Branches) repeat the extended metaphor of life as a
journey, stressing the presence of a silent God—object of impassioned
quest—as essential to the voyage. An earlier theme—Woman as
unheeded prophet—reappears late in this collection. *Elegías para un*
álbum (1982; Elegies for an Album) uses family photographs (figures
from the past) to create intersecting time planes, blending nostalgia with
metaphysical and existential concerns. *La Paloma* (1982; The Dove), consisting of traditional songs, contains five sections with respective common themes. Later works are *Más allá de la soledad* (1984; Beyond
Solitude), *Con el arco a punto* (1984; With the Bow Bent), *En la rueda del*

viento (1985; In the Wheel of the Wind), and *Segunda trilogía* (1986; Second Trilogy). The selections included in *Las Diosas blancas* come from two presumably unpublished collections, *El Telar* (The Loom) and *Cuando el amor es sólo vuelo* (When Love Is Only Flight).[4]

Concha de Marco

Concha de Marco (b. 23 May 1916 in Soria) lived as child and adolescent in the Mediterranean port of Figueras (Gerona), later obtaining a natural sciences degree from the University of Madrid. She married art critic Juan Antonio Gaya Nuño and traveled extensively, serving in Puerto Rico as visiting professor. After the war she began translating books and writing stories and essays. Her poetry collections, published relatively late and in rapid succession, include *Hora 0.5* (1966; Half-Past Midnight), *Diario de la mañana* (1967; Morning Newspaper), *Acta de identificación* (1969; Ceremony of Identification), *Congreso en Maldoror* (1970; Meeting in Maldoror), and *Tarot* (1972), which won the Juan Ramón Jiménez Prize in 1973. *Las Hilanderas* (1973; The Spinners) was followed by the undated *Cantos del compañero muerto* (Songs for a Dead Companion) and *Una Noche de invierno* (1974; One Winter Night).

Marco's usually brief poems use varied metrical forms, from the sonnet (hendecasyllables or Alexandrines) to free verse and the prose poem, with abiding concern for time evinced in various titles. Such motifs as calendars and clocks appear frequently, and precise hours are referred to. The first part of *Una Noche de invierno* contains 13 poems whose titles give the time every quarter-hour from 6:00 to 9:00 P.M., then an "Intermezzo with Story." The second part's dozen poems are titled from 9:15 to midnight. *La Mujer española del Romanticismo* (Spanish Women during Romanticism) treats historical themes—especially the sixteenth and seventeenth centuries—and reflects the poet's interest in women. Frequently interred in nunnery or palace, sequestered from life, nature, and sunshine in "opulent sepulchres" (e.g., the Descalzas Reales convent with its perpetual mortification and penance), the Hapsburg women endured stone slabs for beds and twice-daily prayers, without joy, warmth, or love. Marco inquires whose sins these royal nuns were expiating, whether God was truly served by these "blue-eyed shades in somber mourning . . . erased from the world." Her concern with time subsumes history, but Marco also paints typical events and humble people overlooked by historians (cf. Unamuno's "intrahistory"), connecting with "social poetry." Set in historical epochs as part of time's implacable flow, anonymous quotidian anecdotes link existential temporality to abstract philosophical meditations. Thus, watching construction excavations—removing archaeological layers of prior habitation along with coffins or ghetto remains—she perceives the past as palpable in the present.

Travel provides another thematic nucleus, recalling Puerto Rico, Russia, Montreal, Stockholm, Vienna, and Amsterdam. Tropical zephyrs contrast with intense cold winds and ice in her native Soria. Marco expresses nostalgia for trips not taken, places never visited (but not for luxury hotels with their pretentious clientele, tedium, alienation, and lack of communication; she prefers her own home—humble but beloved surroundings).

Diario de la mañana echoes mid-century "social poetry," depicting daily happenings, usually reported in newspapers. Well received by critics for its naturalness, irony, and compassion, *Diario* begins with epigraphs from D. H. Lawrence: "The essence of poetry in this inflexible, severe, naked epoch—this disagreeable present—tends to severity, lacking even shade for resting." Marco considers her present more severe, cruel, and unjust than Lawrence's; her social poems denounce daily violence and the injustice of ordinary events. "Palabras, palabras" (Words, Words)—the stuff of newspapers—shows how words are soiled, cheapened by use in lies, becoming empty rhetoric and clichés. Elsewhere, language is a jungle, the poet a tiger, hunting and evading traps. José Luis Cano[5] identifies echoes of Bécquer and Antonio Machado in Marco's melancholy, solitude, and profundity and her motifs of silence, time, and falling rain. Poems recalling childhood, studies, and homework in Soria and love of books link her further with Machado; Marco expresses anguish for books she lacks time to explore: treatises on astrology, star charts, lapidaries, graphics, and "all the other books I'll never read." Elsewhere, she reflects that "the best part of my life is the part that never was," conversing with the son she never had. Mirror motifs (reflections of youth and forgotten happenings) also recall Machado.

Marco's concern with creativity and esthetics appears rarely, as limited experimentation. For instance, in "It's 8:45" ancient Oriental pearls—once worn on a young body and warm neck—are now cold, faded, dying with the moribund owner; experimental typography outlines the breaking string and falling hand of the dying wearer. Existential preoccupation with death and life's limits appears often, as in "It's 9:15," which contemplates a funereal statue in a convent, a mute relic of a body that "lived death to the fullest," its soul's senses awakened at dawn by Gregorian chants to resume an existence of prayer and penitence while

desiring infinite life. Reiterated concerns with aging link Marco's feminist and existential preoccupations. Nearing midnight, *Una Noche de
invierno* hints repeatedly of approaching death but ends with a celebration of life.

Una Noche de invierno recalls youthful aspirations and illusions—things
the poetic persona has left behind. River and moonlit street—symbolizing time and life's passing—frame the beloved house where the poet
once lived, simply, almost in poverty, but "sweet, full, vast poverty" nostalgically recalled. Cleaning closets, reordering female forebears' needle-
work (grandmother's comforter, mother's embroidered sheets), rereading
great-grandmother's recipes, the poetic persona folds her husband's
shirts, finding nothing of her children or grandchildren. The daughter
she never had and mother she never knew feel more comfortable with
each other than with her; she senses their reproaches, their perceptions of
her as strange. Regrets for her childlessness echo Spanish expectations
that women produce offspring, expressing frustration that all she has
accumulated in life will mean nothing to anyone after her death.
Relatively "liberated" as pedagogue and writer, she struggles futilely
against patriarchal values internalized during her socialization. Her poetry eloquently expresses dilemmas common to intelligent women of her
generation.

In *Acta de identificación* Marco identifies with her historical
Mediterranean heritage. "Mujer de Piedra" (Stone Woman), the first part,
treats the Roman conquest of Spain's prehistoric Celt-Iberian inhabitants,
while the second part consists of love poems, viewing love as suffering
and victimization (much as Spain was victimized by Rome). *Congreso en
Maldoror* incorporates ambients and vocabulary of professional conferences; subsections include "Lectures" (29 titles arranged alphabetically)
and "Discussions" (29 "refutations," "conclusions," "affirmations," "argu-
ments," and "retorts").

Susana March

Susana March Alcalá (1918–93), born to a middle-class family in
Barcelona, studied music, painting and foreign languages during lapses
in her schooling occasioned by illnesses. She began publishing in periodicals before her fifteenth birthday; *Rutas* (1938; Itineraries), written during adolescence, was privately printed during the Civil War. In 1940 she
married novelist Ricardo Fernández de la Reguera, with whom she had
one son. They collaborated on 11 historical novels, twentieth-century

echoes of Galdos's re-creations of recent national history. March also wrote short stories, five novels, and various "potboilers." She credits early readings of Juan Ramón Jiménez with awakening her lyric vocation; Antonio Machado (to whom she dedicates the poem "Compañeros" [*La Tristeza*]) and later Carmen Conde became major influences. March shared Aleixandre's conviction that poetry is, above all, communication.

Feminine protagonists or speakers characterize March's largely auto-biographical poetry and fiction, privileging themes of love, motherhood, feminine identity, or mother-daughter bonds. March's works and interviews protest women's inequality—their inferior education and domestic cloistering, Spain's discriminatory work laws and salaries. Various poems denounce class and gender conventions that repress individuality, destroy relationships, and stifle emotions or indict conventional standards of "good taste" that impede communication and victimize both men and women—especially women, for whom violence may result. Frequent lyrics express pessimism, frustration, sorrow, disappointment, and bitterness (engendered by wartime experiences and postwar difficulties); idealism, rebellion, melancholy, and loss underlie many poems. A contemporary of Fuertes, March restrains her language more but incorporates colloquial registers and (like "social poets" generally) portrays daily life. Selected poems have been translated to French, English, Italian, Swedish, Russian, Portuguese, and Dutch.

Poemas de la Plaza Real (1987; Poems of Royal Square), composed in 1944, remained unpublished for over four decades; the title refers to the address where March was born.[6] Intimate, very lyrical, and introspective, these pieces recall her beloved childhood home, youthful encounters with nature, the forest, sunlit mornings, dreams, discovering the interrelatedness of creation, and the emotional stirrings of first love. Romanticizing liberty and love of freedom, the poetic persona fantasizes an impossible, vagabond life. Early poems combine rhyme with irregular line lengths, many similes and repetitions; subsequently the poet uses unrhymed Sapphic odes and sonnets. An especially enduring theme is aging, with many poems commemorating birthdays, the poet's first gray hairs and other bodily changes, and laments for time's passing without having realized her dreams.

La Pasión desvelada (1946; Passion Unveiled) contains love poems, some unrhymed, varying line lengths from heptasyllables and octosyllables to ponderous Alexandrines. Passion, life's beauty, and strong erotic undercurrents result in exalting the lover's perfection, viewing even eternity as erotic; these alternate with laments and forebodings of death (which means losing the beloved). Other poems celebrate motherhood and the dawning life, perceptions, and consciousness of the poet's son. One poem foreseeing the poet's death affirms that her heart will still desire to retain its identity. *Ardiente voz* (1951; Burning Voice) treats fraternity and collective concerns, incorporating ingredients of "social poetry." *El Viento* (1951; Wind) and *La Tristeza* (1953; Sadness), using assonantal octosyllabic quatrains, blend social concerns and pastoral visions with strong personal motifs of broken dreams, mortality, and remembrance. March's aged mother, evoked in "Mi madre y yo" (Mother and I), is shown still treating the poet like a little girl, leaving her daughter desolate at the thought of losing her. Gray-haired adults are the saddest orphans of all, the poet affirms; if her mother could live forever, March would never grow old. Poems treating her son's childhood, innocence, games, instinctive wisdom, and ability to dream alternate with laments for unspecified lonely suffering, society with its hate and fratricidal conflicts, beggars and misery, hypocrisy and poverty. Other poems express anguish, guilt, Romantic rejection of order and moderation, anticipations of death, depression at the thought that the poet's son, too, will die, and occasional longing for death as release. *Antología poética* (1957) incorporates selections from the first five collections.

Esta mujer que soy (1959; The Woman I Am), a self-portrait, emphasizes melancholy, grave eyes, unfulfilled longings, indolence, poverty, and dignity. Repetitive motifs—lost youth, aging, sorrow, and rebellion— evolve, as poems to March's son now depict his adolescence; social poems portray male-female social inequality, lamenting the difficulty of friendship without coquetry, the impossibility of being treated "like a man." "Una Señora" (A Lady) protests those things "ladies" cannot say, being "wrapped in cellophane" by scruples, dogmas, and the social clichés imposed by "good upbringing." The persona struggles to keep herself from shouting out humiliating secrets, from voicing despair and rebellion; a related poem affirms that she is "fed up," ending "to hell with everything." The sonnet "Me lanzaré a la calle cualquier día" (I'll Run into the Street Any Day Now) reiterates desires to cry aloud things the poet feels constrained to suppress. Familiar presentiments of death appear as leavetaking of everything around; religious motifs include prayers to the Virgin, a dialogue with God (imagined as bored at man's hypocrisy and violence), and prayers of supplication for hope, faith, and charity and something solid, "something that will console me / Lord, for ever being born." *Poemas* (1966) reprints all previous collections, while *Los Poemas del hijo* (1970; Poems to My Son) apparently comprises previously published poems to her son plus later ones commemorating his transition to manhood and fatherhood. Her well-defined poetic personality, clearly delineated nuclear themes, and strong emotional impact place Susana March among the best lyric voices of her generation.

A Poet in Exile

Nuria Parés, born in Barcelona on 12 May 1925, accompanied her parents to exile in Mexico in 1943. An art critic, essayist, and translator, she spent her childhood in Madrid, attended the Instituto Escuela, and, following the war, studied classical guitar at the Paris Conservatory of Music, performing as concert guitarist in the major cities of Europe and the United States and in Cuba and Mexico. She abandoned her concert career early, however, and collaborated with literary supplements of the Mexican newspapers *Novedades* and *Excelsior,* publishing books of art criticism and essays. Her experiences as one of the 15,000 to 25,000 Spanish Republican exiles in Mexico inspire many poems; most exiles remained unintegrated in Mexican society, conflicting with pro-Franco elements among the older Spanish colonists and awaiting the moment of return. "Canto a los míos" (Song to My People), included in Susana Rivera's anthology,[7] affirms that "our lives themselves were borrowed; we didn't live." Parés voices the alienation of the exiles' children: belonging neither to Spain nor Mexico, lonely, estranged, uprooted, theirs is a generation without a country. Exile means living in limbo on both sides of the Atlantic, as the native land censors any mention of exile works and the country where one writes and publishes negates one's existence, excluding non-natives from anthologies and literary histories.

Parés's work, published in Mexico and almost unknown, consists of *Romances de la voz sola* (1951; Ballads for Unaccompanied Voice), *Canto llano* (1959; Plain Song), and *Colofón de luz* (1987; Colophon of Light), incorporating "Canto llano" and other previously unpublished poems. The titles' obvious musical references recur in individual poems, often titled as songs, ballads, and cantos; other pieces have no titles, only Roman numerals. Major poetic devices are repetition, cadence, assonance, and the *estribillo* (tag line). One "ballad" repeats the tag line "This voice which is not mine," communicating alienation, problems of identity, the difficulties of finding and expressing oneself in exile. A second tag line, "¿A quién diré mi canto?" (To Whom Shall I Sing My Song?), evokes medieval balladry but also the exile's lack of his or her own audience (Rivera, 73). An eminently lyrical plaint, using unaccustomed consonant rhyme, affirms that "Y no hay dios, ni creencia, ni destino / no hay tampoco estandarte ni bandera / . . . / ¿Te lo han robado todo, peregrino . . . ?" ("And there's no God, belief, or destiny; Nor is there standard, nor a flag / . . . Has it all been taken from you, pilgrim?" [Rivera, 74]).

Elsewhere Parés depicts the poetic persona as naked—a tree without roots or migratory bird—still hoping to find the road's end. In another poem solitary docks and shadowy ships on a rainy night provide self-images; the poet characterizes herself as "transit," "body without a face," torn shreds of shadow. "El Grito" (The Cry) from *Canto llano* protests the exile children's somber heritage of blood, violence, and conflict that they cannot renounce. "Dicen" (They Say) evokes the name "España peregrina" (Pilgrim Spain), euphemistically applied by sympathizers to the exiles: what a lovely name for drifting about the world, the poet muses, but the name doesn't fit—pilgrims eventually reach the shrine and return home. Exile's negative impact on personal identity appears with immense drama in "Canto a los míos" (Song to My People) as Parés voices the lament of her "lost generation"—condemned to be spectators of their parents' lives and deaths, with nothing of their own, not even youth: "They were the voice / we the echo / they the flame / we the smoke / they the image of life / we the mirror" (80). Another poem presumably written after the long-awaited return to Spain ends pathetically: "Canción de la patria pequeña" (Song for a Second Homeland) discovers the land of exile was the real home; now only a memory, the distant refuge is truly hers, hers alone.

María Elvira Lacaci

María Elvira Lacaci, born (ca. 1925) and raised in the Galician seaport of El Ferrol, apparently has no collections in Gallego, but Elisa Vázquez de Gey considers her Galician.[8] Little is known of Lacaci's life before she moved to Madrid in 1952, presumably to pursue literary interests; soon afterward, she began publishing poetry. Lacaci married novelist and filmmaker Luis Buñuel. *Humana voz* (1957; Human Voice), containing 38 poems, won the Adonais Prize. Most of her work appeared during the vogue of "social poetry," and she is usually classed with that movement, although she departs from its Socialist ideology with occasional metaphysical preoccupations and subjective themes and techniques. Her devoutly Christian poetic persona does express solidarity with suffering humanity, sympathizing with the poor and downtrodden (sung by "social poets"), but her fundamentally religious poetry seeks God against backgrounds of existentialist doubt and postwar despair. Unlike true existentialists, she believes in a loving, protective God, whose presence she perceives in the humble things of daily life and transcendent religious experiences.

Humana voz, like "social poetry" generally, contains deliberately "unpoetic" material, including public charity, urban scenes of crowded mass transport, poverty, and foul-smelling neighborhood houses. Lacaci's poetry, lacking rhetorical adornment and ingenious devices, was written entirely in Madrid, the setting for many compositions; Galicia appears in memories of childhood, a village by the sea with its fishermen's church and cemetery (cf. "El Regreso" [The Return]), the pines and *orballo* (drizzle). General melancholy and specific motifs of suffering and sadness evoke Rosalía de Castro, but technique and style diverge. Fundamental themes include grief, angst, death, desolation, and the suffering soul in need of light (usually God) and salvation. Urban scenes place in the foreground the homeless, the humble, and the dispossessed. Other themes include love, death, patience, loneliness, self-pity, and confession of private sentiments.

Sonido de Dios (1962; Sound of God), containing the title poem and 39 more, treats the poetic persona's quest for God, painting search, epiphany, encounter, and illumination in typically unpretentious style and conversational lexicon. Seeking salvation, the poetic persona—a mask of Lacaci—clings to God's hand. Divine presence fills this entirely religious collection but recedes to the background of *Al este de la ciudad* (1963; East of the City), Lacaci's longest collection, which includes her most "social" (critical) compositions together with religious pieces in registers ranging from meditative to mystic to existential. *Al este* depicts shantytowns at Madrid's edge in naturalistic detail, with quotidian rhythms, sounds, and voices raised in anger or hate. Precise geography evokes specific Madrid locations: bus, trolley, and metro stops and *barrios* such as Cuatro Caminos, Vallecas, Puerta del Sol, and Gran Vía. Temporal realism highlights waiting in line for buses, the subway, and government rent controls; women (re)selling metro tickets and lottery vendors hawking their numbers; and covert begging.

Like Fuertes, Lacaci wished to communicate with everyone, including the largely illiterate poor; thus, anti-esthetic attitudes sometimes combine with intuitive style. Direct, colloquial language, scant imagery, sobriety, and few metaphors produce simplicity verging on linguistic poverty (as the poet recognized). Absence of color (as in other "social poetry") and deliberate minimizing of beauty and lyric devices result from such adornments being considered upper-class privileges. In "El Traje nuevo" (The New Suit [*Humana voz*]) Lacaci confesses inability to dress poems in "Sunday best" words; "La Palabra" (Words), introducing *Al este,* affirms that her "naked" poetry is as she wants it, even though—like poor urchins pressing their faces against shop windows—she admires beauties destined for others. Lacaci portrays the poet as worker, poetry as labor. José Luis Cano's "Dios y el suburbio en la poesía de María Elvira Lacaci" appropriately emphasizes the poet's two salient motifs.[9]

Julia Uceda

Julia Uceda Valiente (b. 1925 in Seville) received her doctorate in philosophy and humanities from the University of Seville with a dissertation on the life and work of poet José Luis Hidalgo. She has taught Spanish language and literature at the Universities of Seville and Cádiz, at Michigan State University (1966–73), and briefly in Ireland. She has also resided in Oviedo and Albacete. With Manuel Mantero, she founded and directed the poetry review *Rocío* and published in *Insula, Cuadernos Hispanoamericanos,* and *Revista de Occidente.* Selected poems by Uceda have been translated to English, with some published in *American Poetry, Prairie Schooner,* and *New Orleans Review.* Since returning to Spain, she has lived in Galicia, where she founded the "Esquío" poetry collection. Uceda authored critical studies on Jorge Guillén and Hidalgo, and traces of Hidalgo have been detected in her poems; she also reflects influences of fellow Sevillean Luis Cernuda, especially his existential themes and poetry of expatriation.

Preoccupations with life as being-toward-death, repetitive focus upon her own death, and concern with existential authenticity connect with identity themes recalling Unamuno. Postsymbolist elements include reiterated use of such motifs as ashes, mist, shadows, steamy window-panes, smoke, fog, foam, and twilight; distant sounds or music, echoes, confused words or voices, objects far away in time or space, words such as *indefinable, inaudible, interminable, unintelligible*—all with evident ontological and epistemological implications. Occasionally surrealistic—in events and effects perhaps more than techniques—Uceda uses what Bousoño terms "visionary metaphors" (re Aleixandre) and the hallucinatory techniques of José Hierro's *Libro de las alucinaciones,* as noted by Valis (Galerstein, 320). Many poems should be understood as dreams—

controlled and lucid dreams, revelatory of hidden reality, ultimate truths concealed within chaotic, quotidian exteriors.

Although usually considered part of the same "generation" as Gloria Fuertes, Uceda has maintained her independence. Social preoccupations, including concern for social inequities and injustice, inspire the dedication of *Extraña juventud* (1962; Strange Youth) to "mankind in my time," denouncing repression and (implicitly) the abusive Franco regime. This second collection contains existential motifs, as the poetic persona questions her own identity, authenticity, and existence, expressing feelings of strangeness, alienation, and isolation. Subjective, personal, contemplative veins run throughout Uceda's work, with growing ontological, epistemological, and metaphysical concerns. Strong, intimate love poetry in her first collection, *Mariposa en cenizas* (1959; Butterfly in Ashes), blends the erotic and existential, combining sexuality with death and alienation. While the love theme dominates, these strange, sometimes mysterious poems arouse faintly Gothic echoes, suggesting multiple personalities derived from reincarnation without totally forgetting prior identities.

Death is an enduring concern, both the poet's own demise and ancient links between Eros and Thanatos, passion and death, disturbingly implicit in many elliptical erotic pieces. Yet Uceda also writes with depth, clarity, and lyrical intellectualism. *Sin mucha esperanza* (1966; Without Much Hope) revisits the question of identity, treating alienation, dehumanization, and loss of contact with one's past, together with problems of existential freedom, becoming more metaphysical and introspective. Awareness of human and sociopolitical problems persists, but collective concerns are balanced by individual loss—of freedom, of childhood (youth, innocence)—and by integration into the social body, leading to exile (a metaphor for alienation) and death. Baroque themes of reality versus illusion, dream states, the profoundly mysterious nature of everyday things, alternate with recurring images of exile and death.

Poemas de Cherry Lane (1968), 14 brief, dense free-verse compositions written largely during residence in the United States, advances the poet's ontological quest, her search for answers to ultimate questions, her ongoing struggle with identity. Many poems are directed to a mute interlocutor called Charlie, putative friend and companion in exploring the mysteries of death and nature of reality. Several poems (e.g., "Diálogo," "El Retrato" [The Portrait], and "Cita con una sombra" [Date with a Shadow]) suggest other-worldly encounters and the porosity of boundaries between past and present existence. Uceda's experience in the United States sometimes produces nightmarish, psychedelic imagery.

Campanas en Sansueña (1977; Bells in Sansuena) anticipates *Viejas voces secretas de la noche* (1981; Ancient, Secret Voices of the Night) in its visionary search for metaphysical answers to ultimate questions. The poet seeks light in darkness, symbolic light with solidity and substance, recasting traditional mystic poetry (the dark night of the soul) or images referring to the soul's "dark side." The title, as Valis suggests, alludes to Luis Cernuda with his probing of reality's appearances in "Resaca en Sansueña" and "Ser de Sansueña." Baroque sentiment (*desengaño*, disillusionment), paradox, chiaroscuro, and labyrinthine twists accompany the poet's contemplation of Spain, distant in time or space. In the brief, five-part collection "Ancient Voices," Uceda waxes still more intimate and personal, pursuing her metaphysical quest for revelation amid further images of light and darkness, dreams and perils, false gods and almost palpable luminosity. The most extensive anthology and study of Uceda's poetry is *Julia Uceda: Poesía* (1991), edited by Francisco J. Peñas-Bermejo. His thematic introductory essay concentrates upon the Sevillean roots and traditions represented by Uceda and her love poetry, social preoccupations, existential influences, use of dreams, and development of personal style. This edition adds selections from Uceda's most recent collection, *Del camino de humo* (From the Road of Smoke), in press when Peñas-Bermejo's book was published.

A Pacifist Activist

Angelina Gatell (b. 1926) moved from Barcelona to Valencia as an adolescent. There she completed her *bachillerato,* published her first book, and bore her first child. Active in noncommercial theater, she scored several successes as an actress, founding one of Spain's first chamber theaters with her future husband. She moved to Madrid in 1959. Gatell's poetry offers outspoken testimonials reflecting her activism in peace movements. *El Poema del soldado* (1954; The Soldier's Poem), a dramatic monologue, commemorates the death of Miguel Hernández, Republican soldier-poet, imprisoned by Franco. The soliloquy denounces war, violence, and injustice. Considered a "social poet" by anthologists, Gatell apparently does not write in Catalan. The Civil War, experienced in childhood, colors her work. Like others of her generation, she identifies with Franco's intellectual opponents, writing largely in realistic, denunciatory tones. *Esa oscura palabra* (1963; That Obscure Word) protests lack of political freedom, justice, and equality.

Unusually open criticism, defying censorial constraints, typifies Gatell's committed art, seen also in *Las Claudicaciones* (1969; Surrenders), considered her most moving and forceful denunciation. Focusing upon the plight of those who lost the Civil War (but remained in Spain), *Las Claudicaciones* reiterates themes of injustice and lack of freedom characterizing Gatell's works during the 1950s and 1960s. Gatell opposed not only Francoist oppression and abuse but also the patriarchal society behind the dictator. Often using feminist perspectives, she spoke out in favor of liberation. Other poems paint her generation's dreams, treating discouragement, waiting, the Vietnam War, solitude, mankind's future, trains, and a daughter's accidental death.

As co-founder of various independent literary groups, Gatell lectured and gave poetry recitals and became literary critic for *Poesía española*. She produced scholarly essays on Pablo Neruda, Delmira Agustini, and Alfonsina Storni and wrote children's books—including *Mis primeras lecturas poéticas* (n.d.; My First Poetry Readings), *Mis primeros héroes* (n.d.; My First Heroes), and *El Hombre del acordeón* (1984; The Accordion Man)—and short stories for juvenile audiences.

Acacia Uceta

Born in Madrid in 1927, Acacia Uceta lived through the Civil War as a child; she studied sketching and painting after finishing secondary school, obtaining a diploma in Spanish-American history and art. Uceta worked as a commercial artist and began publishing in major Spanish literary reviews in the late 1950s. Selections of her work have been translated to Portuguese, French, Italian, Arabic, and English. She has received several regional prizes for her poetry and novelettes and creative writing fellowships from the Juan March Foundation (1968) and Spain's Ministry of Culture (1981). She married poet Enrique Domínguez Millán and is the mother of one of Spain's youngest women poets, Acacia Domínguez. Uceta has written several plays (produced for radio and television) and various unpublished novels. Most of her literary culture is "anarchical" and autodidactic; she disclaims specific influences in her poetry.

Solitude—personal solitude, experienced as cosmic and irreparable—figures among Uceta's most profound and enduring themes. One poem speaks of solitude's beginning at her birth when placed alone in her crib. In an interview with Victoria Urbano,[10] Uceta mentions "accompanying herself," an ability considered an important asset. Time is likewise an especially significant theme, as is the ancient topos of life's brevity and fugacity (experienced not as cliché but as rebellion against death). Time—envisioned as that which exists between birth and death—appears in its biological aspects, united to nature and the life cycles of all creation from plants to planets. Another poetic preoccupation—human liberty—connects with existential freedom and the quest for life's meaning in face of doubt, fear, and emptiness. Her vitalism, originating in the struggle to survive war's terrors and the early postwar years, accompanies an underlying faith and orthodoxy; Uceta does not experience solitude as metaphysical. Her free-verse compositions offer no difficulties for the reader; usually serene and optimistic, sometimes expressing plenitude and satisfied love, her lyrics are essentially chaste, straightforward, and unadorned. Major devices include prosopopeya, repetition, metaphors, and parallelism.

El Corro de las horas (1961; The Race of Hours), Uceta's first collection, depicts her subjective confrontation with time, along with society's "race" to success, materialistic triumph, and consumerism, sacrificing human values and trampling upon the weak. *Frente a un muro de cal abrasadora* (1967; Facing a Burning, Whitewashed Wall) suggests with its image of a blind alley the difficulties faced by women in Spanish society, organized by and for men, lacking rights and services taken for granted elsewhere. Although Uceta terms herself feminist, few overt or aggressive statements appear in her work; excepting occasional insinuations so general that they lack gender specificity, she expresses satisfaction with her roles as wife and mother. *Detrás de cada noche* (1970; Behind Each Night), written during the tenure of her March Foundation grant, contains five sections whose subtitles reiterate preoccupation with time: "Morning," "Noon," "Afternoon," "Night," and "Dawn." This collection celebrates hope as humanity's ally in justifying existence in face of doubt, hardship, and death. Uceta's essential optimism asserts itself despite adversity.

Al sur de las estrellas (1976; South of the Stars), celebrating an essentially happy, fulfilled marriage and serene family life, was followed by *Cuenca, roca viva* (1980; Cuenca, Living Rock), commemorating the poet's links with the city of Cuenca and its poetic circle. Modest experimentation includes homages to the picturesque city with its "hanging" houses built above the gorge and to its artistic colony. *Íntima dimensión* (1983; Intimate Dimension) consists of 36 poems divided into three 12-poem sections. Their geometric subtitles ("Sphere," "Circle," "Spiral") suggest the "dehumanized" mode of prewar vanguard years, but this is misleading; Uceta again celebrates hope and happiness, proclaiming the power of optimism to triumph over obstacles and organize one's personal existence. The "intimate dimension" of her own subjectivity—firmly under her control, closed to sorrow, pessimism, and despair—rests upon hope, love, and perhaps an act of will.

In *Arbol de agua* (1987; Water Tree) Uceta continues blending the personal and autobiographical with broader collective concerns. Her style—intense, transparent, and intimate—changes little, but this collection presents clearer religious preoccupations, suggested by the titles of its five parts: "Love," "The Absolute," "Science," "Beauty," and "The Encounter." Each implies focus on different facets of the divine essence. Christ is the nucleus of Uceta's complete vision, culminating in mutual presence of the transcendent being and the searching individual whose freedom remains unmitigated (rather than being mystically fused with the Godhead). Thus Uceta paints in clear and profound terms a mystery in which humanity participates without losing individual identity, communicable despite its mystic elements.

Aurora de Albornoz

Aurora de Albornoz, born in Luarca (Asturias) in 1926, was a poet, critic, and professor of Spanish literature. Her family moved to Puerto Rico in the early 1940s, where she lived for many years and did her university studies. She subsequently obtained a doctorate from the University of Salamanca and lived in the United States and in Paris, studying comparative literature at the Sorbonne. She held a chair at the University of Puerto Rico and taught contemporary humanities at the Universidad Autónoma in Madrid, where she died in 1990. Her criticism includes books on Antonio Machado, Juan Ramón Jiménez, Miguel de Unamuno, Pablo Neruda, and José Hierro. With marked fondness for narrative modes, she frequently treats autobiographical materials, contemplating life, existence, and historical time from within her own anguished consciousness. Her cultural activities included founding reviews and seminars, collaborating in numerous Spanish and foreign periodicals (*Insula, Revista de Occidente, Sur, Triunfo, La Torre, El Urogallo*), and lecturing.

Influenced by Machado and Jiménez, Albornoz favored prose poems, lyric prose, and free verse, liberally sprinkled with dedications to other poets and critics and allusions to modern and contemporary literature and twentieth-century history. *Brazo de niebla* (1957; Arm of Mist) was followed shortly by *Prosas de París* (1959; Paris Prose), evoking the poet's French experiences. *Poemas para alcanzar un segundo* (1961; Poems to Catch a Second) contains a prologue and six subsections, each treating part of Albornoz's life. Painting her quest for self-realization and ultimate answers (destiny, death, God, the meaning of existence), she revisits childhood, especially the Civil War, and—in a confessional mode—discusses personal feelings. Commentators note Proustian influences in this collection and its predecessor. The fourth section celebrates women—one real (her sister Sonia) and three literary (Emma Bovary, Anna Karenina, and Ophelia).

Por la primavera blanca (1962; Through the White Springtime) consists of 10 lyric tales or vignettes. *En busca de esos niños en hilera* (1967; In Search of Those Lined-up Children), whose leitmotiv is childhood, evokes Albornoz's own (interwoven with the present), addresses childish interlocutors, tells stories, and interprets literature. *Palabras desatadas* (1974; Unbound Words), less subjective and autobiographical, precedes *Palabras reunidas* (1983; Collected Words), treating more universal themes in a progressively more impersonal fashion, recalling "pure poetry."

When she died, Albornoz left three book manuscripts: two poetry collections and one of lyric prose. *Canciones de Guiomar* (1990; Guiomar's Songs) laments lost love via systematically alternating revelation and concealment. Albornoz attributes the text to Machado's "Guiomar," while she herself poses as critic-commentator, authoring the Prologue. Although entitled "Songs," these are prose poems, written years before, recounting a vague, elliptical history whose only indisputable fact is pain. Sensations and emotions—the internal landscape—are veiled by intertextual citations representing poets from Lope de Vega to Juan Ramón Jiménez and François Villon, allusions to fictional characters and real persons, including Claude Debussy and Georges Sand. The poetic persona (Guiomar) addresses as putative interlocutor the dead Machado; Albornoz's adoption of the heteronyms recalls the latter's *Juan de Mairena*. Her apocryphal "critical Prologue" terms the work a response to Machado's "Songs to Guiomar." The fragmentary prose poems express disillusion, despair, solitude, desolation, and lifelong efforts to recover the past and relive lost love.

Croniliricas (1991), subtitled "Collages" and difficult to classify, blends aspects of the memoir, narrative, and intimate conversation with criticism and lyric meditation. Written in 1979–90, the brief essays are both lyrical and reportorial, including several appreciations inspired by the deaths of Blas de Otero, Celso Emilio Ferreiro, Salvador Allende, Alejo Carpentier, José Bergamín, Concha Meléndez, and Tierno Galván— mostly poets and/or exiles. Five pieces treat literary or imaginary travels; two comment on films by Luchino Visconti and Roberto Rossellini; others depict memories of Puerto Rico and Juan Ramón or evoke Madrid encounters with contemporary poets.

Cristina Lacasa

Cristina Lacasa (b. 1929 in Tarrasa) lived since childhood in the isolated, mountainous Catalan provincial capital of Lérida, where her poetry— necessarily personal and independent—was composed and published. Lacasa worked in isolation, occasionally enunciating testimonial "social" themes. But her testimony—individual and personal rather than collective—surprises with its positive tone. Sincerity, tenderness, love, and rebellion against injustice inform her denunciations of human pain and sorrow. Primarily a lyricist, Lacasa also produced three volumes of prose.

La Voz oculta (1953; Hidden Voice), post-Romantic and autobiographical, echoes Bécquer's concern with love and poetry. This apprenticeship effort contains aspects characteristic of Lacasa's later lyricism and an optimistic depiction of humanity's trajectory. *Los Brazos en estela* (1958; Arms in the Wake), a positive celebration of life, uses childhood memories as its point of departure, elaborating present dreams and hopes of future fulfillment. Both joy and sorrow appear, with more rejoicing than pain. *Un Resplandor que no perdonó la noche* (1961; A Fiery Glow that Didn't Pardon the Night) further probes life's sorrows and joys, combining emotion, perception, and thoughtful meditation. Fresh, consistently optimistic, and profoundly lyrical, Lacasa's testimonial poems avoid both abrasiveness and sentimentality.

Con el sudor alzado (1964; With Sweat Raised), autobiographical and confessional, emphasizes ambitions and failures as the poet presents her life, dreams, and inward self. *Poemas de la muerte y de la vida* (1966; Poems of Death and Life) traces another subjective, introspective trajectory, serenely questing for selfhood and understanding. Considered a high point of Lacasa's production, this collection enunciates eternal poetic themes: life, death, and love. Profoundly pacifistic, *Encender los olivos como lámparas* (1969; To Light Olive Branches like Lamps) proclaims opposition to war, devastation, violence and brutality without ceasing to be eminently lyrical and personal. Insisting on peace and fraternity, Lacasa protests injustice while voicing hope and joy; as in *Ha llegado la hora*

(1971; The Time Has Come), she affirms positive values—beauty, love, and understanding—which become weapons to combat pain, anguish, and despair.

Lacasa produced two poetry collections for which I have found only titles and dates: *Mientras crecen las aguas* (1977; While the Waters Rise) and *El Viaje* (1981; The Voyage). *Opalos del instante* (1982; Opals of the Instant) re-creates aspects of the poet's past, tracing her life up to the present and attempting to use her personal experience to interpret the enigmatic human condition. Somewhat somber and disillusioned, these mature poems nonetheless voice serene, positive acceptance of existence. Each of the 17 poems treats part of the human body, ending with a poem to the soul. *En un plural designio* (1983; In a Plural Design), one of Lacasa's most idealistic works, moves her closer to activism as she writes of children's vulnerability and difficult position in the often insensitive adult world. Frequently citing the Declaration of the Rights of Children and authors treating child abuse and neglect, Lacasa addresses aspects of child-rearing in an unmistakably feminine voice. Her pacifist stance and defense of the defenseless logically precede *Ramas de la esperanza (Poemas ecológicos)* (1984; Boughs of Hope [Ecological Poems]), wherein Lacasa takes nature's part against exploitation by an aggressive, phallocentric civilization. Indicting pollution and nuclear testing, she denounces the destruction of forests and waters, the plight of endangered species and wilderness areas, sacrificed in the name of progress or "conservation." Lacasa consistently presents the spoilers as male, the victims as female, thereby incorporating feminist dimensions to her outpouring of anger over man's traditional exploitation of virgin ecological areas.

Considerable diversity characterizes postwar women poets, although most combine personal and autobiographical veins with collective concerns, echoing the blend found in Figuera and Fuertes. Diverse in age (born over the first three decades of this century), most fall short of full-blown feminism; "seniors" who came to maturity under the Republic are sometimes more outspoken than younger women educated under the repressive and reactionary Franco regime. The Franco censorship's severity during the first quarter-century after the Civil War partially explains their restrained expression, comparably chaste treatment of eroticism, preference for conventional topoi, and prominent religious motifs. Most avoid much sentimentality, perhaps fearing criticism of lachrymose, pathetic or passionate outbursts; examples by the Generation of 1927 in controlling emotional and autobiographical content may increase restraint. Existential and testimonial veins attest to the popularity of such themes among Peninsular poets of both genders during these years and to emphasis on *engagement*. Nevertheless, the majority of these poets succeed in conveying their specific personalities, developing voices that, if not entirely unique, reveal individuality, altruism, and femininity.

Chapter Eight

Postwar Poets in Galician and Catalan

Although the Franco regime repressed cultural and literary expression in all of the Peninsula's vernaculars, only Galician and Catalan had undergone post-Romantic rebirth, producing numerous twentieth-century literary representatives. Other vernaculars (Andalán or Aragonese, Leonese, Bable or Asturian, Valencian and Majorcan) are essentially dialects of Castilian or Catalan, whereas Basque literature historically belonged to the oral tradition. These minority languages thus had no literature to suppress, while Catalan and Gallego enjoyed a nineteenth-century cultural Renaissance. These vernaculars differ linguistically, socially, and economically; Catalan's political and economic base overshadows Galician. Galicia, a traditionally impoverished, backward land of emigrants and tiny family farms, lacked Cataluña's literacy, capitalistic development, and industrialization. Without modern, standardized grammars of Galician or wealthy cultural patrons to underwrite semi-clandestine publications during the early Franco decades, Gallego—its practitioners and literary tradition—approached extinction. Closer to Castilian than Catalan, Galician was at greater risk of assimilation. But the same peasantry that preserved medieval oral traditions learned by Rosalía de Castro in her youth perpetuated Gallego in remote rural areas; some educated speakers clung to Galician because it symbolized regional autonomy.

Perhaps because of Galician lyric traditions, poets are surprisingly numerous. Current dynamic poetic production leads some observers to postulate another Golden Age. Many contemporary Galician poets are women, as evinced by two recent anthologies of Galician women poets.[1] Elisa Vázquez de Gey organizes her anthology chronologically, by birth dates; Kathleen March's organizational principle is alphabetical. Vázquez samples 33 and March 34 women poets; they agree on 12. Fifty-five poets are represented (some included by Vázquez write in Castilian, including María Elvira Lacaci and Blanca Andreu). March cites several more, pushing the total above 60; however, some are beginners, with publications only in periodicals. Both anthologists include poets with only one book. Seeking twentieth-century Galician women poets with at least one book published, Vázquez indicates that she located 54 names, eliminated those who had died (listing 14 names "In Memoriam"), but found 30 more with important unpublished lyrics. She concludes that "in this century, there have been some seventy women working in the area of poetry in Galicia" (9). Several names mentioned by Vázquez but not included are anthologized by March, making the estimate of 70 appear reasonable. Relative youth and late publication place most in the post-Franco era.

Catalan women in recent years have produced considerably more fiction than work in other genres, although some are known to have written poetry that remained unpublished. Few Catalan women writers are primarily poets. Major poetic anthologies in Catalan[2] contain few women: they coincide in representing Clementina Arderiu and Maria Antònia Salvà; Joan Triadú adds Rosa Leveroni. David Rosenthal's *Postwar Catalan Poetry* (1991) includes no women. Joaquim Marco and Jaume Pont's bilingual anthology, *La Nueva Poesía catalana* (1984) revises and expands the 1980 edition, adding six poets for a total of 21, including only two women—Maria-Mercè Marçal and Marta Pessarrodona, whose first book appeared in 1969. Given traditional omission of women from canonical works, such paucity might merely indicate "standard" underrepresentation. Significantly, however, there are no specialized anthologies of Catalan women poets, although several exist in Castilian, with the two mentioned above in Galician and even one in Basque. Poetic activity by Catalan women thus appears comparably less frequent and less intense.

Minor Poets in Galician

Herminia Fariña e Cobián (1904–66) spent most of her life in Santiago de Compostela and wrote both in Spanish and Galician. Her literary activity began early with her first book of lyrics, *Cadencias* (1922; Cadences), written in Castilian. She wrote plays in Galician (staged in Vigo) and published *Seara* (1924; Harvest), her only volume of Galician verse, Romantic in content but influenced formally by modernism. After marriage, she lived in South America, collaborating in periodicals there and in Spain. Other books include *Hosanna* (1931) and *Por España y para España* (1937; For Spain's Sake, Written to Spain). Like Rosalía, she prefers depicting rural Galicia, emphasizing the folkloric and picturesque.

Carmen Prieto Rouco (1901–70) was born and died in Vilalba. A successor of Rosalía de Castro, Prieto produced subjective lyrics describing rural Galicia, protesting against its rigid social structure and the peasants' marginal existence. Prieto seldom treats love or the confessional vein, although she does portray woman's condition, especially in her theatrical works (more numerous than her poetry collections). She is important largely for representing the situation of women writers in Galicia. Prieto was interested in Galician politics, and some poems criticize the power and abuses of *caciques* (local political bosses) in rural areas. Deeply concerned for Galicia's backwardness and poverty, she could be bitter and abrasive. Frequent poems use monologue or dialogue forms. Prieto's poetry collections include *Horas de frebe* (1926; Feverish Hours), *Violetas* (1954; Violets), and *Lluvia menuda* (1956; Fine Rain).

Dora Vázquez Iglesias (b. 1913), poet, playwright, and short-story writer, has published both in Castilian and Galician. A longtime schoolteacher in her birthplace of Orense and its surrounding villages, she collaborated assiduously with the periodical press, primarily in Galicia but also in the rest of Spain and Latin America. Didacticism appears often; much of her writing is directed to children. Nature looms large in her poetry, playing important roles in her dramas, as do religious values and traditional morality. The work ethic, family values, and conservative and patriarchal norms underlie most of her works, including *Palma y corona* (1946; Palm and Wreath), *Un Poema cada mes* (1969; A Poem Each Month), *Irmá: Poemas de ausencia* (1970; Sister: Poems of Absence), *Campo e mar aberto* (1975; Field and Open Sea), *Augas soltas* (1979; Unleashed Waters), and *Oración junto al camino* (1985; Prayer along the Road).

María Mariño Carou (1918–67) lived in several provincial Galician towns (Noia, Santiago, La Coruña, El Ferrol) and later in Vizcaya. From age 29 onward, she resided in the village of Parada de O Courel, where her husband was a rural schoolmaster and where Galician poet Uxío Novoneyra lived. She began writing a decade later (in 1957), but given her isolation and writing in Gallego, she has been largely ignored despite lyrics considered "perfect" and impeccably crafted (an early death from leukemia cut short her production). Major poetic influences are Rosalía de Castro and Novoneyra. Occasionally echoing Rosalía's tragic tones (perhaps because of her fatal illness), she sometimes treats nature similarly and pursues her predecessor's occasional mystic vein, although her treatment is more negative and disturbing. The sea and waves alternate with fields and rocks, expressing a Romantic sense of self, a suffering soul identified with nature and Galicia.

Mariño's linguistic experiments included twisting and forcing her syntax, making portmanteau words (in the manner of Joyce), and seeking new effects with alliteration and internal rhyme. Other techniques include repetition, anaphora, parallelisms, chaotic enumeration of natural elements and efforts to maximize the sonority of Gallego. Reiterated struggles between mind and body externalize her subterranean existential anguish. Her collections of verse—*Palabra no tempo* (1963; The Word in Time) and *Verba que comenza* (n.d.; The Beginning Word; also listed as *Verbo no ar*)[3]—constitute not protest poetry but serene contemplation of her surroundings, especially the mountains, reverently described, and of simple, traditional Galician peasant constructions—the timeless landscape and country roads. Intimate and understated, her lyric voice is private and profound.

Pura Vázquez

Pura Vázquez Iglesias, born in Orense on 31 March 1918, writes poetry and prose in both Galician and Castilian. A teacher by profession, she married and lived for several years in Venezuela. In 1949 she was elected to the Royal Galician Academy. She has frequently collaborated with her older sister, Dora, and shares Dora's didactic bent, cultivation of children's literature, moralizing tendencies, religious themes, and propagation of traditional family values. Her lyrics, however, reveal contact with contemporary esthetics and philosophical currents (touches of vanguardism and existential preoccupations). Her primary genre is poetry, but she also has written novels, short stories, essays, and plays for children. Having acquired some prestige, she figures in several anthologies and in reference books.[4]

Pura Vázquez began to write at 14, winning several prizes. Like Rosalía de Castro, with whom she is often compared, she is preoccupied with Galician ambients—the mountainous landscape, the sea, *orballo* (mist), and emotion. Her concept of the lyric—sentimental and Romantic—lacks constraint and attention to form, yet she is one of few Galicians to use closed forms such as the sonnet. Also like Rosalía, her poetry contains notable autobiographical substrata, defies those who criticize Galicia, expresses desire for justice, and projects melancholic dark shadows (death, self-destruction, evil, suffering, injustice, sensuality, grief). Influences mentioned include Vicente Aleixandre and Carmen Conde.

En torno a la voz (1948; Around the Voice) echoes Romanticism and Rosalía; the persona searches for the ineffable, aspiring to absolutes, seeking poetic perfection and obsessed with musicality. *Madrugada fronda* (1951; Leafy Dawn) contains a dozen poems organized around existential concerns, stressing life's precariousness and authenticity. Unlike many existentialists, the poet neither struggles with the divine nor anguishes over the passing of time. *Desde la niebla* (1951; From the Fog) contemplates the mystery of poetry—divine, prodigious passion—and the joys of poetic expression. Several key poems with similar themes elaborate romantic visions of poetic inspiration, writing as searching for answers to transcendent questions. *Tiempo mío* (1952; My Time) presents passionate love themes (not then in fashion), especially in "Three Sonnets to One Love." Vitalist and optimistic in the face of her own mortality, independent of current poetic fashion with its concentration on socioeconomic injustice and suffering, Vázquez expresses her own intimate joy. In *Mañana del amor* (1956; Morning of Love), which uses an erotic and mystic vocabulary with universal resonances, she seeks personal and romantic plenitude, exulting in creativity, enthusiasm, and her impassioned imagination. *13 poemas a mi sombra* (1957; 13 Poems to My Shadow) reiterates earlier poetic visions and techniques, using an interstellar voice with cosmic resonances and proclaiming victory over existential or metaphysical anguish. Influence of "social poetry" appears in the mention of specific time (conveyed by historical objects).

Repetitive motifs include hearth and fire, cabin or cottage, burning love, rural figures (shepherd child, wagoneer, plowman), Romantic longing for rest or escape, sensuality, marine imagery (ships, sails, gulls, waves, and watery horizons), and fog and night. Pura Vázquez writes solid, traditional lyrics with little experimentalism or trendiness. A solitary and independent poet, Pura Vázquez is remote from contemporary social preoccupations and esthetic conventions. Mirta Camandone links her with an erotic tradition in Spanish verse initiated by Delmira Agustini, suggesting antecedents among women of the previous generation, including Ernestina de Champourcín and Carmen Conde.[5] Eugenio de Nora (cited by Camandone, 404) criticizes Vázquez's "sentimental verse," impugning absence of social themes and colloquialisms, scornfully referring to "marbleized language" and criticizing her subjectivity and esthetic preoccupation. Whether or not these constitute defects, they aptly characterize Pura Vázquez's poetry.

Luz Pozo Garza

Born 21 June 1922 in Ribadeo (Lugo) near the Asturian border, Luz Pozo Garza became well acquainted with the work of Galician poet Luis Pimentel (a Lugo native), later publishing critical essays on his poetry. When she was seven, her family moved to Vivero; Fascist persecutions during the Civil War took them to Lugo and then Morocco. In 1940 she returned to Galicia, where she married writer Eduardo Moreiras; her three children were born in Vivero. An artist and musician as well as a writer, Pozo became a secondary-school teacher of Spanish language and literature and co-director of the critical review *Nordés*. Her critical interests focus on Galicia: writers Rosalía de Castro, Alvaro Cunqueiro, Luis Seoane. With Tomás Barros she compiled *Antoloxia da poesia galega actual*. Pozo also published a critical edition of medieval Galician poet Martín Codax's work, *As Siete Cantigas* (1987; Seven Canticles).

Pozo's first published poetry collections were in Castilian: *Anfora* (1949; Storage Vessel) and *El Vagabundo* (1952; The Wanderer). Her poems make generous use of musical motifs, and critics have detected early thematic influences of Gerardo Diego (González Garcés [149] disagrees), along with classical allusions and echoes of Juan Ramón Jiménez and Vicente Aleixandre (especially Aleixandre's fusion of cosmic and natural elements). Generally overlooked are postsymbolist influences that have led to generous use of fog, mist, melancholy, ambiguity, twilight forest depths, and distant memories (González attributes these to the impact of Pimentel [149]). Constant concerns are time (including being-toward-death), love (a major quest), feminine intimacy, subtle eroticism (reflecting complete communication and a gratifying relationship with the masculine Other). The pair of lovers appears central to the poet's being and identity. Later works (*O páxaro na boca* [1952; Bird in Mouth], whose overpowering theme is love, and *Cita en el viento* [1962; Date in the Wind]) expand their focus to meditate upon life's broader meanings, contemplating vital cycles (birth, maturation, death, rebirth) with serene acceptance of natural processes.

Solitude—a constant—is not loneliness but productive introspection, meditation, and analysis, leading to epiphanies. In *Ultimas palabras/verbas derradeiras* (1976; Final Words) Pozo approaches the problem of poetics, exploring principles based on progressive deletion (fewer words each day), spurred by the semantic insufficiency of words—their inadequacy in expressing death, nothingness, and aging, with its inevitable message of mortality. Occasional melancholy or existential sadness notwithstanding, basic security and stable emotional relationships prevail. *Concerto de outono* (1981; Autumn Concert) celebrates the symphony of seasons, incorporating rural music and neopopular song, and treats themes ranging from freedom and rebellion to love of country, death, and the quest for beauty.

Pozo has earned praise for her musicality and her "perfect" verses, with their abundant imagery, condensation, synthesis, refinement, and felicitious metaphors. While social or testimonial themes are not entirely absent, the reader notes more abundant word play, impressionistic depictions, and strong vitality in her renderings of Galicia, often humanized with its birds, streams, foliage, and typical figures such as the *gaitero* (bagpipe player) and Rosalía. Motifs of silence and memory, roads, night, and rain distantly echo Machado, but more immediate influences include French and medieval poetry (the latter inspiring *Códice calixtino* [1986], with its allusion to Martín Codax, an intertextual interlocutor). March notes that Pozo refracts medieval male courtly love lyrics, deriving feminine perspectives from the formulaic encounters and establishing a woman's presence usurped during earlier centuries. *Códice* also incorporates surrealist elements, exhibiting ingredients found in the *novísimos* (neo-*culteranista* allusions to Rimbaud, Ophelia, Tristan) and various neovanguard touches, including intertextual homages to other Galician poets. González Garcés points out the connection with Juana de Ibarbarou (pseudonym of Galician-born Juana Fernández)—her sensuality, paganism, use of mythology, and Galician elements (148).

Maria do Carme Kruckenberg Sanjurjo

Born in Vigo in 1926, Maria do Carme Kruckenberg Sanjurjo (whose father was a conservative Mexican of German ancestry) began studying in the city's private German School but never finished her *bachillerato,* wanting only to read and travel. She wrote poetry from adolescence, participating in the Alameda "tertulia" from 1945 to 1949. Married in 1949, she lived four years in Buenos Aires, returning to Galicia in 1953. During the next three decades she worked in Madrid and Vigo as representative of a pharmaceuticals company, traveling in 34 European and American countries. In addition to poetry (including the children's book *Farol de aire* [1958; Lantern of Air]), she has published prose fiction, translated the poems of Rilke, and collaborated assiduously with the press and radio. Her Galician identity is firmly established, although she writes more in Castilian than Gallego. She even wrote a book on bullfighting, *Tauromaquia en línea y verso* (1964; Bullfighting in Line and Verse), illustrated with her avant-garde drawings.

While critics have detected echoes of several male Hispanic poets and (inevitably?) of Rosalía de Castro, Kruckenberg—like Pozo—has been attracted by the medieval *cantigas,* as in *Cantigas do vento* (1956; Canticles of the Wind). Several of these pieces—including *Cantigas de amigo a Ramón González Sierra do Pampillón* (1972; Love Plaints for Ramón González Sierra do Pampillón)—she composed for a friend, returning to the form again with *Cantigas pra un tempo esquencido* (1986; Ballads for a Diminished Time). These imitations of medieval balladry and popular songs draw motifs from folklore and oral tradition, echoing their elliptical presentation and achieving that haunting air of timeless mystery found in such songs from the troubadours through Lorca's *Romancero gitano.*

Kruckenberg's early books center on love and defense of Galician identity, occasionally enunciating social and testimonial themes without renouncing the poetic persona's own intimate life: these include *Las Palabras olvidadas* (1956; Forgotten Words), *Los Parajes inmóviles* (1956; Motionless Landscapes), *Rumor de tiempo* (1957; Sound of Time), *Poemas inevitables* (1960; Inevitable Poems), *Poemas y canciones de aquí y de allá* (1962; Poems and Songs from Here and There), and *Memoria de mi sueño* (1964; Memoir of My Dream), often printed at the author's expense. *Canaval de Ouro* (1962) portrays a woman's unrequited love. Metaphors of nails, needles, thorns, and other sharp objects fixed upright have obvious phallic connotations but also have been seen as symbolizing women's painful search for knowledge (March, 15). Kruckenberg frequently addresses feminist topics, usually treating them with humor and a light touch but with self-assurance, reworking masculine literary conventions and reclaiming the usurped feminine viewpoint (as in her *cantigas*).

Kruckenberg deems *A sombra ergueita* (1976; Erect Shadow) her best book in Galician; it also happens to be her most testimonial, raising the battle cries of various groups, proclaiming their independence and resistance, accusing and denouncing, and affirming the poetic persona's integrity, rights, and determination. Placed in historical context, the volume belongs to the struggle for regional autonomy that followed the dictator's death. Galician culture had been especially ill-treated by the Franco regime. *Cantares de mi silencio* (1980; Songs of My Silence) plumbs more subjective, emotional veins, using occasionally powerful metaphors drawn from the natural environment to express her emotions.

Minor Poets in Catalan

Roser Matheu (b. 1892 in Barcelona), the daughter of poet Francesc Matheu, published two collections of poems before the Civil War—*La Carena* (1935) and *Cançons de Setembre* (1936; September Songs). Her wartime sufferings, both physical and emotional, fill postwar works, as seen in *Poems a la filla* (1949; Poems to My Daughter), expressing ethical concerns, and *Poems de la fam* (1953; Poems of Hunger), more directly painting wartime suffering. Matheu was apparently a friend of Palmira Jacquetti i Isant (1895–1963; pseudonym of P. de Castellvell), whose poetry consists of *L'Estel dins la llar* (1938; Stars in the Fireplace) and *Elegies* (1955), plus unpublished works. Carme Montoriol i Puig (1893–1966) and Concepció Maluquer i González (b. 1918), both of whom cultivated other genres, were significant presences on the Catalan literary scene. A successful translator, novelist, and playwright, Montoriol began her literary career late, after devoting years to music. Politically and culturally active in Barcelona before the war, she lapsed into complete silence afterward. Her poetic activity is mentioned by several sources without listing titles.[6] Maluquer, who lived in Barcelona, was primarily a novelist but won the municipal prize in 1957 with her long poem, *La Creu dels vents* (Cross of the Winds), wherein the city dialogues with the winds—spirits whose paths of intersection form an enormous cross. *La Ciutat y les hores* (1960; The City and the Hours) features 24 feminine characters personifying the hours, flowing in endless rhythm.

"Simona Gay"

Simona Pons (1898–1969), born in Illa del Riberal in the region of Roselló, near the border with France, belongs to the modernist sphere of Riba, Arderiu, Marià Manent, Sagarra, and Rodoreda.[7] She was the sister of Josep Sebastià Pons, a postsymbolist Catalan poet who facilitated her acquaintance with several other literary figures, especially Tomás Garcés, who supplied the Prologue for her first book, *Aigües vives/Eaux vives* (1932; Living Waters). Marià Manent provided the Prologue for her third and last book, *La Gerra al sol,* posthumously published in 1965. At 19, she married León Gay and moved to Paris, where her husband was a jurist. She adopted his name, living and writing in Paris during the 1930s, and her poems appeared in bilingual editions. Studies of Latin and readings of French and English writers during those years account for neo-Parnassian and modernist elements in her verse. With the outbreak of World War II she returned to her family's rural home, where primitive conditions and agricultural chores eventually undermined her health.

Aigües vives, a slim and simple collection of generally brief poems, documents moments of a woman's life from the prelude to love to "Engagement Song," from poems of conjugal life to those dedicated to the poet's children. Other compositions are more tenuous and enigmatic, as in the melancholic "Friendship." The second part depicts the Roselló countryside, now distant but lovingly evoked, where the Pyrenees gaze across Carbera, Sant Pere del Bosc, Casafabra, and L'Aspre and their forests and rocky outcroppings (depicted in "Canta Perdiu" [Lost Song]). Gay's enchanted, motionless landscape, with its rarefied atmosphere and deserted air, recalls some forgotten time of solitude and silence.

La Lluita amb l'angel/Lutte avec l'ange (1938), likewise in two parts, begins somberly, its titles connoting pessimism and melancholy: "Mal vent" (Evil Air), "Platja del silenci" (Beach of Silence), "El Gorg negre" (Black Gorge), "Vall fosca" (Forbidding Valley), and "Soledat" (Solitude). The poetic persona contemplates hostile destiny, unable to perceive what awaits her or to find a single pole to help her across the frightful chasm. Fear and trembling, uncertainty and hesitation are finally overcome by struggling against the shadows—the "wrestling with the angel" that provides the title. Rather than metaphysical, the struggle is one in which the secret, ineffable self tries its strength against spiritual darkness, ending renewed and fortified and thereby winning the return to light, joy, and companionship. The collection, chronologically and thematically heterogeneous, also contains miscellany whose common denominator is the Catalan landscape. Girona, Andorra, and the Valley of Aran inspire compositions, plus elegiac evocations of times past, customs lost, lands now deserted. The book was completed in somber times, during Spain's Civil War and on the eve of World War II in Paris.

La Gerra al sol (1965; Root-Cellar in the Sun) evokes the ancient roads and misty byways of the mountain village of Illa del Riberal and Gay's childhood years there—her far-off youth among the solitary heights, giant boulders, streams, and passes—recollecting songs now almost forgotten, hearing ancestral voices of aged peasants pronouncing dying proverbs. The poet recalls her family's privileged situation—their country manor with its walled garden, herself refined and smiling as she gathered fruits and flowers. The 27-year lapse between her second and third volumes brought maturation, changed attitudes, and sober, classical purity of expression. Describing foggy landscapes after a rain, a tree or peasant building with minute, amorous detail, Gay stresses the sense of time, the weight of centuries, and the past's almost palpable presence, rendering chronological flux nearly visible as she depicts her homeland's changing seasons, the planting and harvest, vineyards and the sea. Her close relationship with her brother, Josep Sebastià Pons, inspired elegiac poems written after his death, dedicated to her "big brother in poetry and blood." His January burial on the white slopes of Canigó she described in austere, dignified, yet emotion-filled verse.

Celia Viñas

Celia Viñas Olivella (1915–54) was born in Lérida and grew up speaking Catalan (she wrote one collection in Catalan). Viñas is associated with Almería, the Mediterranean port where she spent her adult life and celebrated in her lyrics. This provincial capital considered her its official poet, dedicating a small plaza and bust with her name after her early death (she died when expecting her first child). Viñas completed a university degree in modern Romance philology, married educator-writer Arturo Medina (editor and publisher of her posthumous works), and became a teacher. Primarily a poet, she also wrote short stories, vignettes, and plays. Poetry collections published before her death include *Trigo del corazón* (1946; Wheat from the Heart), *Canción tonta en el sur* (1948; Silly Song in the South), *Palabras sin voz* (1953; Words without Voice), and (in Catalan) *Del foc i la cendra* (1953; Of Fire and Ashes). Posthumous poetry collections are *Como el ciervo corre herido* (1955; As the Deer Runs Wounded), *Canto* (1964; Song), *Antología lírica* (1976; Lyric Anthology), and *Poesía última* (1980; Last Poems). Prose works include *Estampas de la vida de Cervantes* (1949; Scenes from Cervantes's Life), *El Primer Botón del mundo y trece cuentos más* (1976; The World's First Button and Thirteen Other Stories), and the play *Plaza de la Virgen del Mar* (1974; Plaza of Our Lady of the Sea).

Viñas especially loved Mallorca, and many poems express that attachment. Another thematic nucleus centers on her teaching experience, celebrating children—their games and laughter, innocence, questions, and wide-eyed attention to stories—and the classroom itself. Viñas, who adored children, favors implicit dialogue form with frequent rhetorical questions, addressing interlocutors (usually children or the beloved) in the familiar "tú" (thou), creating enormously intimate effects. Ardently religious, she professed Franciscan poverty, gentleness, humility, and love of living things, humanizing all creation. Elements of neopopular song, fantasy, and notes of children's games combine with personification of flora and fauna, attribution of life or sentiments to inanimate objects (almonds, wine), and expressions of religiosity.

Viñas's generally unrhymed poetry follows no discernible metric or strophic pattern; she prefers shorter syllabic forms (*arte menor*), but occasional sonnets appear. Her major lyric devices—repetition, cadence, alliteration, and metaphor—include some truly remarkable, original imagery (a spider with a bridal veil; swallows with little musical bones; the wind with desert whiskers of broken glass and dead silver; yellow words hanging like ripe fruit; a simple stone wearing work-clothes; the enamored heart as an aquarium filled with honey and sugar-candy fish). Freshness, simplicity, deceptive naïveté, and echoes of Spanish popular tradition counterbalance occasional cosmopolitan intertextuality (allusions to Heine, for example), creating a most personal, profoundly lyric voice. The posthumously produced *Antología lírica* (1976) from her out-of-print and generally unavailable collections is the best source for sampling Viñas's works.[8]

Rosa Leveroni

Rosa Leveroni (1910–86), of Italian ancestry, was born in Barcelona, where she lived throughout her life. She studied library science at the Escola de Bibliotecaries in Barcelona, having poet Carles Riba (husband of Clementina Arderiu) among her professors. His influence, and that of famed Catalan poet Salvador Espriu heightens the presence of Catalan modernism (*noucentisme*) in Leveroni's work. Both Riba and Espriu wrote prologues celebrating her poetic excellence. Following graduation in 1933, she was employed by the Autonomous University until it was closed in 1939, thereafter suffering the rigors of "internal exile" and repression of Catalan culture. Leveroni never married, apparently bowing to familial pressure, but abundant erotic motifs in her work suggest she did not renounce love; ultimately, however, she felt deceived by men and retreated into intellectual isolation, distant from both genders. She researched Ausiàs March and translated T. S. Eliot, contributing stories and poems to the periodicals *Ariel* and *Poesia*. She conceded special importance to women's writing, translating poems by Christina Rosetti and Edith Sitwell and stories by Katherine Mansfield. The epigraph to her first book was from the Countess de Noailles, and that to her second was from Elizabeth Barrett Browning; she also professed great admiration for Emily Dickinson.

Epigrames i cançons (1938; Epigrams and Songs), with a Prologue by Riba, uses principally hendecasyllabic quatrains of epigrammatic brevity and concentration in the "Epigram" section; the "Songs" group, of eight to sixteen lines with the subtitle "Absence," treats love and solitude, especially love's joy and the pain of first passion. Personal and intimate in tone, Leveroni writes with classic restraint, concisely rendering subtle emotions via analogies with nature, the sea, night, and stars. *Presència i record* (1952; Presence and Memory), which reprints the first collection along with new work, begins with a dozen haikus, followed by a group of five-line Oriental tankas, whose themes include meditations upon the changing round of seasons, recollections of landscapes, travel impressions, and dreams. Still personal, intimate, classic, and circumspect, Leveroni treats her dreams, solitude, and love in melancholy, elegiac tones. Elegies, comprising the largest subgroup, evoke night, sorrow, and distant love. Yet another subgroup, "Les Notes greus" (Gray Notes), uses God as interlocutor for the poet's pain, questioning, and suffering. Metaphysical preoccupation and existential notes (including the silence of God, one's consciousness of passing time, angst, solitude, and alienation) become more pronounced, often recalling Antonio Machado, with whom Leveroni shares such motifs as memories, dreams, melancholoy landscapes, distant love, the topos of the road and journey, and symbolically empty houses and gardens.

Poesia (1981; Poetry), with its Prologue by Maria Aurèlia Capmany, incorporates Leveroni's two earlier books, plus a third section ("Altres poemes" [Other Poems]) of previously uncollected poems. The most complete collection of Leveroni's poetry to date, this is the only accessible edition. The growing desperation of postwar poems continues in "Cinc poemes desolats" (Five Poems of Desolation), recognized by an award at the 1956 Jocs Florals in Cambridge, England. (Jocs Florals, a traditional contest for poetry in Catalan usually held in Catalonia, was held in France and elsewhere during the Franco years because of the government's banning of the vernacular.) Themes of pain, wandering, and exilic quest proliferate, together with motifs of barriers, hostile destiny, and frustrated desire, as the best Romantic tradition is adapted to express the alienation suffered by Catalan intellectuals.

Although Leveroni participated in clandestine postwar efforts to maintain Catalan's cultural viability (such as the reviews *Ariel* and

Poesia), she does not adopt the ideology, anti-estheticism, or registers of popular discourse characterizing postwar "opposition" poets in Castilian; her tone is always classic, dignified, grave, chaste, harmonious and discreet—slightly solemn, with clearly perceptible cultural underpinnings. Her imagery, reelaborated and controlled, subsumes the entirety of European poetic tradition from the Renaissance to symbolism but owes most to *noucentisme* and immediate precedents in Catalan. Her philosophic bent, elegiac tones, and use of bees, flowers, the seasons (preferring spring and fall), afternoon and evening, and light and shadow likewise evoke Machado. Nevertheless, Leveroni is simultaneously feminine and intensely personal in her simplicity and authenticity; her angst and her language are very much her own.

María Beneyto

María Beneyto Cunyat (b. 1925 in Valencia) writes poetry, fiction, and literary criticism in Spanish and Catalan. Little information is available on Beneyto, whose family moved to Madrid before the war and apparently lived afterward in Venezuela, possibly in exile. Beneyto began writing in the periodical press, first publishing stories and critical essays. During the 1950s, despite harsh treatment of the minority tongues, she began publishing poems in Valencian (a Catalan dialect), helping to pioneer Catalan's postwar rebirth. *Altre veu* (1952; Another Voice) was followed by *Ratlles a l'aire* (1956; Lines in the Air), which won the City of Barcelona Prize. *La Dona forta* (1967; The Strong Woman), a novel, depicts a domineering matron's smothering of her weakling son. *Vidre ferit de sang* (1976; Blood-Wounded Glass), Beneyto's last (and slim) collection of Catalan verse, received the Ausias March Prize.

Beneyto's Castilian poetry includes *Canción olvidada* (1947; Forgotten Song); *Eva en el tiempo* (1952; Eve in Time); *Criatura múltiple* (1954; Multiple Child), which won the Valencia Prize; *Tierra viva* (1956; Living Earth); and *Poemas de la ciudad* (1956). The anthology *Poesía, 1947–1964* (1965) incorporates selections from the foregoing. Published during the heyday of social poetry, most of these collections treat urban social problems, portraying collective dehumanization, public transportation, factories, neglected children, hunger, poverty, suffering and the absence of compassion. In her essay "Poética" (which precedes selections in Leopoldo de Luis's *Antología de poesía social*) she proclaims *engagement* an inescapable moral obligation, defends artistic freedom, and seeks dialogue with the reader.

Beneyto's focus is not limited to the city; she also depicts rural scenes and treats other more subjective and personal themes: melancholy, solitude, lost love, the search for religious and existential answers, and women's condition. She prefers long lines and long poems, writing of the many women within herself and the multiple roles women must play; while protesting women's past margination, she offers man companionship, collaboration, and her strength to begin again. Hers is a vision in which woman is durable and nourishing, stronger than man (who is exhausted by war). Critics have praised her landscape artistry, sincerity, and mastery of form, and Beneyto has won regional and national prizes for both prose and poetry. Later works include *Vida anterior* (1962; Previous Life), *El Agua que rodea la isla* (1974; The Water Surrounding the Island), and *Biografía breve del silencio* (1975; Short Biography of Silence).

The relative dearth of Catalan women poets in the postwar era and the absence of poets of major productivity and significance contrasts with women's notably more vigorous lyric activity in Galicia. Attempts to explain the discrepancy (Catalan preference for other genres, difference in traditions, etc.) would be merely conjecture. A sufficient number of women have written recent vernacular poetry in both languages to prevent lapses into silence, even maintaining continuity for a modest feminine poetic canon. It remains to be seen whether women's writing in the vernaculars will continue as viable in the next century, especially with the homogenizing influence of the European Union. Meanwhile, increased numbers of poets and more aggressive poetry in Castilian and various minority tongues reflect sweeping social change as well as the effects of feminism and women's enhanced access to education, the media, and publication.

Conclusion

Women drawn to poetry throughout the centuries have had little choice but to imitate the masculine canon. We learn by precept and example, and when precepts are not available, one parodies the example. Denied access to formal education until the present century, women have of necessity been largely autodidactic; usually without instruction in prosody, rhetorical complexities, and poetics, they were obliged to derive such principles intuitively from male-authored models or to devise ways of achieving similar results—in other words, to play the game without knowing the rules. This explains the high degree of orality in women's poetry; the popularity of relatively free, unstructured forms such as free verse and the prose poem; and the comparable paucity of women poets using consonant rhyme or rigid structures such as the sonnet. While a few women have been praised for the formal perfection of their lyrics or their metric virtuosity, such cases are the exception, as are women who use esoteric, hermetic lexicon, Baroque complications, elaborate conceits, or extensive learned allusion.

The historical development of women's poetry in Spain reflects the history of the genre per se (i.e., the masculine canon) as concerns major periods and movements with their distinguishing themes and formal characteristics, but most women poets accord less importance to form than to substance. Women's writing features more straightforward vocabulary, including domestic and colloquial registers, and emphasizes communication. Thus women's language, insofar as it exists, consists in absence or reduction (of the formal, pretentious, confining, and artificial) as much as in presence (of greater naturalness, simplicity, and freedom).

Women's poetry throughout most of its development has treated canonical themes—the universal, eternal themes of all great poetry, emphasizing those motifs most relevant to woman's experience. Reluctant to treat topics alien to their experience, women have with few exceptions avoided the epic—the treatment of battles, exploration, conquest, military fame, or adventures—preferring love, religion, death, memory, nature, and personal or confessional themes. While often adopting masculine conventions of the genre, women poets began early to adapt and subvert them—for example, subverting masculine courtly love conventions by adapting them to express the female persona's desire for intellectual freedom, fame, or escape from male domination, or satirically subverting the same courtly love conventions through burlesquing men's love of food or other mundane objects. Parodic inversion of masculine models (often reversing expected outcomes) allowed women writers to express ideas that might otherwise have incurred masculine censure. Use of gender-neutral language and images, of dreams, irony, and cross-gender writing (i.e., a pseudo-masculine narrator), communicated the woman's viewpoint, obliquely protesting without directly challenging patriarchal norms.

Besides religiosity or faith, "safe" topics included the Nativity, the Eucharist, convent life, church holidays and celebrations, pilgrimages, ascetic and mystic strivings, rejection of vanities (the world and its pleasures), nostalgia, melancholy, meditations, landscapes, and the poetry of circumstance. Love-related themes were most often treated in the context of plaints or laments addressed to a feminine confidante regarding inconstancy, disenchantment, rejection, or unrequited love; extramarital relationships, if not platonic, were treated circumspectly, attributed to others, portrayed as legend, history, or dreams.

By the eighteenth century protests against unjust treatment of women had begun to transcend the love plaint, decrying physical abuse and defending woman's intellectual capacity, their right to education, and their spiritual equality. During the eighteenth and nineteenth centuries poems to the Virgin Mary became more numerous, with the saint functioning either as interlocutor, muse, or miraculous defender of victims of wife and child abuse. Religious sentiments included charity, love of humanity, search for peace, and broadening philosophical reflections. Protests against woman's lot and masculine brutality soon broadened to encompass disenfranchisement and disempowerment, viewing gender as slavery. Antislavery (abolitionist) and antiwar sentiments, part of victims' advocacy, accompanied introduction of marginal social types with the realization that women shared common problems and common interests with slaves and social outcasts. Growing social and political consciousness accompanied the introduction of themes related to national politics (not circumstantial, patriotic, or civic poems, but concern for the decadent economy, impoverished peasantry, and emigration).

Regional cultures and regional autonomy movements likewise furnished significant themes. Women poets commenced writing of the insults inflicted on women writers, burlesquing clichéd discourse, satirizing misogyny, and dialoguing with prevailing gender codes. Mother-daughter bonds, biological and literary sisterhood, maternity and maternal love, and the loss of children and childhood innocence (significant "feminine" themes scarcely suggested in Golden Age poetry) appeared together with the "war of the sexes," examination of alternatives to traditional gender roles and alternative lifestyles (urban vs. rural life, *costumbrismo,* travel), and the introduction of increasingly problematic, conflicting meditations: metaphysical uncertainty, doubt, and despair. Some women reaffirm patriarchal values (chastity, fidelity, self-abnegation) and faith, but these themes and idyllic motifs do not exclude feminine vindication and awareness of social change.

Turn-of-the-century writers increase the emphasis on gender, portraying female heroism; they also reflect scientific and technological progress and the spirit of the international labor movement (praising the dignity of work, depicting mining accidents and the like), revealing awareness of expanding choices for women elsewhere in poems treating unrealized ideals, tedium, and anger. A significant didactic vein accompanies expanding horizons, with women's access to international travel, museums, and art expositions.

With the twentieth century women poets show significant increase in theoretical awareness, and technical preoccupations grow in the vanguard years, paralleling the rising cultural level of women and bringing such themes as classrooms and texts, specialized study experience, and creativity. Women's homages to contemporary literati proliferate, but so do poems celebrating domestic life, women's daily routines, feminine joys and sorrows, the family ambient, and home interiors. As respectable alternatives to matrimony begin to become available, women poets show less hesitation in portraying conjugal bliss. Pregnancy and birth are treated much more concretely, as are carnal encounters (no longer mystic, these are usually depicted metaphorically while leaving no doubt as to their specificity). War's violence and devastation, its effects on women and families, the resulting trauma, and exile and hardships appear as part of personal experience.

Women poets acknowledge identity crises and problems of aging, frustrated maternal urges and the erotic deprivation of widowhood, silence and solitude, and depression and drugs. Extramarital relationships, some platonic and others adulterous, are no longer disguised as dream, legend, or someone else's experience; the suffering and problems they create for women are movingly portrayed. Along with increasing existential alienation, anguish, incommunication, and isolation, some women poets write of humiliation, abandonment, and unfulfilled dreams and ambition or express defiance of traditional gender roles and patriarchal values. Some write of futility, fatigue, the contradictions of Spanish society's double standard and cult of the Virgin juxtaposed to feminine disempowerment.

The trajectory from "pure" to "impure" lyrics, from art for art's sake to *engagement* that characterizes twentieth-century poetry as a whole, likewise involves women poets. "Social poetry's" veiled political protest—the denunciation underlying depictions of economic injustice, inequities of the class structure, and wealth versus poverty—expressed in deliberately "unpoetic" language coincides with more direct rhetoric as women poets begin specific mention of body parts, use metaphors of procreation and genesis from the feminine perspective, and increase the number of "unpoetic" subjects (beggars, prostitutes, mutilated bodies, exploded children). "Timeless constants" evolve similarly: God, death, love, romance, and matrimony are demystified, while formerly veiled feminine intimacy (daily toilettes, self-loathing, thoughts of suicide, fears, and malaise) is exposed to public view. Women poets focus on inequality in the workplace, the "polite" conventions stifling women, and women's multiple roles, as well as such broader contemporary problems as political corruption, nuclear power and weaponry, pollution, and ecological endangerment.

Despite problems of generalization when numerous writers, several generations, and an enormous poetic corpus are involved, it can be said that women poets share preferences for certain techniques and avoidance of others. Exceptions notwithstanding, most use little rhyme (unless for humorous effect) and often avoid fixed strophic structures, preferring repetition or reiteration with variation and parallelisms. Cadence, often subtle, appears more often than marked rhythms, and dialogue forms are favored, including rhetorical questions and interrogation. Metaphor, irony, condensation, and ellipses are used by most, with prosopopeya and symbols. Several poets use ekphrasis extensively; others use shifting perspectives or multiple voices. Colloquial registers and tag lines are popular, and most women use conventional topoi, sometimes subverting or rewriting for revisionist effects. If these techniques have anything in common, it is that none is peculiar to poetry.

Spain's women poets have increased in number, have expanded their horizons, and have collectively become more prolific, cosmopolitan, and versatile. Passing from pseudo-conformity and veiled subversion to open

protest, women's poetry currently enjoys a visibility and attention probably unequalled at any past time. Younger, more activist and aggresive
poets of the post-Franco era (to be treated in the sequel to this study) are
challenging norms, boundaries, and convention. Meanwhile, women
poets in Spain today have yet to recover their past, connect with their
roots, and gain entry to the canon.

Notes and References

Preface

1.   Bloom summarizes and paraphrases Vico, adding his own conclusions; difficulty arises in determining where Vico ends and Bloom begins. See Harold Bloom, *Poetry and Repression* (New Haven, Conn., and London: Yale University Press, 1976).

2.   Fetterley's concept of the "inmasculation" of women readers applies to Spanish women of past centuries, limited to a rigidly traditional, patriarchal, masculine canon. See Judith Fetterley, *The Resisting Reader: A Feminist Approach to American Fiction* (Bloomington: Indiana University Press, 1978).

3.   Culler suggests that the phrase "a woman reading as a woman" is abstract and subject to dizzying deconstruction. See Jonathan Culler, "Reading as a Woman," in *On Deconstruction: Theory and Criticism after Structuralism* (Ithaca, N.Y., and London: Cornell University Press, 1982).

4.   Simone de Beauvoir, *The Second Sex,* trans. H. M. Parshley (1952; New York: Vintage Books, 1974). De Beauvoir argues in *Force of Circumstance,* summarized by her in *Toute Compte Fait* (Paris: Gallimard, 1972), that "all male ideologies are directed at justifying the oppression of women, and that women are so conditioned by society that they consent to this oppression" (462–63).

5.   Introduction to *Women in Hispanic Literature: Icons and Fallen Idols,* ed. Beth Miller (Berkeley: University of California Press, 1983), 15.

6.   See Andrew P. Debicki, "Introduction: Critical Perspectives on Contemporary Spanish Poetry," and José Olivio Jiménez, "Fifty Years of Contemporary Spanish Poetry (1939–1989)," *Studies in 20th Century Literature* 16, no. 1 (Winter 1992): 5–13 and 15–41; special issue on contemporary Spanish Poetry, 1939–90.

7.   No critical consensus exists as to which poets comprise the Generation of 1927 aside from four or five nuclear figures. See Janet Pérez, "On Misapplications of the Generational Label," *La Otra cara del 27: La Novela social española, 1923–1939,* ed. Víctor Fuentes, *Letras Peninsulares* 6, no. 1 (Spring 1993): 31–50. Several dozen writers mention 20-odd male poets writing in Castilian, but no women, and no vernacular poets, thereby perpetuating exclusivity in canon formation. Yet Clementina Arderiu, Rosa Chacel, and Ernestina de Champourcín "belong" in the Generation of 1927 on the basis of dates of birth and publication, esthetic affinities, and social contacts with male members of the "generation" (meaning that traditional definitions of literary generations fail to justify their exclusion).

8.   See Sharon Keefe Ugalde, *Conversaciones y poemas: La Nueva Poesía femenina española en castellano* (Madrid: Siglo Veintiuno de España, 1991); hereafter

cited in text. Most women interviewed did not place themselves in any generation, sometimes because of beginning to write late in life, sometimes because of relative isolation.

9.   Women's exclusion from literary histories, anthologies, and reference works accompanies exclusion from "generations"; such exclusions, resulting from gender bias, obviously should be remedied. But two eminent poetry specialists have already challenged generational schemata; even if the concept does not disappear from the critical repertoire, it does not adequately represent women's experience. Chronological categories, however, need no explanation.

Prologue

1.   Ugalde interviews seven women poets born between 1931 and 1966 in *Conversaciones y poemas: La nueva poesía femenina española en castellano.*

2.   Angel Flores and Kate Flores, eds., *The Defiant Muse: A Bilingual Anthology* (New York: Feminist Press, 1986), xiv; hereafter cited in text.

3.   Julián Olivares and Elizabeth Boyce, *Tras el espejo la musa escribe: Lírica femenina de los siglos de Oro* (Madrid: Siglo Veintiuno de España, 1993), 66–67; hereafter cited in text.

4.   Electa Arenal and Stacey Schlau, *Untold Sisters: Hispanic Nuns in Their Own Works* (Albuquerque: University of New Mexico Press, 1989), 1; hereafter cited in text.

5.   Juan Pérez de Guzmán y Gallo, *Bajo los Austrias: La Mujer española en la Minerva castellana* (Madrid: Tipografía Salesiana, 1923); cited by Ana Navarro, ed., *Antología poética de escritoras de los siglos XVI y XVII* (Madrid: Castalia/Instituto de la Mujer, 1989), 92, 106; hereafter cited in text.

6.   Howard Mancing, "A Consensual Canon of Hispanic Poetry," *Hispania* 69, no. 1 (March 1986): 53–81.

7.   Víctor García de la Concha, "La Renovación estética de los años sesenta," in *El Estado de las poesías* (Oviedo: Caja de Ahorros de Asturias, 1986), 10–23.

8.   Interestingly, this comes from a male expert in sociolinguistics. See Adam Jaworski, *The Power of Silence* (Newbury Park, Calif.: Sage Publications, 1993), 119. Jaworski's fourth chapter, "The Politics of Silence," studies uses of silence to dominate and oppress, seeing women as paradigmatic of the "societal silencing of dominated groups" (118), further explored on pp. 119–29.

9.   Here Jaworski paraphrases M. Daly, *Beyond God the Father: Toward a Philosophy of Women's Liberation* (Boston: Beacon Press, 1973), 93.

10.   Allusion to Dale Spender, *Invisible Women: The Schooling Scandal* (London: Writers & Readers, 1982), n.p. Jaworski paraphrases Spender that a feminist "tradition exists but has been concealed in the workings of a male-dominated education system" (120).

Chapter One

1. Clara Janés, *Las Primeras Poetisas en lengua castellana* (Madrid: Editorial Ayuso, 1986), represents 41 women poets writing in the sixteenth and seventeenth centuries.

2. Janés's introduction provides several sources for such poems, including Emilio García Gómez, *Poemas arabigo-andaluces* (Madrid: Espasa Calpe, 1946); Heri Pérez, *Esplendor de al-Andalus* (Madrid: Ediciones Hiperión, 1983); Mahmud Sobh, *Poetisas arabigoandaluzas* (Granada: Diputación Provincial, 1985); and Teresa Garulo, *Diwan de las poetisas de al-Andalus* (Madrid: Ediciones Hiperión, 1986). Not mentioned by Janés, given the date of publication, is María Jesús Rubiera Mata, *Poesía femenina hispano-andaluza* (Madrid: Castalia/Instituto de la Mujer, 1989).

3. Elvira Gangutia, "Poesía griega de amigo y poesía arábigo-española," *Emerita* 40 (1972), 329–96; cited by Rubiera.

4. Classic Hispano-Arabic poetry (not visibly feminine, even when attributed to women, as it is implicitly homoerotic) adopts a masculine voice praising feminine beauty—or that of an ephebe—in neoplatonic, courtly love terms. Women poets turn to satire, depicting lovesickness, tears, and langour. The self-portrait, self-praise (a classical Arabic theme), and love's locus amoenus appear repeatedly, as does the occasional panegyric.

5. Examples appear in Flores and Flores 1986 and these editors' *Poesía feminista del mundo hispánico (desde la edad media hasta la actualidad)* (Mexico: Siglo Veintiuno, 1984), which contains some two dozen poems. See also Luzmaría Jiménez Faro's *Panorama Antológico de Poetisas Españolas (siglos XV al XX)* (Madrid: Torremozas, 1987). Jiménez Faro surveys 44 women poets, emphasizing the twentieth century, but adds two more fifteenth-century women poets, María Sarmiento and Isabel de Borja (for a total of four from the Golden Age). A more important anthology of women poets in *cancioneros* is that of Miguel Angel Pérez Priego, *Poesía femenina en los cancioneros* (Madrid: Castalia/Instituto de la Mujer, 1990). Isabel Segura's *Romances de señoras* (Barcelona: Editorial Alta Fulla, 1981) contains facsimile reproductions of 55 eighteenth- and nineteenth-century *romances de ciego* (blind beggars' ballads). The compositions are not by but *about* women, reflecting what society expected of them and thus allowing reconstruction of the epoch's ideal female prototype. These anonymous, popular ballads by generally uneducated composers reveal only three choices for women: nun, spinster, and wife. With the transition to an industrialized society (neither the nun nor spinster [re]produces), woman's contribution is reduced to reproduction.

6. Peter Broad, "Florencia Pinar y la poética del *Cancionero*," in *La Escritora hispánica,* ed. Nora Erro-Orthmann and Juan Cruz Mendizábal (Miami: Ediciones Universal, 1990), 26–35.

7. These include *Cancionero de poesías varias* (MS 617 de la Biblioteca

Real de Madrid, 1986); *Cancionero de Pedro de Rojas* (MS 3924 de la Biblioteca Nacional de Madrid, 1988); *Cancionero de poesías varias* (MS 3902 de la Biblioteca Nacional de Madrid, 1989); *Cartapacio de Francisco Morán de la Estrella* (MS 531 de la Biblioteca Real de Madrid, 1989); *Cartapacio de poesías varias* (MS 2803 de la Biblioteca Real de Madrid, 1989); *Poesías del Maestro León y Fray Melchor de la Serna y Otros (S. XVI)* (MS 961 de la Biblioteca Real de Madrid, 1991); and *Tabla de los principios de la poesía española (siglos XVI–XVIII)* (1993). Besides a forthcoming critical edition of *Cancionero de poesías varias* (MS 1587 de la Biblioteca Real de Madrid, 1994), further newly accessible material includes Diego Hurtado de Mendoza's *El Cancionero sevillano* (MS B-2486, Hispanic Society of America), *Romancero de Palacio* (MS 996 de la Biblioteca Real de Madrid), and *Cancionero autógrafo de Pedro de Padilla* (MS 1579 de la Biblioteca Real de Madrid).

    8.   Electa Arenal and Georgina Sabat de Rivers, *Literatura conventual femenina: Sor Marcela de San Félix, hija de Lope de Vega: Obra completa* (Barcelona: Publicaciones de la Universidad, 1988), 16.

    9.   Compare the word *virago,* which in the late fifteenth century designated women of superior strength, learning, and accomplishments (e.g., Queen Isabel and Santa Teresa); after five centuries of deprecating feminine learning, insulting connotations include mean-tempered, spiteful, and so forth.

    10.   Compare Malón de Chaide, *La Conversión de Magdalena* (Madrid: Espasa-Calpe, 1958).

    11.   Emily James Putnam, *The Lady: Studies in Certain Significant Phases of Her History,* cited by Arenal and Schlau, 5.

    12.   Several women interviewed by Ugalde in *Conversaciones y poemas* mention avoiding gender-specific language; others adopt masculine voice.

    13.   Cruz and Whitnall, 44–45.

    14.   Julia Otxoa, *Emakume Olerkariak/Poetas vascas* (Madrid: Ediciones Torremozas, 1990), provides an introductory historical overview, bibliography of basic references, and bilingual anthology of five recent women poets in Euskera and fourteen of Basque culture writing in Castilian.

    15.   Jon Kortázar, "La Poesía vasca actual," in *El Estado de las poesías* (Oviedo: Caja de Ahorros de Asturias, 1986), 132–39.

Chapter Two

    1.   Susan Kirkpatrick focuses on Romanticism proper in Spain in *Las Románticas: Women Writers and Subjectivity in Spain, 1835–1850* (Berkeley: University of California Press, 1989); hereafter cited in text. She treats Carolina Coronado, Gertrudis Gómez de Avellaneda, and "transitional" novelist "Fernán Caballero" (pseudonym of Cecilia Böhl de Faber). Kirkpatrick's Introduction to *Antología poética de escritoras del siglo XIX* (Madrid: Castalia/Instituto de la Mujer, 1992) accompanies poems representing three "generations" and some 30 writers. The first generation, born 1810–30, includes 14 women; the second, born 1831–49, includes nine; and the third, born 1850–69, six.

2. See Elena Catena's Introduction to *Gertrudis Gómez de Avellaneda: Poesías y epistolario de amor y amistad* (Madrid: Castalia/Instituto de la Mujer, 1989), 20.

3. My translation from María del Carmen Simón Palmer, "Escritoras españolas del siglo XIX o el miedo a la marginación," *Anales de Literatura Española* 2 (1983): 477–83.

4. See *Antología poética de escritoras del siglo XIX*. The women's biographies coincide in (1) loss of children, arousing outpourings of maternal grief; (2) liberal leanings (except for Grassi and Sinués); and (3) abolitionism.

5. See *Carolina Coronado: Poesías. Edición, introducción y notas de Noël Valis* (Madrid: Castalia/Biblioteca de Escritoras, 1991), 7–41. Using Coronado's second lyric collection (1852), Noël Valis incorporates the 37 poems of the 1843 collection, adding 182 others, plus some 40 poems published in periodicals. Fernando Manso Amarillo, *Carolina Coronado: Su obra literaria* (Badajoz: Diputación Provincial, 1992), provides a detailed biography and study of Coronado's poetry.

6. My translation from Gregorio Torres Nebrera, *Carolina Coronado* (Mérida: Editora Regional de Extremadura, 1986), 4.

7. Hartzenbusch's Prologue to Coronado's *Poesías* (Madrid, 1843), cited by Isabel María Pérez González, *Carolina Coronado* (Badajoz: Diputación Provincial, 1986).

8. Bridget Aldaraca treats this stereotype in *El Angel del hogar: Galdós and the Ideology of Domesticity in Spain* (Chapel Hill: University of North Carolina Press, 1991).

9. See Donald L. Shaw, *Historia de la literatura española: El siglo XIX* (Barcelona: Ariel, 1973), 80. Noël Valis indicates that, in 1877, 81 percent of Spanish women were illiterate (30, n34).

10. Angel Fernández de los Ríos, "La Señorita Doña Carolina Coronado," *Semanario Pintoresco Español* 15 (April 1850); quoted by Pérez González *Carolina Coronado*, 36.

11. Novels by Coronado include *Jarilla* (Madrid: M. Tello, 1873), reprinted as *Jarilla: Páginas de un diario; Adoración* (Madrid: Biblioteca Universal, 1951); *La Sigea*, 2 vols. (Madrid: Anselmo Santa Coloma, 1854); *La Rueda de la desgracia: Manuscrito de un conde* (Madrid: M. Tello, 1873). Her *Poesías completas* (Mexico: Librería Hispano-Mexicana, 1884) contained a Prologue by Emilio Castelar, for whom Coronado obtained royal pardon.

12. S. García, *Las Ideas literarias en España entre 1840–1850* (Berkeley: University of California Press, 1971), 8; cited by Gregorio Torres Nebrera, *Carolina Coronado: Treinta y nueve poemas y una prosa (Antología Poética 1840–1904)* (Mérida: Editorial Regional de Extremadura, 1986), 42.

13. J. M. Díez Taboada, *La Mujer ideal: Aspectos y fuentes de las "Rimas" de Bécquer* (Madrid: CSIC, 1965), 6; cited by Torres 1986, 44.

14. Ricardo Navas Ruiz, *El Romanticismo Español*, 3d ed. rev. (Madrid: Cátedra, 1982), 365–66.

15. Vicente Llorens, *El Romanticismo Español* (Madrid: Fundación March/Castalia, 1979), 580–86.

16. Gerardo Diego, "Primavera poética de Carolina Coronado," *Boletín de la Biblioteca Menéndez Pelayo* 38 (1962): 385–409.

17. Liliana Trevizan, "Carolina Coronado y el canon," *Monographic Review/Revista monográfica* 6 (1990): 25–35.

18. Published in *La Ilustración: Album de las Damas* 8 (2 November 1845); formerly *La Gaceta de las Mujeres,* directed by Avellaneda.

19. Originally included in *Poesías de la señorita Doña Carolina Coronado* (Madrid, 1852).

20. Valis cites Emily Dickinson as one for whom "poetess" was an unpleasant epithet (twentieth-century connotations are still insulting).

21. Valis cites Alberto Castilla, *Carolina Coronado de Perry* (Madrid: Ediciones Beramar, 1987). These three are James Cortada, "An Isabeline Poet: Carolina Coronado," *Revista de estudios hispánicos* 12 (1978): 313–20; Monroe Hafter, "Carolina Coronado as a Novelist," *Kentucky Romance Quarterly* 30, no. 4 (1983): 403–18; and Noël Valis, "The Language of Treasure: Carolina Coronado, Casta Esteban, and Marina Romero," in *In the Feminine Mode: Essays on Hispanic Women Writers,* ed. Noël Valis and Carol Maier (Lewisburg, Pa., and London: Bucknell University Press, 1990), 246–72.

22. See Ricardo Navas Ruiz, *Maria Josepa Massanés: Antología poética* (Madrid: Castalia, 1992), and Kirkpatrick, *Antología poética de escritoras del siglo XIX.*

23. María del Carmen Simón Palmer, *Escritoras españolas del siglo XIX: Manual bio-bibliográfico* (Madrid: Castalia, 1991), demonstrates dramatic increases in women's writing after Romanticism.

24. Selected poems were published by Josefina Romo, *Poetas románticas desconocidas* (Madrid: Librería Internacional, 1979), plus Romo's study, *Concepción Estevarena: Poetisa romántica* (Madrid, 1965).

25. The major English source is Hugh A. Harter, *Gertrudis Gómez de Avellaneda* (Boston: G. K. Hall/Twayne Publishers, 1981). Other data on Avellaneda's life come from Catena, *Gertrudis Gómez de Avellaneda.*

26. *The Love Letters,* trans. Dorrey Malcolm; introduction by José A. Portuondo (Havana: Juan Fernández Burgos, 1956).

27. Raimundo Lazo, *Gertrudis Gómez de Avellaneda: La Mujer y la poetisa* (Mexico: Editorial Porrúa, S. A., 1972).

28. Both Victoriano García Martí ("Rosalía de Castro o el dolor de vivir," Preface to the sixth edition of her *Obras completas* [Madrid: Aguilar, 1966], 16; hereafter cited in text as *OC*) and Benito Varela Jácome (ed., *Rosalía de Castro: Obra poética* [Barcelona: publisher, 1972], 15) state that María Francisca Martínez (a servant) acted as godmother and foster parent. Marina Mayoral (*La Poesía de Rosalía de Castro* [Madrid: Brugera, 1974], 572–73) and Juan Barja (ed., *Cantares gallegos* and *Follas novas* [Madrid: Akal, 1985]) say the caretaker was Teresa Martínez Viojo.

29. Marina Mayoral (ed., *Rosalía de Castro: En las orillas del Sar* [Madrid: Castalia, 1976]) believes orthographic manuscript errors owe to insufficient schooling (13).

30. Mayoral (cited by Kathleen Kulp-Hill, *Rosalía de Castro* [Boston: G. K. Hall/Twayne Publishers, 1977]) states that the second child was Aura (1868), followed by twins Gala and Ovidio (1871), Amara (1873 or 1874), and Honorato Alejandro, who died at 18 months. Valentina was stillborn (1877).

31. Ramón Piñeiro's Prologue to Matilde Albert Robatto, *Rosalía de Castro y la condición femenina* (Madrid: Ediciones Partenón, 1981), mentions Rosalía's "supposed frustrations . . . because of her husband's matrimonial infidelities" (xvi).

32. Rof Carballo, cited by Albert (10), suggests having no father explains the strange cruelty of Castro's fictional males in *Flavio* and *El Caballero de las botas azules*.

33. *Rosalía de Castro: Antología,* ed. Matilde Albert Robatto Basilio Losada (Estela [Navarra]: Salvat Editores, 1985), 1, 18; hereafter cited in text.

34. Albert, Alonso Montero, Díaz, and Fiorentino stress her advocacy of victims.

35. Clearly, Murguía was a key figure in Rosalía's literary development, although Mayoral (577–80) questions his influence, as does Alonso Montero (24–25). Others term the marriage stable, although conflictive (Fermín Bouza Brey, Prologue, *Cantares gallegos* [Vigo: Galaxia, 1970], 12; Ricardo Carballo Calero, "Contribución ao estudo das fontes literarias de Rosalía," *Sobre lingua e literatura galega* [Vigo: Galaxia, 1971], 9–78; Juan Naya Pérez, *Inéditos de Rosalía* [Santiago: Patronato de Rosalía de Castro, 1953], 75–89). Albert argues that only serious marital problems explain Murguía's destruction of Rosalía's correspondence.

36. *En las orillas del Sar* (Barcelona: TAIFA, 1984), 44; hereafter cited in text.

Chapter Three

1. Kathleen N. March, *Festa da Palabra* (New York: Peter Lang Publishing, 1989), 10.

2. *Women Writers of Spain: An Annotated Bio-Bibliographical Guide,* edited by Carolyn L. Galerstein (Westport, Conn.: Greenwood Press, 1986). The contributors of the Herrera entry indicate that she was "antifeminist" but offer no evidence.

3. March includes Herrera ("Galician Literary Foremothers"), affirming that "no other woman [except Pardo Bazán] has achieved the position of official academician in Galicia" (8). Casanova, however, was elected to the Royal Galician Academy in 1906.

4. Biographical information on Casanova comes principally from Ofelia Alayeto, *Sofía Pérez Casanova (1861–1958): Spanish Poet, Journalist and*

Author (Potomac, Md.: Scripta Humanistica, 1992). See also Ofelia Alayeto, "Sofía Casanova: A Bibliography," *Bulletin of Bibliography* 44, no. 1 (1987): 46–61. I am indebted to Alayeto for photocopies of Casanova's inaccessible poetry.

5. Sofía Casanova, *Poesías* (Madrid: Imprenta de A. J. Alaria, 1885).
6. *Fugaces* (Coruña: Andrés Martínez, Editor, 1898).
7. Ofelia Alayeto, "The Poetry of Sofía Casanova" *Monographic Review/Revista monográfica* 6 (1990 [1991]): 36–45.
8. A second edition of *El Cancionero de la dicha* was published the following year (Madrid: R. Velasco, Impresor, 1912).

Chapter Four

1. I cite from the most complete edition of Chacel's poetry: *Poesía (1931–1991)* (Barcelona: Tusquets Editores, 1992), including authorial forewords to the 1978 *Versos prohibidos* and 1985 *A la orilla de un pozo*. Quotation is from p. 240 of *Poesía (1931–1991)*.
2. José Corredor-Matheos, Prologue, *Clementina Arderiu: Antología* (Barcelona: Plaza y Janés, 1982), 12; hereafter cited in text as *Antología*. Other biographical data come from Robert Saladrigas, "Monólogo con Clementina Arderiu," *Destino* 1840 (6 January 1973): 32–33.
3. Cèlia Viñas Olivella (1915–1954), considered one of Catalan poetry's most promising new voices, died at 39 (see Chapter 8).
4. Little information exists on Méndez (omitted from Galerstein 1986); I am indebted to Julia Otxoa (1990) and Catherine Bellver, "Exile and the Female Experience in the Poetry of Concha Méndez," *Anales de la literatura española contemporánea* 18, nos. 1–2 (1993): 27–42. Bellver cites Margery Resnick, "La Inteligencia audaz: Vida y poesía de Concha Méndez," *Papeles de Son Armadans* 88, no. 263 (1978): 131–46, which I have not seen. Mirta Camandone in *Escritura sin fronteras: Poesía española desde 1936* [first part, 1936–44] (New York: Lang, 1992) briefly mentions Méndez (p. 61). I have been unable to examine Paloma Ulacia Altolaguirre, *Concha Méndez: Memorias habladas, memorias armadas* (Madrid: Mondadori, 1990).
5. Otxoa (31) gives different dates on some titles by Méndez: *Surtidor* (1926), *Inquietudes* (1927), *Canciones de mar y tierra* (1931), *Vida a vida* (1932), *Niño y sombras* (1935), *Poemas, sombras y sueños* (1944), and *Vida o río* (1979).
6. Carlos Murciano, "Presencia de Antonio Machado en la poesía de Pilar de Valderrama" (22), Prologue, *De Mar a Mar* (Madrid: Torremozas, 1984).
7. See Valderrama's posthumous *Sí, soy Guiomar (Memorias de mi vida)* (Barcelona: Plaza y Janés, 1981). Earlier she confided in Concha Espina, who published *De Antonio Machado a su grande y secreto amor.*
8. *In the Feminine Mode: Essays on Hispanic Women Writers,* ed. Noël Valis and Carol Maier (Lewisburg, Pa.: Bucknell University Press, 1990), 11.

Both editors treat Romero; Maier offers personal reminiscences, and Valis emphasizes *Sin agua, el mar* (1961) in "The Language of Treasure." Camandone briefly mentions Romero (113).

9. Anthologized by Francisco Carenas, *Poetas españoles en U.S.A.* (Madrid: Rialp, 1972), 61–66 (including Jorge Guillén, Manuel Durán, Germán Bleiberg, Marina Romero, Concha Zardoya, Ana María Fagundo, and Julia Uceda).

10. Marina Romero, *Honda raíz* (Madrid: Torremozas, 1989), 21.

11. Julia Otxoa's bilingual anthology *Emakume Olerkariak/Poetas vascas* (Madrid: Torremozas, 1989), concentrating on post-Franco writers, considers culture more important than language of expression; women born in Basque areas or of Basque parentage are considered Basque poets even when writing in Castilian.

12. Biographical data come from José Angel Asunce, *Ernestina de Champourcín: Poesía a través del tiempo* (Barcelona: Anthropos, 1991); Luzmaría Jiménez Faro's Introduction to the Torremozas anthology; Arturo del Villar's articles "Ernestina de Champourcín" (*La Estafeta Literaria* 556 [15 January 1975]) and "La Vida con la palabra de Ernesta de Champourcín" (*Alaluz* 2 [Fall 1986]: 5–9); and various interviews with Champourcín cited by Asunce. Andrew Debicki ("Una Dimensión olvidada de la poesía española de los '20 y '30: La Lírica visionaria de Ernestina de Champourcín," *Ojáncano* 1, no. 1 [1988]: 48–60) adapts Carlos Bousoño's concept of the "visionary" metaphor. See also Biruté Ciplijauskaité, "Escribir entre dos exilios: Las Voces femeninas de la Generación del 27," in *Homenaje al profesor Antonio Vilanova* (Barcelona: Universidad, 1989), 119–26.

13. See Galerstein, *Spanish Women Writers*. Landeira omits the then-unpublished *Huyeron todas las islas,* which Asunce combines with *La Pared transparente* to create his fourth and final division.

14. Highlighted in Juan Cano Ballesta, *La Poesía española entre pureza y revolución 1930–1936* (Madrid: Gredos, 1972), 69–71.

15. All quotations come from the Asunce edition, *Poesía a través del tiempo,* the most nearly complete poems.

16. While never as much of an esthete as her husband, Champourcín reacts with disgust to the neorealist and neonaturalist content of Spanish "social poetry," suggesting she would rather quit than write in that vein.

Chapter Five

1. On the inconsistent critical roster of "official" membership in the Generation of 1927, see Janet Pérez, "On Misapplications of the Generational Label," *Letras Peninsulares* 6, no. 1 (1993): 31–50.

2. Taped interviews by Zenaida Gutiérrez-Vega and Marie-Lise Gazarian-Gautier, *Carmen Conde, de viva voz* (Montclair, N.J.: Senda Nueva de Ediciones, 1992), 47; hereafter cited in text as *Voz.*

3. Proliferation of putative generations—those of 1925, 1927, 1930

(if Conde's entry is accepted), and 1936—undermines critical credibility and usefulness.

4. Recent bibliography appears in *Voz,* listing 92 books plus eight records and cassettes; the latest work published under Conde's name is dated 1987 (142–47). Conde's total is difficult to determine: manuscripts are cited interchangeably with published works. See *Obra poética, 1929–1966* (Madrid: Biblioteca Nueva, 1979) (hereafter cited in text as *OP*) and *Memoria puesta en olvido* (Madrid: Torremozas, 1987), subtitled "Personal Anthology" and containing work from early postwar years not included in *Obra poética.* Conde changes titles without explanation: *El Escorial* (1940; *Memoria puesta en olvido,* 25–35) first appeared in *Obra poética* as *Mío; Enajenado mirar* (written 1962–64) is represented by a partial selection (*Memoria puesta en olvido,* 157–90), like *Desde nunca (Memoria puesta en olvido,* 251–75), published only in part. Reference to *Signo de amor* (1945) appears only in Leopoldo de Luis's Introduction to the 1985 reedition of *Mujer sin Edén.*

5. In *The Dictionary of Literary Biography* (vol. 108, *Twentieth-Century Spanish Poets: First Series,* ed. Michael Perna, 88–99 [New York: Bruccoli, Clark, Layman, 1991]) biographer Pilar Martín indicates that Conde was born in 1901, citing *Por el camino viendo sus orillas.* The cover "blurb" (vol. 3 of *Por el camino*) gives the year customarily given: 1907. *Empezando la vida* states that upon the family's financial ruin in 1913, Conde's father was 39, her mother 34, and their daughter six (*Obra poética,* 123).

6. Josefina Inclán in *Carmen Conde y el mar/Carmen Conde and the Sea* (Miami: Ediciones Universal, 1980) investigates oceanic language and the symbolic dimensions thereof. Conde describes the sea's effects upon her, infusing vitality, strength, joy, will, and self-confidence, while rocky interior landscapes achieve the opposite effects (cf. *Por el camino viendo sus orillas,* 3: 49–50, 52–53).

7. Rubio Paredes found no evidence of publication but reproduces a homage (1953) mentioning a novelette, *El Reino de los que sufren* (The Kingdom of Those Who Suffer), ca. 1925 (23–25).

8. All quotations from Conde, unless otherwise indicated, are from *Obra poética, 1929–1966;* hereafter cited as *OP,* with my translations.

9. Candelas Newton, "El Discurso heroico de Carmen Conde," *Monographic Review/Revista Monográfica* 6 (1990): 62.

10. María Concepción Ruiz Abellán (in *Cultura y ocio en una ciudad de retaguardia durante la guerra civil {Murcia, 1936–1939}* [Murcia: Real Academia de Alfonso el Sabio, 1993], 178–81) makes no mention of Conde's wartime writings; works by obscure provincial intellectuals (all male) are cited.

11. *Mi libro de El Escorial* (1949; My Book of the Escorial), inspired—like *Mío*—by residing there (1940), provides personal reactions to Castile. With only the title changed, Conde reprinted it in *Memoria puesta en olvido* (1987).

12. Leopoldo de Luis, Prologue to Carmen Conde, *Mujer sin Edén* (Madrid: Torremozas, 1985), 12. Discussion of *Woman* refers to this most accessible edition.

13. Concha Zardoya, "*Mujer sin Edén,* poema vivo de Carmen Conde," *Poesía española contemporánea,* 637ff.

14. Víctor García de la Concha, "Pasión de Carmen Conde" and "Dramaticamente arraigada," in *La Poesía española de 1935 a 1975,* 2: 517–27.

15. Judith Richards, "The World without End: Mythic and Linguistic Revision in Carmen Conde Abellán's *Mujer sin Edén,*" *Monographic Review/Revista Monográfica* 6 (1990): 71–80.

16. Manuel Alvar, Introduction ("Tras los símbolos y los mitos en unos poemas de Carmen Conde") to Carmen Conde, *Cráter* (Madrid: Editorial Biblioteca Nueva, 1985).

Chapter Six

1. Ricardo Gullón, "Dos grupos generacionales de posguerra," *Historia de la literatura española: Epoca contemporánea, 1939–1950;* Carmen Conde, *Poesía femenina española (1939–1950)* (Barcelona: Bruguera, 1970); Angel del Río, *Historia de la literatura española: Desde 1700 hasta nuestros días;* José Luis Cano, *Lírica española de hoy* (Madrid: Gredos, 1975); *El Tema de España en la poesía española contemporánea* (Madrid: Revista de Occidente, 1964); and *Poetas del 50: I. Antología de la lírica femenina actual* (Madrid: Coculsa, 1969).

2. Mercedes Rodríguez Pequeño (in *La Poesía de Concha Zardoya* [Valladolid: Universidad, 1987], 36) cites an interview from *La Estafeta Literaria* 589 (June 1976).

3. Rodríguez Pequeño lists these unpublished works: *Violencia del duelo* (1937–38), *Memorial de la guerra, Agreste voz, Sólo el amor,* and *Loas y elegías a una rosa,* indicating that Zardoya decided never to publish her "immature efforts."

4. Among 120 entries in the secondary bibliography, 30 are anthologies mentioning Zardoya or including samples of her work: the remainder are "critical evaluations"—mostly book reviews in newspapers of Spain and Latin America. More significant criticism appears in *Sin Nombre* (San Juan, Puerto Rico [October–December 1978]), dedicated to Zardoya. Manuel Durán, Andrew Debicki, Biruté Ciplijauskaité, and Ana María Fagundo have written insightfully on Zardoya.

5. H. Ernest Lewald, review of Concha Zardoya's *Corral de vivos y muertos,* in *Books Abroad* (1966): 323.

6. In *Alaluz* 4, no. 1 (Spring 1972): 37–38.

7. See Ana María Fagundo's "Poetas femeninas españolas siglo XX: 1900–1940," *Alaluz* 20, nos. 1–2 (Spring–Fall 1988): 17.

8. John C. Wilcox, "A Reconsideration of Two Spanish Women Poets: Angela Figuera Aymerich and Francisca Aguirre," *Studies in 20th Century Literature* 16, no. 1 (Winter 1992): 65–92.

9. Besides the Wilcox essay, see Santiago Daydi-Tolson, *The Post–Civil War Spanish Social Poets* (Boston: Twayne Publishers, 1983), 93–99; Nancy Mandlove, "*Historia* and *Intra-historia:* Two Spanish Women Poets in Dialogue

with History," *Third Woman* 2, no. 2 (1984): 84–93; Roberta Quance's Introduction to Figuera's *Obras completas* (Madrid: Hiperión, 1986), 11–19; Robert Saladrigas, "Monólogo con Angela Figuera," *Destino,* 23 November 1974, 48–49; and Eleanor Wright, *The Poetry of Protest under Franco* (London: Tamesis, 1986), 154–57. Selected poems appear in *Recent Poetry of Spain: A Bilingual Anthology,* ed. and trans. Louis Hammer and Sara Schyfter (Old Chatham, N.Y.: Sachem Press, 1983), 140–49, including "My Lover's Flesh," "Insomnia," "Women of the Market," "The Jail," "When My Father Painted," "If You Haven't Died for an Instant," and "Symbol."

10.   In *Poesía hispánica, 1939–1969: Estudio y antología* (Barcelona: El Bardo, 1970), 89. This critic also includes Fuertes, but no additional women.

11.   Cited by Pablo González Rodas, Introduction, *Historia de Gloria: Amor, humor y desamor,* 4th ed. (Madrid: Cátedra, 1983), 33–34; hereafter cited in text as *HG*.

12.   Gloria Fuertes, *Obras incompletas* (Madrid: Cátedra, 1984), 41; hereafter cited in text as *OI*.

13.   Arturo del Villar, "Gloria Fuertes, poeta para todo (y de guardia)," *La Estafeta literaria* 580 (15 January 1976): 12–14.

14.   Brenda Logan Cappuccio, "Gloria Fuertes frente a la crítica," *Anales de la literatura española contemporánea* 18, no. 1 (1993): 89. Besides reviews or short "blurbs" in some 20 anthologies or general surveys, criticism on Fuertes includes some 20 critical essays—see Cappuccio's bibliography—a master's thesis and doctoral dissertation. Cappuccio also published "Hambre y poesía: Una breve biografía de Gloria Fuertes" in the same issue (323–44). Selected poems by Fuertes appear in *Recent Poetry of Spain,* 150–63, including "Biographical Note," "Let's Not Waste Time," "The Man's Departure," "Look at Me Here," "I Fell," "Old-Age Asylum for the Poor," "Homage to Rubén Darío," "The Truth Inside the Lie," and "Don't Run Away from Pain."

15.   In *After the War: Essays on Recent Spanish Poetry,* ed. Salvador Jiménez-Fajardo and John Wilcox (Boulder, Colo.: SSSAS, 1984), 47–54. Stycos notes also Zardoya's expanding intertextuality in *Los Ríos caudales,* requiring readers to be familiar with works of the poets of 1927 as well as the relevant literary criticism (52–53).

16.   See *Poesía española contemporánea: Las Generaciones de postguerra* (Madrid: Guadarrama, 1974), one of several anthologies by Cano, who includes proportionately more women and figures among the critics who have most thoroughly studied Fuertes. Leopoldo de Luis, *Poesía social: Antología, 1939–1964* (Madrid: Alfaguara, 1965), includes four women: Figuera, Fuertes, Lacaci, and Beneyto, but only Figuera achieves mention—a scant half-dozen lines—in his introductory essay.

17.   Andrew Debicki (in "Gloria Fuertes: Intertextuality and Reversal of Expectations," *Poetry of Discovery: The Spanish Generation of 1956–1971* [Lexington: University Press of Kentucky, 1982], 81–101) notes that Fuertes's use of intertexts and her epistemology resemble aspects of younger poets and

classes her with José Angel Valente, Claudio Rodríguez, Francisco Brines, and others of the Generation of 1956–71.

18. This poet (included in *Joven poesía española,* ed. Concepción G. Moral and Rosa María Pereda [Madrid: Cátedra, 1980]) coincides with Fuertes in his use of irony and humor, cultivation of erotic themes, love poetry, and "surprise" endings. This anthology contains 17 male poets and no women.

19. Silvia R. Sherno (in "Gloria Fuertes' Room of Her Own," *Letras Femeninas* 16, nos. 1–2 [1990]: 85–99, and "Gloria Fuertes and the Poetics of Solitude," *Anales de la literatura española* 12, no. 3 [1987]: 311–26) emphasizes interconnected themes of solitude and the void, noting Fuertes's bizarre guises and confontation of loneliness. Sherno lists three forthcoming essays on Fuertes, of which I have seen one—"Weaving the World: The Poetry of Gloria Fuertes," *Hispania* 72, no. 2 (May 1989): 247–55, which stresses Fuertes's awareness of her individuality, noncomformity, "outlandish character," and marginality and solitude. Sherno notes the poet's emphasis on marginality, affirming that Fuertes regards her solitude placidly (248), although she apparently lives in a house full of ghosts and spirits, "in an eerie atmosphere where odd things are the norm" (249). See also Nancy Mandlove, "Oral Texts: The Play of Orality and Literacy in the Poetry of Gloria Fuertes," *Siglo XX/20th Century* 5, nos. 1–2 (1987–88): 11–16, where she analyzes "consciously cultivated secondary orality: orality mediated and transformed by literacy" (12). Mandlove's "Used Thread: The Transparent Language of Gloria Fuertes and Angel González" (published by Margaret A. Persin, Andrew P. Debicki, Mandlove and Robert Spires under the joint title "Meta-Literature and Recent Spanish Literature," *Revista Canadiense de Estudios Hispánicos* 7, no. 2 [1983]: 297–309) examines how Fuertes manipulates "clichés so that they again must be taken literally" (302), returning used language to pristine condition. Mandlove treats Fuertes's quest for communication—poetry accessible to all—in "The Letter-Poems of Gloria Fuertes," *Letras Femeninas* 10, no. 1 (Spring 1984): 33–38, noting the frequency of linguistically commonplace, incongruous, or inappropriate contexts, requiring readers to resolve ambiguities or create new meaning. See also Margaret Persin, "Gloria Fuertes and (Her) Feminist Reader," *Revista/Review Interamericana* 12 (Spring 1982): 125–32, and Vicente Araguas, "Un Poco de Gloria," *Antípodas* 2 (December 1989): 141–47. Similar observations appear in Candelas Newton, "La Palabra 'convertida' de Gloria Fuertes," *Letras femeninas* 13, nos. 1–2 (Spring–Summer 1987): 1–11, which emphasizes "frases hechas, canciones, refranes, y otras fórmulas archiconocidas" (2). Newton traces how Fuertes reelabora clichés via substitutions, creating original and surprising poetic artifacts, revitalizing language that had lost its semantic charge.

Chapter Seven

1. See Andrew Debicki, *Poetry of Discovery* (Lexington: University of Kentucky Press, 1983), and José María de Castellet, *Nueve novísimos poetas*

españoles (Barcelona: Barral Editores, 1970). Castellet's lengthy introduction constitutes the first critical analysis of this emerging trend, evincing replacement of "social" esthetics and the "postwar" mentality.

2.   José Ortega's essay "Tiempo de soledad en la poesía de Elena Martín Vivaldi," *Monographic Review/Revista monográfica* 6 (1990): 105–12, views solitude as preceding confrontation between the Self and Other; it reflects not lack of social and familial relationships but lack or loss of the Other (105–106). Solitude facilitates self-encounter (107) but may be exacerbated by the impossibility of return to the past, before loss of the Other (108–109). Silence, night, and dreams intensify solitude (110).

3.   See María Dolores de Asís, "El Sentimiento de soledad en la poesía de Elena Martín Vivaldi," *Antípodas* 2 (1989): 129–40.

4.   Ramón Buenaventura, ed., *Las Diosas blancas,* 2d ed. (Madrid: Hiperión, 1986).

5.   *Poesía española contemporánea: Las Generaciones de postguerra,* "Concha de Marco y su *Diario de la mañana*" (Madrid: Guadarrama, 1974), 188–92.

6.   Susana Cavallo (in "The Quiescent Muse of Susana March" (*Monographic Review/Revista monográfica* 6 [1990]: 81–92) recapitulates March's publishing history, exclusion from "definitive" anthologies, marginality, surprising versatility, the significant presence of a male interlocutor or Other (lover, husband, son), and important silences or deletions.

7.   Susana Rivera, ed., *Ultima voz del exilio (El grupo poético hispano-mexicano): Antología* (Madrid: Hiperión, 1990). Of 10 poets included, Parés is the only woman.

8.   Elisa Vásquez de Gey, *Queimar as meigas* (Madrid: Torremozas, 1988), considers as Galician those born in Galicia, regardless of language of expression.

9.   *Poesía española contemporánea: Las Generaciones de postguerra* (Madrid: Guadarrama, 1974), 181–87. The title *Molinillo de papel* (Paper Windmill), attributed to Lacaci, appeared without publication data.

10.   "Entrevista a Acacia Uceta," *Letras Femeninas* 12, nos. 1–2 (1986): 121–30.

Chapter Eight

1.   Elisa Vázquez de Gey, *Queimar as Meigas* (Madrid: Torremozas, 1988), and Kathleen March, *Festa da Palabra* (New York: Peter Lang, 1989). Vázquez's work, subtitled "Galicia: 50 Years of Women's Poetry," emphasizes the half-century after the Civil War.

2.   See J. M. Castellet and Joaquim Molas, *Poesía catalana del segle XX,* 2d ed. (Barcelona: Ediciones 62, 1978), and Joan Triadú, *Nova antologia de la poesia catalana (De Maragall als nostres dies),* 2d ed. (Barcelona: Editorial Selecta, 1973).

3. March lists this variant title (11). Miguel González Garcés, *Poesía gallega de posguerra (1939–1975)* (Coruña: Ediciones del Castro, 1976), terms *Verba que comenza* unpublished, written during Mariño's final year of life (55–67).

4. For instance, *Diccionario de autores ilustres, The World Who's Who of Women,* and *The International Authors and Writers Who's Who.*

5. Mirta Camandone de Cohen, "De pasión y belleza: De pasión por la belleza: La Poesía de Pura Vázquez," *Actas do segundo congreso de estudios Galegos: Homenaxe a José Amor y Vázquez* (Vigo: Galaxia, 1990), 397–404.

6. M. Angels Anglada (in "Carme Montoriol," *Literatura de Dones: Una visió del Mon* [Barcelona: La Sal, 1988]) states that a collection of unpublished love poems was found after Montoriol's death.

7. I am indebted to Cristina Enríquez de Salamanca for furnishing photocopies of Gay's poems as well as essential biographical data.

8. See Celia Viñas, *Antología lírica* (Madrid: Rialp, 1976).

Selected Bibliography

Albert i Paradis, Caterina (pseudonym of Víctor Català). *Els cants dels mesos.* Barcelona, 1901.
———. *El Llibre blanc.* Barcelona, 1951.
———. *Quatre monòlegs.* Barcelona, 1901.
Albornoz, Aurora de. *Brazo de niebla.* Santander: Isla de los Ratones, 1957.
———. *Prosas de Paris.* San Juan, Puerto Rico: 1959.
———. *Poemas para alcanzar un segundo.* Madrid: Rialp, 1961.
———. *Palabras desatadas.* Málaga, 1974.
———. *Hacia la realidad creada.* Barcelona: Península, 1979.
———. *Palabras reunidas (1969–1979).* Madrid: Ayuso, 1983.
Arderiu i Voltas, Clementina. *Cançons i elegies.* Barcelona: La Revista, 1916.
———. *L'Alta llibertat.* Barcelona: Catalana, 1920.
———. *Cant i paraules.* Barcelona: Lira, 1936.
———. *Sempre i ara.* Barcelona: Societat Aliança d'Arts Gràfiques, 1946.
———. *Poesies completes.* Prologue by Salvador Espriu. Barcelona: Selecta, 1952.
———. *Es a dir.* Barcelona: Ossa Menor, 1959.
———. *Antologia poètica.* Bilingual text. Madrid: Rialp, 1961. 2d ed. (enlarged), Barcelona: Plaza y Janés, 1982.
———. *L'Esperança encara.* Prologue by Joaquim Molas. Barcelona: Edicions 62, 1969.
———. *Obra poètica.* Prologue by Joan Teixidor. Barcelona: Edicions 62, 1973.
Armengol de Badia, Agnes. *Ramell de semprevives. Poesies.* Sabadell: Imprenta M. Torner, 1891.
———. *Redempció.* Sabadell: Biblioteca Sabadellenca, 1925.
———. *Sabadellenques i altres poesies.* Sabadell: Oradors de Joan Sallent, 1925.
———. *Els dies clars.* Sabadell: Tallers de Joan Sallent, 1926.
———. *Rosari Antic, tradicions i records.* Sabadell: Tallers de Joan Sallent, 1926.
Becker, Angélicka. *Figuras y meditaciones.* Madrid: Rialp, 1965.
———. *Definiciones.* Madrid: Cultura Hispánica, 1968.
Beneyto Cunyat, María. *Canción olvidada.* Valencia, 1947.
———. *Altre veu.* Valencia: Torre, 1952.
———. *Eva en el tiempo.* Valencia, 1952.
———. *Tierra viva.* Madrid: Adonais, 1956.
———. *Poemas de la ciudad.* Barcelona: Joaquín Horta, 1956.
———. *Ratlles a l'aire.* Valencia: Torre, 1956.
———. *Antología general.* Caracas: Lírica Hispana, 1956.
———. *Vida anterior.* Caracas: Lírica Hispana, 1962.
———. *Poesía, 1947–1964.* Barcelona: Plaza y Janés, 1965.

————. *La Gent que viu al món.* Valencia: L'Estel, 1966.

————. *El Agua que rodea la isla.* 1974.

————. *Biografía breve del silencio.* 1975.

————. *Vidre ferit de sang.* Gandia: Ajuntament, 1976.

Casanova de Lutoslawski, Sofía. *Poesías.* Madrid: A. J. Alaria, 1885.

————. *Fugaces.* La Coruña: A. Martínez, 1898.

————. *El Cancionero de la dicha.* Madrid: Imprenta de Regino Velasco, 1911.

Castro, Rosalía de. *La Flor (Poesías).* Madrid: "La Crónica," 1861.

————. *A mi madre.* Vigo: J. Compañel, 1863.

————. *Cantares gallegos.* Vigo: J. Compañel, 1863.

————. *Follas novas.* Prólogo de Emilio Castelar. Madrid: Biblioteca de la Propaganda Literaria, 1880.

————. *En las orillas del Sar.* Madrid: Imprenta de Ricardo Fe, 1884.

————. *Obras completas.* Madrid: Aguilar, 1966.

Chacel, Rosa. *Versos prohibidos.* Madrid: Caballo Griego para la Poesía, 1978.

————. *Poesía (1931–1991).* Barcelona: Tusquets, 1992.

Champourcín, Ernestina de. *En silencio.* Madrid: Espasa Calpe, 1926.

————. *Ahora.* Madrid: León Sánchez Cuesta, 1928.

————. *La Voz en el viento.* Madrid: Artes Gráficas, 1931.

————. *Cántico inútil.* Madrid: Aguilar, 1936.

————. *Presencia a oscuras.* Madrid: Rialp, 1952.

————. *El Nombre que me diste.* Mexico: Finisterre, 1960.

————. *Hai-kais espirituales.* Mexico: Finisterre, 1967.

————. *Cárcel de los sentidos.* Mexico: Finisterre, 1964.

————. *Cartas cerradas.* Mexico: Finisterre, 1968.

————. *Poemas del ser y del estar.* Madrid: Alfaguara, 1974.

————. *Primer Exilio.* Madrid: Rialp, 1978.

————. *La Pared transparente.* Madrid: Los libros de Fausto, 1984.

————. *Huyeron todas las islas.* Madrid: Torremozas, 1988.

Conde Abellán, Carmen. *Brocal.* Madrid: La lectura, 1929.

————. *Júbilos.* Prologue by Gabriela Mistral. Murcia: Sudeste, 1934.

————. *Soplo que va y no vuelve* (pseudonym of Florentina del Mar). Madrid: Alhambra, 1944.

————. *Mujer sin Edén.* Madrid: Ed. Jura, 1947.

————. *Sea la luz.* Madrid: Mensaje, 1947.

————. *Iluminada tierra.* Madrid, 1951.

————. *Ansia de la gracia.* Madrid: Adonais, 1952.

————. *Mientras los hombres mueren.* Milan: Editorial Disalpino, 1953.

————. *Vivientes de los siglos.* Madrid, 1957.

————. *Empezando la vida.* Tetuán, Morocco: Al-Motamid, 1955.

————. *Mi fin en el viento.* Madrid: Adonais, 1957.

————. *Los Monólogos de la hija.* Madrid, 1959.

————. *En un mundo de fugitivos.* Buenos Aires: Losada, 1960.

————. *En la tierra de nadie*. Murcia: El Laurel, 1960.

————. *Derribado arcángel*. Madrid: Revista de Occidente, 1960.

————. *Su voz le doy a la noche*. Madrid, 1962.

————. *Los Poemas del mar menor*. Murcia: Universidad, 1962.

————. *Jaguar puro inmarchito*. Madrid, 1963.

————. *Obra poética (1929–1966)*. Madrid: Biblioteca Nueva, 1967.

————. *A este lado de la eternidad*. Madrid: Biblioteca Nueva, 1970.

————. *Corrosión*. Madrid: Biblioteca Nueva, 1971.

————. *Cita con la vida*. Madrid: Biblioteca Nueva, 1976.

————. *Días por la tierra*. Madrid: Nacional, 1977.

————. *El Tiempo es un río lentísimo de fuego*. Barcelona: Ediciones 29, 1978.

————. *La Noche oscura del cuerpo*. Madrid: Biblioteca Nueva, 1980.

————. *Derraman su sangre las sombras*. Madrid, 1983.

Coronado, Carolina. *Poesías*. Madrid: Alegría y Charlain, 1843.

————. *Poesías de la señorita Doña Carolina Coronado*. Madrid: 1852.

————. *Poesías completas*. Prólogo por Emilio Castelar. Mexico: Librería Hispano-Mexicana, 1883.

————. *Poesías*. Preface by Julio Cienfuegos Linares. Badajoz: Biblioteca de Autores Extremeños, 1953.

Figuera Aymerich, Angela. *Mujer de barro: Poemas*. Madrid: SAETA, 1948.

————. *Soria pura*. Madrid: Jura, 1949.

————. *Vencida por el ángel*. Alicante: Verbo, 1950.

————. *El Grito inútil*. Alicante: Ifach, 1952.

————. *Víspera de la vida*. Madrid: Neblí, 1953.

————. *Los Días duros, Vencida por el ángel, Víspera de la vida, El grito inútil*. Madrid: Aguado, 1953.

————. *Belleza cruel*. Mexico: Compañía General de Ediciones, 1958.

————. *Primera Antología*. Caracas: Lírica Hispana, 1961.

————. *Toco la tierra: Letanías*. Madrid: Rialp, 1962.

————. *Antología*. Monterrey: Sierra Madre, 1969.

————. *Antología total, 1948–1969*. Madrid: Videosistemas, 1973.

Fuentes Blanco, María de los Reyes ("Reyes Fuentes"). *Sonetos del corazón adelante*. Arcos de la Frontera, 1960.

————. *Elegías del Uad-el-Kebir*. Seville, 1961.

————. *Romances de la miel en los labios*. Seville: La Muestra, 1962.

————. *Elegías Tartessias*. Orense: Comercial, 1964.

————. *Oración de la verdad*. Jerez: Grupo Atalaya, 1965.

————. *Acrópolis del testimonio*. Seville: Ayuntamiento, 1966.

————. *Pozo de Jacob*. Seville: Ayuntamiento, 1967.

————. *Aire de amor*. Madrid: Rialp, 1977.

Fuertes, Gloria. *Isla ignorada*. Madrid: Musa Nueva, 1950.

————. *Aconsejo beber hilo*. Madrid: Arquero, 1954.

————. *Antología y poemas del suburbio*. Caracas: Lírica Hispana, 1954.

————. *Todo asusta*. Caracas: Lírica Hispana, 1958.

————. *Que estás en la tierra . . .* Barcelona: Colección Colliure, 1962.

————. *Ni tiro, ni veneno, ni navaja*. Barcelona: El Bardo, 1966.

————. *Poeta de guardia*. Barcelona: El Bardo, 1968.

————. *Cómo atar los bigotes del tigre*. Barcelona: El Bardo, 1969.

————. *Antología poética, 1950–1969*. Prologue by Francisco Ynduráin. Barcelona: Plaza y Janés, 1970.

————. *Sola en la sala*. Zaragoza: Javalambre, 1973.

————. *Historia de Gloria*. Madrid: Cátedra, 1983.

————. *Obras incompletas*. Madrid: Cátedra, 1984.

Gatell, Angelina. *El Poema del soldado*. Valencia: Diputación, 1954.

————. *Esa oscura palabra*. Santander: Isla de los Ratones, 1963.

————. *Las Claudicaciones*. Madrid: Biblioteca Nueva, 1969.

Gay, Simona. *Aigües vives*. 1932.

————. *La Lluita amb l'angel*. 1938.

————. *La Gerra al sol*. 1965.

Grassi de Cuenca, Angela. *Poesías*. Madrid: Campo-Redondo, 1871.

Gutierrez Torrero, Concepción (pseudonym of Concha Lagos). *Balcón*. Madrid: Gráficas Bachende, 1954.

————. *Los Obstáculos*. Madrid: Agora, 1955.

————. *Al sur del recuerdo*. Madrid: Agora, 1955.

————. *El Corazón cansado*. Madrid: Agora, 1957.

————. *Agua de Dios*. Málaga: Meridiano, 1958.

————. *La Soledad de siempre*. Santander: Cantalapiedra, 1958.

————. *Arroyo claro*. Madrid: Agora, 1958.

————. *Campo abierto*. Madrid: Gráficas Orbe, 1959.

————. *Luna de enero*. Arcos de la Frontera: Alcarabán, 1960.

————. *Tema fundamental*. Madrid: Agora, 1961.

————. *Golpeando el silencio*. Caracas: Lírica Hispana, 1961.

————. *Canciones desde la barca*. Madrid: Editora Nacional, 1962.

————. *Para empezar*. Madrid: Editora Nacional, 1963.

————. *Los Anales*. Palma de Mallorca: Ediciones de Papeles de Son Armadans, 1966.

————. *Diario de un hombre*. Caracas: Arbol de Fuego, 1970.

————. *El Cerco*. Madrid: Alfaguara, 1971.

————. *La Aventura*. Madrid: Alfaguara, 1973.

————. *Fragmentos en espiral desde el pozo*. Sevilla: Aldebarán, 1974.

————. *Gótico florido*. Seville: Católica Española, 1976.

————. *Antología,1954–1976/Concha Lagos*. Barcelona: Plaza y Janés, 1976.

————. *Por las ramas*. Barcelona: Pozanco, 1980.

————. *Teoría de la inseguridad*. Madrid: Gráficas Orbe, 1980.

————. *Elegías para un álbum*. Madrid: Gráficas Orbe, 1982.

————. *La Paloma*. Alicante: Sinhaya, 1982.

————. *Más allá de la soledad.* Alicante: Sinhaya, 1984.

————. *Con el arco a punto.* Madrid: Instituto Hispano-Arabe, 1984.

————. *En la rueda del viento.* Valladolid: Miñón, 1985.

Herrera Garrido, Francisca. *Sorrisas e bágoas.* Madrid, 1913.

————. *¡Almas de muller. . . Volallas na luz!* La Coruña, 1915.

————. *Flores do noso paxareco.* La Coruña, 1919.

Kruckenberg Sanjurjo, Maria do Carme. *Cantigas a vento.* Vigo, 1956.

————. *Las Palabras olvidadas.* Vigo, 1956.

————. *Los Parajes inmóviles.* Vigo, 1956.

————. *Rumor de tiempo.* Vigo, 1957.

————. *Farol de aire.* Vigo, 1958.

————. *Poemas inevitables.* Vigo, 1960.

————. *Canaval de Ouro.* Vigo: Galaxia, 1962.

————. *Poemas y canciones de aquí y de allá.* Bilbao: Alrededor de la mesa, 1962.

————. *Memoria de mi sueño.* Vigo, 1964.

————. *Tauromaquia en línea y verso.* Vigo, 1964.

————. *Cantigas de amigo a Ramón Gonález Sierra do Pampillón.* Vigo, 1972.

————. *A sombra ergueita.* Vigo, 1976.

————. *Cantares de mi silencio.* Vigo: Acebo, 1980.

Laborda Medir, Clemencia. *Jardines bajo la lluvia.* Madrid: Afrodisio Aguado, 1943.

————. *Ciudad de soledades.* Madrid, 1948.

————. *Retorno a la provincia.* Caracas: Lírica Hispana, 1961.

————. *Tiempo del hombre, tiempo de Dios.* Madrid, 1972.

Lacaci, María Elvira. *Humana voz.* Madrid: Rialp, 1957.

————. *Sonido de Dios.* Madrid: Rialp, 1962.

————. *Al este de la ciudad.* Barcelona: Juan Flors, 1963.

Lacasa, Cristina. *La Voz oculta.* Lérida: Editora Leridiana, 1953.

————. *Los Brazos en estela.* Lérida: Gráficos Artis, 1958.

————. *Un Resplandor que no perdonó la noche.* Barcelona: Atzavara, 1961.

————. *Con el sudor alzado.* Madrid: Agora, 1964.

————. *Poemas de la muerte y de la vida.* Lérida: Diputación Provincial, 1966.

————. *Encender los olivos como lámparas.* Madrid: Agora, 1969.

————. *Ha llegado la hora.* Caracas: Arbol de Fuego, 1971.

————. *Opalos del instante.* Madrid: Rialp, 1982.

————. *En un plural designio.* Cuenca: El Toro de Barro, 1983.

————. *Ramas de la esperanza.* Lérida: Dilagro, 1984.

Lagos, Concha. See Gutiérrez Torrero, Concepción.

Leveroni, Rosa. *Epigrames i cançons.* Barcelona: Gili, 1938.

————. *Presència i record.* Barcelona: Ossa Menor, 1952.

————. *Poesia.* Barcelona: Edicions 62, 1981.

Madera, Asunción ("Chona Madera"). *El Volcano silencio.* Las Palmas de Gran Canaria, 1944.

———. *Mi presencia más clara.* Madrid, 1956.

———. *Las Estancias vacías.* Las Palmas de Gran Canaria, 1961.

———. *Los Contados instantes.* Las Palmas de Gran Canaria, 1961.

———. *La Voz que me desvela.* Las Palmas de Gran Canaria, 1965.

———. *Continuada señal.* Málaga, 1970.

———. *Mi otra palabra.* Málaga: Guadalhorce, 1977.

Maluquer i González, Concepció. *La Creu dels vents.* Barcelona: Ciutat, 1959.

———. *La Ciutat y les hores.* Barcelona, 1960.

March, Susana. *Rutas.* Barcelona: Librería Aviñó, 1938.

———. *La Pasión desvelada.* 1946.

———. *Ardiente voz.* Madrid: Cuadernos del Manzanares, 1948.

———. *El Viento.* Santander: Isla de los Ratones, 1951.

———. *La Tristeza.* Madrid: Adonais, 1953.

———. *Esta mujer que soy.* Madrid: Adonais, 1959.

———. *Poemas (1938–1966).* Santander: Isla de los Ratones, 1966.

Marco, Concha de. *Hora 0.5.* Santander: La Isla de los Ratones, 1966.

———. *Diario de la mañana.* Madrid: Mediterráneo, 1967.

———. *Acta de identificación.* Madrid: Mediterráneo, 1969.

———. *Congreso en Maldoror.* Madrid: Biblioteca Nueva, 1970.

———. *Tarot.* Madrid: Mediterráneo, 1973.

———. *Una Noche de invierno.* Madrid: Rialp, 1974.

Mariño Carou, María. *Palabra no tempo.* Lugo: Celta, 1963.

———. *Verba que comenza.* Lugo: Xerais, 1987.

Martín Vivaldi, Elena. *Arco en desenlace.* Granada, 1963.

———. *Diario incompleto de abril. Homenaje a Gustavo Adolfo Bécquer (1947).* Málaga: Guadalhorce, 1971.

———. *Durante este tiempo. 1965–1972.* Barcelona: El Bardo, 1972.

———. *Primeros poemas (1942–1944).* Introduction by Fidel Villan Ribot. Málaga: Guadalhorce, 1977.

Massanés, María Josepa. *Poesías.* Barcelona: J. Rubió, 1841.

———. *Flores marchitas.* Barcelona: A. Brusi, 1850.

———. *Poesies.* Barcelona: Ilustració Catalana, 1908.

Matheu, Roser. *La Carena.* Barcelona: Editor Altes, 1935.

———. *Cançons de Setembre.* Barcelona: La Revista, 1936.

———. *Poems a la filla.* Barcelona: Editor Arca, 1949.

———. *Poems de la fam.* Barcelona: Editor Barcino, 1953.

Maturana de Gutiérrez, Vicenta. *Ensayos poéticos.* Madrid: Vergés, 1828.

———. *Himno a la luna. Poema en cuatro cantos.* Bayona: Duhart-Fauvet y Maurin, 1838.

———. *Poesías de la señora doña Vicenta Maturana de Gutiérrez.* Paris: Librería de Lecointe y Lesserre, 1841.

Méndez [de Altolaguirre], Concepción (Concha Méndez). *Inquietudes.* Madrid, 1926.

———. *Surtidor.* Madrid, 1928.

————. *Canciones de mar y tierra.* Buenos Aires: 1930.

————. *Vida a vida.* Madrid, 1932.

————. *Niño y sombra.* Madrid, 1936.

————. *Lluvias enlazadas.* Havana, 1940.

————. *Villancicos de Navidad.* Mexico, 1944.

————. *Poemas, sombras y sueños.* Mexico, 1944.

————. *Vida o río.* Madrid, 1979.

Mercader, Trina. *Tiempo a salvo.* Granada, 1956.

————. *Sonetos ascéticos.* Barcelona: Saturno, 1971.

Ojeda, Pino. *Niebla del sueño.* Madrid: Ediciones de la Revista Mensaje, 1947.

————. *Como el fruto en el árbol.* Madrid: Rialp, 1954.

————. *La Piedra sobre la colina.* Las Palmas de Gran Canaria: Tagoro, 1964.

————. *El Alba en la espalda.* Madrid: Torremozas, 1987.

Parés, Nuria. *Romances de la voz sola.* Mexico: Editorial Gráfica Panamericana, 1951.

————. "Canto llano." Mexico: Fondo de Cultura Económica, 1959.

————. *Colofón de luz.* Mexico, 1987.

Penya d'Amer, Victòria. *Poesies.* Barcelona: Ilustració Catalana, 1909.

Pozo Garza, Luz. *Ultimas palabras/verbas derradeiras.* La Coruña: Nordés, 1976.

————. *Concerto de outono.* La Coruña: Ediciones de Castro, 1981.

Prieto Rouco, Carmen. *Horas de frebe: Poesías galegas, Monólogos representabres.* Villalba: El Progreso Villalbés, 1928.

Rincón, María Eugenia. *Tierra secreta.* Valencia, 1962.

————. *Frontera de la sombra.* Madrid: Cultura Hispánica, 1973.

————. *Boca sin tiempo.* León: Provincia, 1974.

Romero Serrano, Marina. *Poemas "A."* Madrid: Aguirre, 1935.

————. *Nostalgia de mañana.* Mexico: Rueca, 1943.

————. *Presencia del recuerdo.* Madrid: Insula, 1952.

————. *Midas: poema de amor.* Madrid: Insula, 1954.

————. *Sin agua, el mar.* Madrid: Agora, 1961.

Romo Arregui, Josefina. *La Peregrinación inmóvil.* Madrid: Gráfica Universal, 1932.

————. *Acuarelas.* Madrid, 1935.

————. *Romancero triste.* Madrid, 1936.

————. *Aguafuertes y otros poemas.* Madrid, 1940.

————. *Cántico de María Sola. 1946–1948.* Madrid, 1950.

————. *Isla sin tierra.* New York, 1955.

————. *Elegías desde la orilla del triunfo.* New York: 1964.

————. *Poemas de América.* Madrid, 1967.

————. *Autoantología.* New York: Academia de la Lengua Española de Nueva York, 1968.

Salvà, Maria Antònia. *Poesies.* Palma: Joan Colom, 1910.

————. *Espigues en flor, Poesies.* Ed. Josep Carner. Barcelona: Imprenta Altés, 1926.

————. *El Retorn: Poemes*. Barcelona: Gili, 1934.

————. *Cel d'horabaixa*. Barcelona, 193?; Mallorca: Moll, 1981.

————. *Lluneta del pagès*. Barcelona, 1948.

————. *Obres de Maria Antònia Salvà*. 6 vols. Majorca: Moll, 1948–55.

————. *Antologia poètica*. Edited by Josep Carner. Barcelona: Selecta, 1957.

————. *Al cel sia!* Prologue by Xesca Ensenyat. Barcelona: Edhasa, 1981.

Santamaria i Ventura de Fabrigues, Joaquima ("Agnes de Valldaura").
    Fullaraca: Prosa y vers. Barcelona: Estampa Peninsular, 1879.

————. *Ridolta: Aplech de poesies*. Barcelona: Roca, 1882.

Silva y Collas, Micaela de (pseudonym of Camila Avilés). *Emanaciones del alma*.
    Madrid: Hijos de Vázquez, 1885.

————. *Un Novio a pedir de boca*. Madrid: Campo Redondo, 1963.

Torre, Josefina de la. *Versos y estampas*. Málaga: Imprenta Sur, 1927.

————. *Poemas de la Isla*. Barcelona: Imprenta Altés, 1930.

————. *Marzo incompleto*. Las Palmas de Gran Canaria: Lezcano, 1968.

Uceda, Julia. *Mariposa en cenizas*. Prologue by Manuel Mantero. Arcos de la
    Frontera: Alcaraván, 1959.

————. *Extraña juventud*. Madrid: Rialp, 1962.

————. *Sin mucha esperanza*. Madrid: Agora, 1966.

————. *Poemas de Cherry Lane*. Madrid: Agora, 1968.

————. *Campanas en Sansueña*. Madrid: Dulcinea, 1977.

————. *Viejas voces secretas de la noche*. El Ferrol: Esquío, 1981.

————. *Del camino de humo*. El Ferrol: Esquío, 1992.

Uceta, Acacia. *El Corro de las horas*. Madrid: Agora, 1961.

————. *Frente a un muro de cal abrasadora*. Cuenca: El Toro de Barro, 1967.

————. *Detrás de cada noche*. Madrid: Nacional, 1970.

————. *Al sur de las estrellas*. Cuenca: Gárgola, 1976.

————. *Cuenca, roca viva*. Cuenca: Los Pliegos del Hocino, 1980.

————. *Intima dimensión*. Cuenca: Los Pliegos del Hocino, 1983.

————. *Arbol de agua*. Madrid: Rialp, 1987.

Valderrama, Pilar de. *Sí, soy Guiomar: Memorias de mi vida*. Barcelona: Plaza &
    Janés, 1981.

Vázquez, Dora. *Palma y corona*. Madrid: Escuela Española, 1964.

————. *Un Poema cada mes*. Orense: La Región, 1969.

————. *Irmá: Poemas de ausencia*. Orense: La Región, 1970.

————. *Campo e mar aberto*. Lugo: Celta, 1975.

————. *Augas soltas*. Orense: La Región, 1979.

————. *Oración junto al camino*. Barcelona: Ronda, 1985.

Vázquez, Pura. *Peregrino de amor*. Larache, 1943.

————. *Márgenes veladas*. Orense: Diputación, 1944.

————. *En torno a la voz*. Orense, 1948.

————. *Madrugada fronda*. Madrid: Palma, 1951.

————. *Desde la niebla*. Segovia: Amigos de Antonio Machado, 1951.

————. *Tiempo mío*. Segovia: Casa Amigos de Antonio Machado, 1952.

————. *Maturidade.* Buenos Aires: Centro Gallego, 1955.

————. *Mañana del amor.* Barcelona: Surco, 1956.

————. *13 poemas a mi sombra.* Caracas: Editorial Arte, 1957.

————. *A saudade e outros poemas.* Vigo: Galaxia, 1963.

————. *Presencia de Venezuela.* Caracas: Lírica Hispana, 1966.

————. *O desacougo.* Vigo: Galaxia, 1971.

————. *Los Sueños desandados.* Bilbao: Editorial CLA, 1974.

————. *Contacto humano del recuerdo.* Barcelona: 1985.

Viñas Olivella, Celia (or Vinyes). *Tierra del sur.* Almería, 1945.

————. *Trigo del corazón.* Almería, 1946.

————. *Viento levante.* Almería, 1946.

————. *Canción tonta en el sur.* Almería, 1948.

————. *Palabras sin voz.* Almería, 1953.

————. *Del foc i la cendra.* Barcelona, 1953.

————. *Como el ciervo corre herido.* Almería, 1955.

————. *Canto.* Madrid, 1964.

————. *Antología lírica.* Madrid: Rialp, 1976.

Zardoya González, María de la Concepción (Concha Zardoya). *Pájaros del nuevo mundo.* Madrid: Hispánica Adonais, 1946.

————. *Dominio del llanto.* Madrid: Hispánica Adonais, 1947.

————. *La Hermosura sencilla.* New York: Hispanic Institute in the United States, 1953.

————. *Los Signos.* Alicante: Ifach, 1954.

————. *El Desterrado ensueño.* New York: Hispanic Institute in the United States, 1955.

————. *Mirar el cielo es tu condena (Homenaje a Miguel Angel).* Madrid: Insula, 1957.

————. *La Casa deshabitada.* Madrid: Insula, 1959.

————. *Debajo de la luz.* Barcelona: Instituto de Estudios Hispánicos, 1959.

————. *Elegías.* Caracas: Lírica Hispana, 1961.

————. *Corral de vivos y muertos.* Buenos Aires: Losada, 1965.

————. *Donde el tiempo resbala (Romancero de Bélgica).* Montevideo: Cuadernos Julio Herrera y Reissig, 1966.

————. *Hondo Sur.* Madrid: Ciencia Nueva, 1968.

————. *Los Engaños de Tremont.* Madrid: Agora, 1971.

————. *Las Hiedras del tiempo.* Madrid: Biblioteca Nueva, 1972.

————. *El Corazón y la sombra.* Madrid: Insula, 1977.

————. *Diotima y sus edades (Autobiografía en cuatro tiempos).* Barcelona: Ambito, 1981.

————. *Los Ríos caudales: Apología del 27.* Madrid: Corcel, 1982.

————. *Manhattan y otras latitudes.* El Ferrol: Esquío, 1983.

Index

189

The Author

Janet Pérez received her M.A. and Ph.D. from Duke University and is Paul Whitfield Horn Professor of Spanish and associate dean of the graduate school at Texas Tech University. She has also taught at Duke University, Trinity College of the Catholic University of America, and the University of North Carolina at Chapel Hill. The editor of the Spanish Literature segment of this series, she is the author of *The Major Themes of Existentialism in the Works of Ortega y Gasset* (1970), *Ana María Matute* (1971), *Miguel Delibes* (1972), *Gonzalo Torrente Ballester* (1984), and *Women Writers of Contemporary Spain* (1988). She is currently at work on critical studies of Spanish women's poetry (1965–95) and Camilo José Cela.

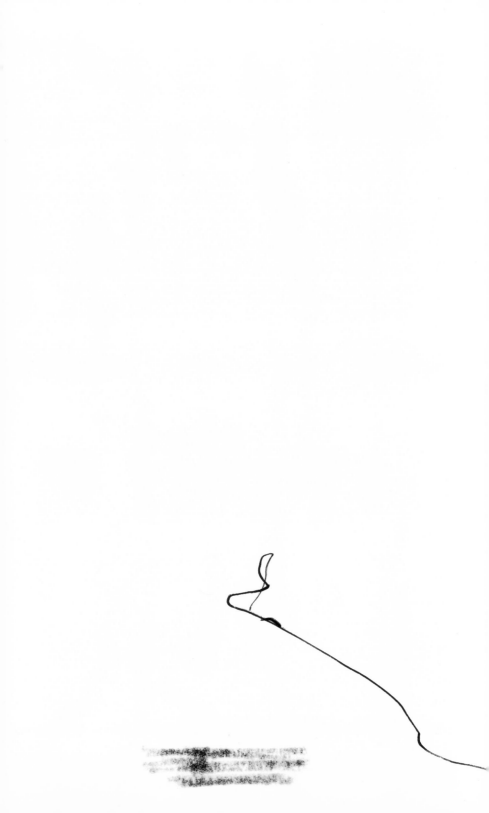